INHALT

* Fakultativ
(wahlfreie Bestandteile)

Differenzierungshinweis

□ Leichtere Übung

■■ Schwierigere Übung

Welcome ...

Hi, I'm Michelle Wilson. I live in the biggest city in the USA.

Hi, my name is Jennifer Sands. My home town is Flagstaff. It's near one of the most famous sights in the USA.

My name is David Chan. I live near the beach. Life is fun in my town – there are lots of things to do.

I'm Rachel Brown. I live about five hours from a very famous national park. I'm going camping there with my family next spring.

My name is Rick Alvarez. My home town is in Texas, not very far from Mexico. I play football at school.

... to the USA!

PLACES

■ **Put the people and the places together.**

Michelle	Flagstaff
Jennifer	New York
David	Brownsville
Rachel	Santa Barbara
Rick	Yellowstone National Park

■ **Look at the map on page 8. Can you find these places?**

W 1, 1a*

* Die blau gedruckten Verweise bezeichnen den frühestmöglichen Einsatzort der Übungen im Workbook.
W 1, 1a = Workbook Seite 1, Übung 1a

The United States of America

The USA is a **BIG** country.

It's 27 times bigger than Germany.

When it's 4 am in Los Angeles, it's 7 am in New York.

■ **Ask a partner.**

YOU When it's 5 am in Flagstaff, what time is it in San Antonio?
A PARTNER 6 am.
YOU When it's … in …, what time is it in …?
A PARTNER …

W 1, 1b-2

American English

American English (AE) and British English (BE) are different.

★ Americans sometimes use different words.

AE	BE
parking lot	car park
apartment	flat
line	queue
movie	film
downtown	town centre
mom	mum
trailer	caravan
9th grade	Year 9
go on vacation	go on holiday

1 ■ Listen to the dialogues.
Which dialogues are from Britain?
Which dialogues are from the USA?

■ What are the blue words in BE?

autumn ▪ underground ▪ shop
torch ▪ rubbish

1 It's dark now.
Do you have your flashlight?
2 My parents have a clothes store.
3 You can travel by bus or subway.
4 Don't leave your garbage in the park.
5 I went to Denver last fall.

★ Americans say some words differently.

2 ■ Listen to these words.

	AE	BE
new, Tuesday, student	uː	juː
little, city, better	d	t
last, dance, ask	æ	ɑː
clock, dog, box	ɑː	ɒ
more, word, car	r	

3 ■ Now listen to these words.
Are they AE or BE?

1 student	6 dance
2 new	7 clock
3 city	8 box
4 little	9 last
5 ask	10 more

★ Americans spell some words differently.

AE	BE
color	colour
center	centre
traveled	travelled

■ Write these AE words in BE.
1 neighbor
2 kilometer
3 traveling

4 ■ AE or BE?
Listen to these five people. Who's from Britain? Who's from the USA? Why do you think so?

UNIT ONE

New York City

Look at the photos.

- Would you like to visit New York? Why? Why not?
- What sights would you like to see?
- Is "Ground Zero" an interesting place for you?
- What would you like to do in New York?

Manhattan is the most exciting part of New York with lots of skyscrapers.

You can walk to the top of the Statue of Liberty.

More than seven million people live in New York.

People from many different countries live in New York.

Chinatown

Little Italy

Some things that tourists do when they visit New York:

Go shopping on Fifth Avenue.

See Times Square at night.

Visit Ground Zero. The World Trade Center stood here till terrorists destroyed it on September 11th, 2001.

W 2, 1

A family in New York

A "Hi, Michelle."
"Hi, Mom. Where are you?"
"I'm at work. Listen, Steve has just phoned me. He isn't going to be home till ten o'clock. Could you look after Sarah tonight, please?"

"But Mom! It's his turn," said Michelle. "I looked after her yesterday. Just because he's 17 and ..."
"I'm sorry, Michelle. I have to go now. Bye!"

Michelle Wilson lives with her mother, sister and brother in Brooklyn, in New York. Mrs Wilson works in a computer shop. She works five evenings a week from 5 till 9 pm. So the older children have to look after Sarah in the evenings.

Michelle's new friend, Laura Smith, has just moved to New York with her mother, father and older sister, Amy. Laura really wants to see Manhattan, the most famous part of New York. Michelle wants to go there with her next Saturday. There's only one problem. Michelle still has to ask her mother ...

? WHAT DO YOU KNOW ABOUT NEW YORK?

- New York is the biggest city in the USA.
  How many people live there?
  a) about 1 million; b) about 7 million;
  c) about 20 million.
- New York isn't the capital of the USA.
  What *is* the capital?
  a) Boston; b) Los Angeles; c) Washington, D.C.
- How many parts does New York have?
  a) three; b) five; c) ten.
- What's Manhattan?
  a) a town; b) a famous street; c) a part of New York.
- When did terrorists destroy the World Trade Center?
  a) on September 11th, 2000;
  b) on September 11th, 2001;
  c) on September 12th, 2001.

W 2, 2; W 3, 3

B On Monday evening Michelle asked her mother about the trip to Manhattan.

MRS WILSON So you want to go to Manhattan with Laura on Saturday afternoon?

MICHELLE Yeah, and we want to see a movie in the evening, too.

MRS WILSON I'm sorry, but the answer is "no". You're only 14. And I have to work on Saturday evening. Somebody has to look after Sarah.

MICHELLE What about Steve? He never has to look after Sarah.

MRS WILSON You know that isn't true. And you know that Steve often has to stay after school for basketball.

MICHELLE But I want to see a movie. Steve went to a dance last week and came home really late.

MRS WILSON That's different. He's three years older than you. And …

MICHELLE And he's a boy. It isn't fair!

What can you do?
Can you go out in the evening / at the weekend?

EXERCISE 1 ■ What do you have to do? Make sentences.

1 (clean my room)
I have to / I don't have to clean my room.
2 (go to bed early every evening)
3 (go to school tomorrow)
4 (look after my brother/sister)
5 (do a lot of homework)
6 (help at home a lot)
7 (stay at home a lot)

C Michelle and Steve have to help at home. Steve has to load and empty the dishwasher. Michelle has to set and clear the table. Michelle and Steve have to look after Sarah when their mother is at work.

EXERCISE 2 ■ Jobs in the Wilson family

Michelle Steve	has to doesn't have to	set the table. clear the table. load the dishwasher. empty the dishwasher. look after Sarah.

W 3, 4

And in your family?
I have to / don't have to …
My brother/sister has to … He/She doesn't have to …
There are/aren't special boys' jobs and girls' jobs in my family.

✔ CHECKPOINT

Was jemand tun muss bzw. nicht zu tun braucht: *have to / has to*

I have to do a lot of homework in the afternoon.
We don't have to get up early on Sundays.
A bus driver often has to work late.
Tom has to be home before 11 o'clock.

D

Michelle talked to Laura on Tuesday.

MICHELLE Mom says I can't go to Manhattan with you. She says I'm too young.

LAURA My parents say the same thing. It's OK for my sister Amy. She's 19.

MICHELLE Hey, look over there. That's my brother, Steve.

LAURA He looks nice. Let's talk to him.

MICHELLE Oh, OK. Steve! This is our new neighbour, Laura. She's from Atlanta.

STEVE Hi, Laura. Do you like New York?

LAURA It's great, but I've only seen Brooklyn. I want to see the sights in Manhattan.

STEVE I know Manhattan really well. You should go there.

You should go up the Empire State Building.

You should visit the Natural History Museum.

You should go for a walk in Central Park.

EXERCISE 3 ■ **What other things should tourists do in New York?**

- visit the Statue of Liberty
- have a meal in Little Italy
- go on a boat trip around Manhattan
- go to Chinatown
- go shopping on Fifth Avenue
- visit Ground Zero

1 They should visit the Statue of Liberty.
2 They should …

W 4, 5

What ideas do you have for tourists in your town?
They should …
visit … ▪ have a meal at … ▪ take photos of …
buy … ▪ go for a walk in … ▪ try a/an … at …

CHECKPOINT

Was jemand (nicht) tun sollte: *should*

You look tired. You should go to bed.
You shouldn't watch so much TV.

We should go to Manhattan. It's exciting.
She shouldn't buy that book. It's boring.

E Later Steve and Michelle were at home.

STEVE I might ask Laura to come to Manhattan with me on Saturday afternoon. What do you think?
MICHELLE Good idea. Err – what are your plans for Saturday evening?
STEVE I'm not sure. I might go to a party with friends.
MICHELLE I might go to Manhattan and see a movie.
STEVE Don't be silly. What will mom say?
MICHELLE It'll be OK if you come with me.
STEVE Go to a movie with my sister? No thanks!
MICHELLE But Laura wants to see the movie, too.
STEVE Laura! That's different. *When's* the movie?
MICHELLE Hey, man! Don't you want to know *which* movie?

EXERCISE 4 ■ What might they do on Sunday?

1 Steve likes sports. He might play basketball.
2 Michelle is a music fan. She might …
3 Mrs Wilson's brother is ill. She might …
4 It's Amy's birthday on Sunday. …
5 Laura has a new camera. …
6 Mrs Smith has a cold. … W 4, 6

stay in bed ▪ have a party
listen to some CDs ▪ play basketball
take some photos ▪ visit him

Write three things that you might do at the weekend.

F On Friday Michelle met Laura in a café. She told her about the trip to Manhattan with Steve. Laura was very pleased. But somebody had to look after Sarah on Saturday evening. Laura had an idea.

LAURA Listen. My sister Amy can look after Sarah.
MICHELLE Are you sure?
LAURA Yeah. She owes me a favour. I cleaned her room last week. This time she can help me.
MICHELLE That's a good idea. Hey! Brothers and sisters are great!

CHECKPOINT

Was vielleicht geschieht: *might*

I might go to the USA next year.
My parents might pay for the trip.
It might rain tomorrow.
If the weather is nice, we might go to Central Park.

STORY

What problems can people have on a trip to a city?

Michelle in Manhattan

After lunch on Saturday Laura, Michelle and Steve walked to the subway station. The girls waited on the special part of the platform where there were lots of lights and a video camera. "It's a lot safer in the subway now," Steve laughed. "Just don't act like a tourist. Act cool. And don't stare at people."

Steve walked along the platform and looked at the subway map. Two men were there, too. One of them asked Steve a question about the map. Five minutes later Laura, Michelle and Steve got on the subway train. Suddenly Steve said, "Oh no! My walkman. It isn't in my backpack."

"Don't worry," said Laura. "Maybe you left it at home."

"Yeah, you might be right," said Steve. But he wasn't really sure.

At 34th Street they left the subway and walked to the Empire State Building. Michelle was worried about the weather. "It's getting very cloudy. It might rain. We won't see anything."

"I'm sure the weather will be OK for the next hour," said Steve. "Don't worry."

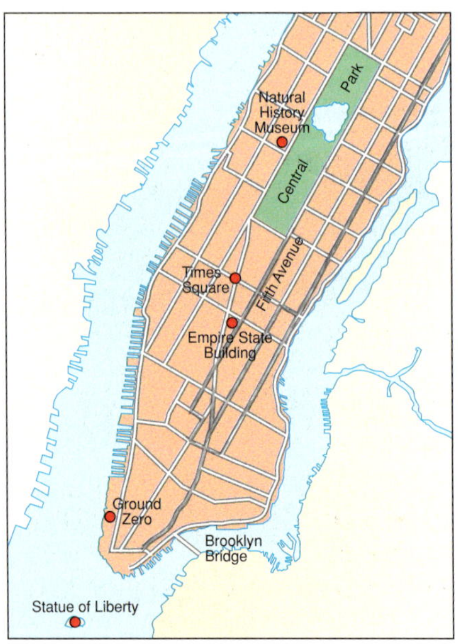

There was a long queue for tickets and another long queue at the lifts. An hour later they were in a lift. It only took three minutes to go up 86 storeys. When they arrived at the top of the Empire State Building, they saw … nothing! It was raining. Michelle didn't look happy, but Laura only smiled. When they got back down to the street, it was still raining.

"We can't go window-shopping on Fifth Avenue now," said Michelle. "This trip is a disaster."

"I think it's a nice trip," said Laura and she looked at Steve.

"I have an idea," said Steve. "There's an exhibition at the Natural History Museum. We can go by bus and look at the stores through the window of the bus. Window-shopping!"

"Ha, ha! Very funny," said Michelle angrily. But Laura laughed.

When they arrived at the Natural History Museum Steve was surprised. There weren't many tourists outside. But there were lots of lights and cameras – and a big sign on the door, "Closed at 2 pm this Saturday."
"What's happening?" Steve asked a camera-woman.
"Don't you read the newspapers?" she said. "We're making a movie in the museum."
"A good New York guide should know things like that," Michelle said. Steve said nothing. But Laura took his hand and smiled.

Then the rain stopped. So they walked into Central Park and bought frankfurters and cokes from a stall there.
"Let's walk through the park," Steve said. "It only takes 20 minutes to get to the other side."

Over an hour later three very tired teenagers came out of Central Park.
"OK, OK. I took the wrong path," said Steve. "Let's take a taxi now. It won't be too expensive."
They stopped a taxi and Michelle told the driver the name of the cinema.
The traffic was terrible and soon the taxi wasn't moving. But the meter in the taxi was moving – very fast. The three teenagers watched the dollars and cents on the meter – $9, $9.50, $10.
"You and your ideas," Michelle said.
Even Laura was worried now.
"Maybe we should get out now," she said. "It's so expensive."
They got out and paid the driver. Then they walked along the busy streets.
"What's the name of the movie?" Steve asked.
Michelle looked at him.
"*Disaster*," she said.

TASK A □ **What are the lines about?**

1 Lines 1 to 15
2 Lines 23 to 28
3 Line 38
4 Lines 40 to 51
5 Lines 55 to 56
6 Lines 64 to 73
7 Line 77

- Steve's idea about the park
- The name of the film
- The trip on the subway
- Problems in the taxi
- Surprises at the museum
- Michelle got angry
- The Empire State Building

TASK B ■ **What were the problems?**

1 Steve's walkman wasn't ... in the backpack
2 At the Empire State Building there was a ... rening
3 At the top of the Empire State Building ... it was raning
4 The museum was closed because ...
5 The teenagers were very tired when they came out of the park, so ...
6 The teenagers were worried in the taxi because ... to exepensiv

TASK C ■■ **How did the day finish?**

What do you think?
Write the end of the story.

W 5, 7-8

ACTIONS Trips in the city

Tracy is at Times Square subway station.

How much does one subway token cost?

TRACY Four tokens, please.
WOMAN That's $6, please. Thank you.

Does Tracy have to change trains?

TRACY Excuse me. Could you tell me which line goes to First Avenue, please?
GIRL Take number 2 to 14th Street. Then change to L.
TRACY Thank you.

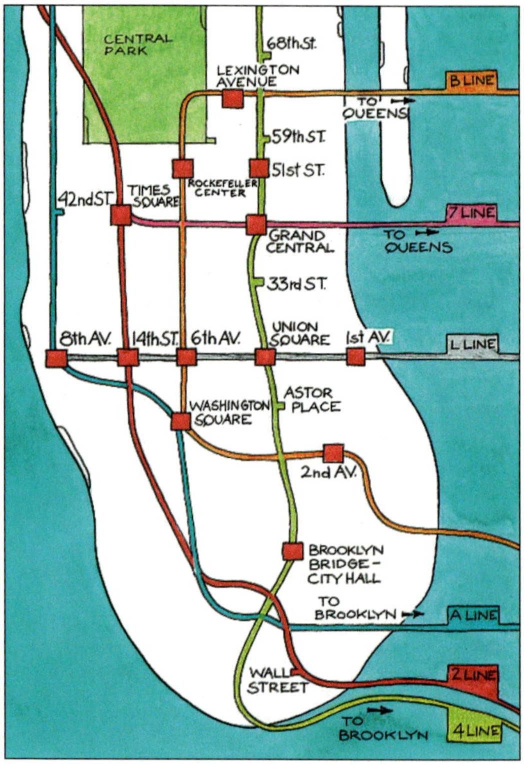

EXERCISE 1 ■ You're at Times Square station. Make dialogues.

YOU Could you tell me which line goes to …, please?
A PARTNER Take …

Tip: The list of numbers on page 154 can help you.

TRIPS IN NEW YORK

- It's easy to travel in New York. There are buses and a subway. You pay for your trips with subway tokens ($1.50) or a Metrocard ($3 – $80). Each trip costs $1.50.
- You have to go through gates to get to the subway trains. You use a token or your Metrocard. You don't get a ticket.
- The **subway** is fast, but it can be dangerous, especially at night.
- **Buses** aren't very fast because of the traffic, but they're safe and very clean.
- **Taxis** are cheaper than in Europe. They're a good idea if you're tired or if three people are travelling together. But ask the driver what the traffic is like first!

Taxi drivers often have useful information.

Is it far to the cinema?

BETH Where can I see a movie near here?
TAXI DRIVER On Times Square.
BETH Is it far?
TAXI DRIVER No, about 10 minutes by taxi. The traffic is OK.
BETH OK. Let's go.

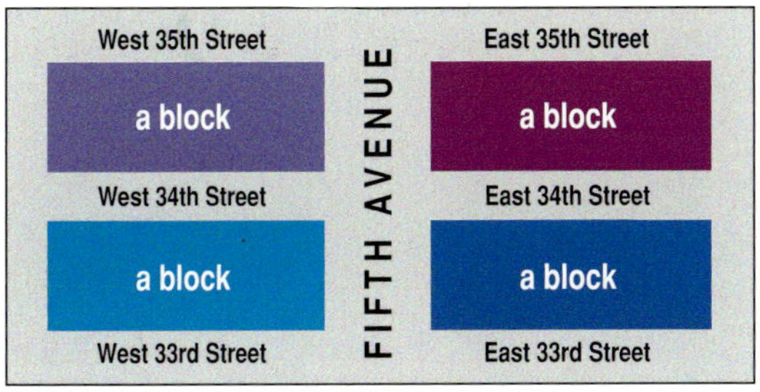

How can Robert get to the shops?

ROBERT Where can I go shopping near here?
TAXI DRIVER On Fifth Avenue.
ROBERT Is it far?
TAXI DRIVER It's 8 blocks from here. That's a long way to walk.
ROBERT OK. Let's go.

EXERCISE 2 ■ Make dialogues with a taxi driver.

YOU Where can I …?
A PARTNER At … / In … / On …
YOU Is it far?
A PARTNER About … minutes by taxi. / It's … blocks from here.
YOU OK. Let's go.

1. have breakfast? at Tom's Café 15 minutes
2. go inline-skating? in Central Park 20 minutes
3. go shopping? on Fifth Avenue 12 blocks
4. find a bank? on 23rd Street 10 blocks
5. buy a hamburger? at Hamburger Harry's 10 minutes
6. go swimming? on West End Avenue 14 blocks

EXERCISE 3 □ Make a dialogue at a subway station.

- Sage, dass du 6 U-Bahn-Münzen haben möchtest.
- Sage, dass das $9 macht.
- Frage nach der Linie zur Brooklyn Bridge.
- Sage, dass er/sie die Nummer 4 nehmen muss.

Tip: The phrases are on page 18.

EXERCISE 4 ■■ Make a dialogue with a taxi driver.

- Frage, ob es hier in der Nähe einen U-Bahnhof gibt.
- Sage, dass der nächste U-Bahnhof fünf Häuserblocks von hier entfernt ist.
- Sage, dass du zum Empire State Building willst. Frage, ob es weit weg ist.
- Sage, dass die Fahrt dorthin nur 10 Minuten dauert. Der Verkehr ist nicht schlecht heute.
- Frage, was die Fahrt kostet.
- Sage, dass sie ungefähr $6 kostet.

W 6, 9-10

* CONTEXTS Information about New York

A

B

C

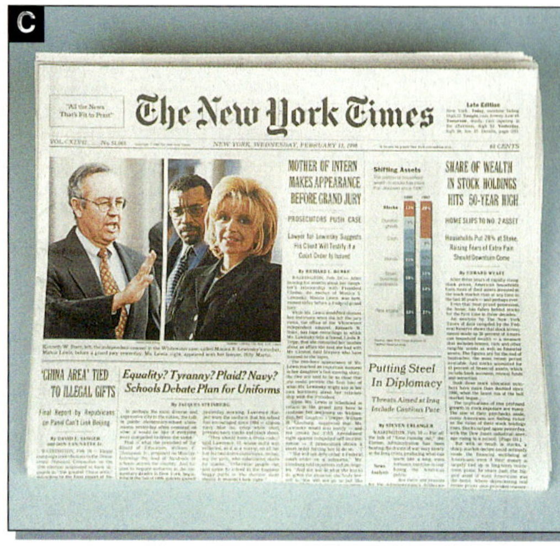

D

E

F

G

H

You need some information, but where can you find it (A-H)?

F 1 You're a tourist in the city, but your English isn't very good.
D 2 You want to see some famous pictures.
C 3 What's the news today? And what's the weather going to be like?
E 4 You want to know which bus goes from Eighth Avenue to Central Park.
H 5 You'd like to read some articles about music, books, exhibitions and films.
B 6 You're planning a cheap holiday in New York and you need lots of information – about hotels, restaurants and shops.
A 7 You want to go on a tour of Manhattan and see some of the sights. Perhaps a boat tour?
G 8 You'd like to play video games.

* SONG Jamaican in New York

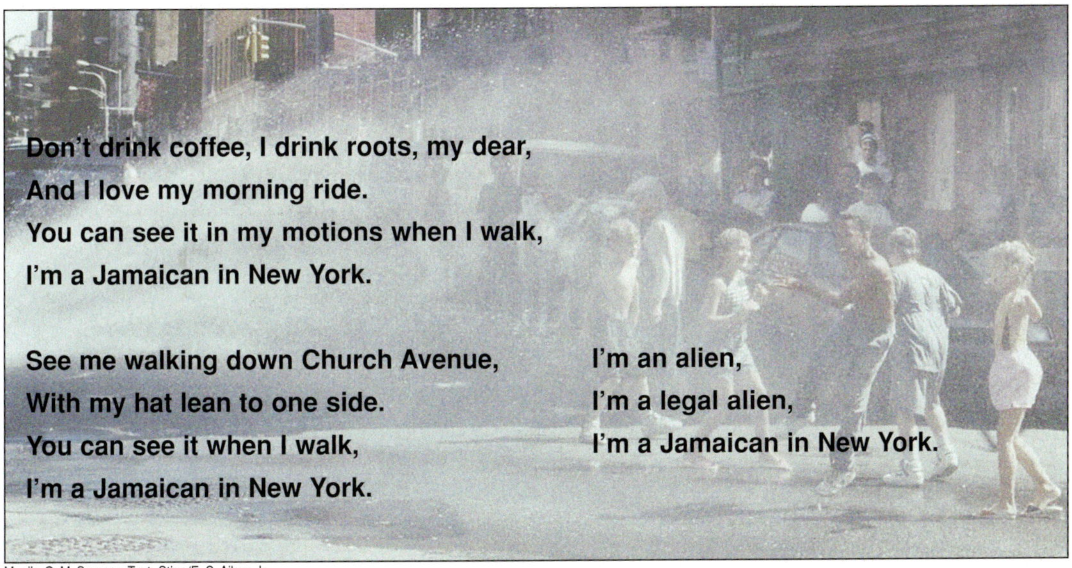

Don't drink coffee, I drink roots, my dear,
And I love my morning ride.
You can see it in my motions when I walk,
I'm a Jamaican in New York.

See me walking down Church Avenue,
With my hat lean to one side.
You can see it when I walk,
I'm a Jamaican in New York.

I'm an alien,
I'm a legal alien,
I'm a Jamaican in New York.

Musik: G. M. Sumner, Text: Sting/E. C. Aiken Jr.

* CLASS PROJECT A bus tour of your town

In New York there are tours on London buses. A tour guide tells you all about the city on the tour.

English-speaking tourists want to visit your town or village or an area near you. Plan a bus tour for them. (It can be a funny tour!)

Work in groups. In your group:
– Make a brochure.
– Write a commentary for the bus tour.
– Record the commentary.

Then the class can listen to the commentaries.

Useful phrases:
- Hallo and welcome to this tour of …
- On the right/left you can see …
- You can/should/have to … here.
- This is the best … in our town/village.
- This is the oldest … in our town/village.
- The … is very beautiful/famous.
- Please don't forget a tip for the guide!

* ACTION CARDS Trips in the city

- Make action cards with useful words and phrases from this unit.

STRUCTURES

EXERCISE 1 ■ When you visit New York: What you should and shouldn't do.

Go to a tourist office and get some information.
Don't do too much on the same day.
Buy a good map.
Try some New York frankfurters.
Don't go to parks in the evening.
Don't take an expensive camera with you.
Wait on the safer part of the subway platform.
Don't stare at people in the subway.

1 You should go to a tourist office and get some information.
2 You shouldn't …
3 …

EXERCISE 2 ■ Ideas for Saturday

to a basketball game
to the shops
in bed ▪ the Internet
some friends ▪ a film

1 I might go to a basketball game.
2 I might stay …
3 I might visit …
4 I might surf …
5 I might watch …
6 I might go …

EXERCISE 3 □ At the top of the Empire State Building

are crossing ▪ is going ▪ are running
is leaving ▪ is waiting ▪ are making

1 A boat … Staten Island.
2 Some cars … Brooklyn Bridge.
3 A bus … along Fifth Avenue.
4 Some people … in Central Park.
5 Some people … a movie.
6 – And everybody … for you!

EXERCISE 4 ■■ Put in the right form – simple present or present progressive.

Welcome to New York Tours!
Let's start on Wall Street. Lots of people (work) in this part of Manhattan Monday to Friday. But it's Saturday today and lots of people (watch) the big football game at Giants Stadium. Over there you can see the boat to Staten Island. It only (cost) 50 cents. We usually (turn) left here, but the road is closed at the moment. A movie company (make) a movie there this afternoon. And now we (go) past Brooklyn Bridge. It's …

EXERCISE 5 ■■ Quiz: Who am I?

Write a text about you and your free time. The other students have to read your text. Do they know who it is?

Who am I?
I'm 14 and I live in Hattingen. In my free time I usually visit my friends. I often watch "Marienhof" on TV. I really like it. I sometimes …

SITUATIONS

Wie sagst du auf Englisch, dass …

1 … etwas nicht wahr ist?
2 … etwas nicht gerecht ist?
3 … du viele Hausaufgaben machen musst?
4 … jemand nicht so viel fernsehen sollte?
5 … du vielleicht zu einer Party gehst?
6 … jemand sich keine Sorgen machen soll?

Tip: Look again at pages 12-19.

WORDPOWER

WORDPOWER 1 ■ Find the words.

WORDPOWER 2 ■ Put the words in the right groups.

department store ▪ frankfurter ▪ frightened
hamburger ▪ happy ▪ market ▪ pizza
pleased ▪ salad ▪ shop ▪ supermarket
surprised ▪ worried

food	how you feel	shopping
frankfurter	frightened	department store
…	…	…

WORDPOWER 3 ■ Michelle and Laura

about ▪ after ▪ at ▪ for ▪ from

Hi, Laura. Listen, when my mom came back … work today, I was looking … an article about a new judo school. It's near the subway station. I showed mom the article. She said, "If you want to do judo, I'll pay … it." What do you think … that? I was really pleased. I have to go now. I have to look … my sister. See you tomorrow.

WORDPOWER 4 □ At home.

What can/can't you do?
What do you have to do?
What don't you have to do?

go to bed late ▪ phone my friends
come home late
look after my brothers/sisters
help in the garden ▪ get up early
watch TV late at night ▪ wash up
do my homework ▪ listen to loud music

I can
I don't have to
I can't
I have to

WORDPOWER 5 ■■ Make a word web.

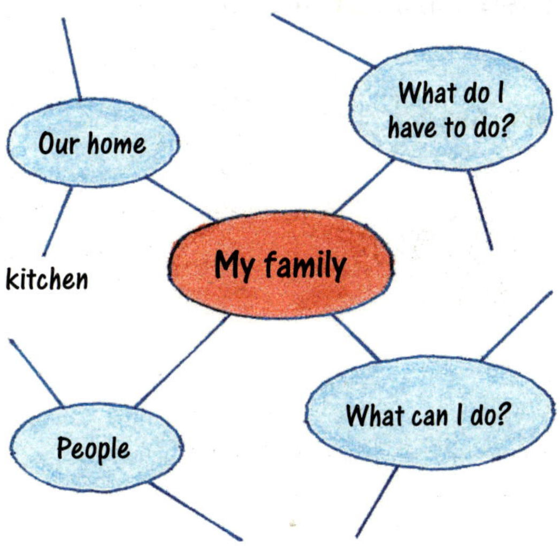

PRACTICE PAGES

READING

BEFORE YOU READ ■ **Is this text a story, an interview in a magazine or a poster?**

My job: New York taxi driver

Pete Delano drives one of New York's famous yellow cabs. He has always been a cab driver. It's an interesting job, but it can sometimes be dangerous.

CITY SCENE What's your day like, Pete?

DELANO I start at 7 am and usually finish at 5 pm. I drive near the large hotels. There are always lots of people who want to go to one of New York's three airports.

CITY SCENE Where do you eat?

DELANO If I'm near East Houston Street, I go to Katz's Delicatessen for lunch. The President has had lunch there, too, you know. There's a letter from him in their window.

CITY SCENE What do *you* eat there?

DELANO Pancakes and sausages.

CITY SCENE That isn't very healthy.

DELANO I know, I weigh too much. You don't get much exercise in a cab!

CITY SCENE What things make you angry?

DELANO Passengers who say, "Go the shortest way. Don't go the long way."

CITY SCENE And you never go the long way?

DELANO Of course not. Well, not often.

CITY SCENE What one major change have you seen in the last 15 years?

DELANO Well, the traffic is much worse now.

CITY SCENE How safe is a cab driver in New York?

DELANO Every cab in New York has an extra yellow light. If it's on, people know I'm having problems with a passenger and they can phone the police.

CITY SCENE Oh, yes. One last question: Are you happy with your job?

DELANO Sure! I love New York. Hey, I have to go now. My shift finishes at 5 pm.

CITY SCENE But it's only 4.15!

DELANO I have to get gas for the guy who drives the next shift. You should see the line of cabs at our gas station on 7th Avenue! See you!

Tip: You can find new words in the *Dictionary* (page 136).

EXERCISE 1 ■ Basic reading: Right or wrong?

1 Delano is a reporter for *City Scene*.
2 Delano always works at night.
3 Delano's job is never dangerous.
4 Delano is happy with his job.

EXERCISE 2 ■ Reading for details: These sentences are wrong. But what's right?

1 Delano starts work at 10 am.
2 There are always lots of people who want to go to Katz's Delicatessen.
3 Delano has pancakes and sausages for breakfast.
4 Delano started his job four years ago.
5 New York taxis have an extra yellow door.
6 Delano has to leave at 4.15 because a passenger wants to go to the airport.

EXERCISE 3 ■ Language tasks Tip: All the words are on page 24.

1 Find: a) the opposite of *safe, short, better, hate;*
b) another word for *taxi, important, stop;*
c) the AE word for *queue.*
2 Find the words for: a) *Pfannkuchen;* b) *gesund;* c) *Fahrgast;* d) *Schicht.*

LISTENING Food in New York

You're going to hear some tourists in New York. They're buying food. Listen.

EXERCISE 1 ■ Which photo (A-D) comes first? Which photo comes next?

EXERCISE 2 ■■ Listen to the dialogues again. Right or wrong?

Dialogue 1: The tourist has to pay $2.
Dialogue 2: The tourist would like some orange juice.
Dialogue 3: The cake isn't very expensive.
Dialogue 4: The tourist wants to buy a cup of tea.

Weitere Fragen: W 52

SUMMARY

* have to / has to

Mit *have to / has to* sagst du, was jemand tun muss bzw. nicht zu tun braucht.

Mrs Wilson often has to work late.

I don't have to go to bed early tonight.

Do I have to buy a ticket?

Do you have to go home now? Musst du jetzt nach Hause gehen?
Sue doesn't have to help at home. Sue braucht nicht zu Hause zu helfen.
Does your brother have to clean his room? Muss dein Bruder sein Zimmer sauber machen?
Most people don't have to work on Saturdays. Die meisten Leute brauchen samstags nicht zu arbeiten.

should

Mit *should* sagst du, was (nicht) geschehen sollte.

You should listen to this.

You shouldn't talk here.

You should be careful in a big city. In einer Großstadt sollte man vorsichtig sein.
The children should go to bed. It's late. Die Kinder sollten ins Bett gehen. Es ist spät.
You shouldn't eat so much chocolate. Ihr solltet nicht so viel Schokolade essen.
Steve shouldn't talk so much. Steve sollte nicht so viel reden.

might

Mit *might* sagst du, was vielleicht geschieht.

I might win lots of money.

Julia might go to New York in summer. Julia fährt vielleicht im Sommer nach New York.
Ken and Ben might visit their grandma. Ken und Ben besuchen vielleicht ihre Oma.
The weather might be nice tomorrow. Morgen ist das Wetter vielleicht schön.

IN DIESER UNIT HAST DU GELERNT, ...

... wie du sagst, was jemand (nicht) tun sollte. → *Children should help their parents. You're ill. You shouldn't go to school.*

... wie du sagst, was vielleicht geschieht. → *I might go to a dance on Saturday. It might rain tomorrow.*

wie du in einer Stadt

... um U-Bahn-Münzen bittest. → *Ten tokens, please.*

... nach einer U-Bahn-Linie fragst. → *Could you tell me which line goes to ..., please?*

... fragst, wo du in der Nähe etwas tun kannst. → *Where can I go shopping near here?*

IN DIESER UNIT HAST DU WIEDERHOLT, ...

... wie du sagst, was jemand tun muss oder nicht zu tun braucht. → *Sally has to clean her room. I don't have to look after my sister.*

... wie du sagst, was jemand (nicht) tun darf. → *I can go to the cinema with my brother. Bob can't visit his father at work.*

UNIT TWO

On the road in Arizona

- Have you ever heard of Arizona?
- Where is it in the USA?
- Look at the photos. Where would you like to go in Arizona?

Arizona is a state in the south-west of the USA.

There's a lot of desert in Arizona.

There are famous sights in Arizona, too, like Monument Valley ...

... the Grand Canyon ...

... the Desert Museum in Tucson.

Many people who travel across the USA use Arizona's interstates.

Some people, especially tourists, like to use the famous old road, Route 66.

Interstate 10 (I10) goes through Arizona's capital, Phoenix.

Be careful! The speed limit on the interstate in Arizona is 75 mph (miles per hour).

Flagstaff is a town on Route 66. It's near the famous Grand Canyon.

W 12, 1-2

Arizona – Grand Canyon state

A Jennifer Sands and her parents live in Flagstaff, Arizona. Flagstaff is near Interstate 40, so people often drive into the town to get gas, food or a motel room for the night. Jennifer's parents have a gas station and Jennifer sometimes helps them there. Jennifer is 15 and is already a good driver. She can drive when her mother or father is with her. She'll be 16 next month and then she can take her driving test.

Jennifer likes hiking and sometimes goes to the Grand Canyon with her church youth group. The Grand Canyon is Arizona's most famous sight and is only two hours from Flagstaff. It's a sight that visitors never forget.

But you have to be careful there, too. Every year lots of people have problems in the canyon. They try to hike too far or they don't take enough water. Many tourists have died in the Grand Canyon.

Grand Canyon

ON THE ROAD IN ARIZONA: WHAT DO YOU KNOW?

- In Arizona you mustn't drive faster than
  a) 60 mph; b) 75 mph; c) 80 mph.
- Young people in Arizona can drive with an adult when they're
  a) 15; b) 16; c) 18.
- What town in Arizona is on a famous road and near a famous sight?
  a) Tucson; b) Phoenix; c) Flagstaff.

Find out:

- How fast is 75 mph in km/h?
- What states are east and west of Arizona?
- What *country* is south of Arizona?

W 12, 3; W 13, 4

B Jennifer is helping two tourists at the gas station.

JENNIFER Is your oil OK?
DRIVER Yes, thanks. I checked it myself this morning.
JENNIFER Are you going far?
DRIVER We started in New York and we're driving to LA.
JENNIFER New York to Los Angeles. What a great trip!
DRIVER Yes. We're really enjoying ourselves.
JENNIFER Why don't you drive on Route 66 for a few hours?
DRIVER Is it near here?
JENNIFER Yes, it is. You're on it now. The part from here to California is great.
DRIVER Good idea – oh, we'd like some coffee, please.
JENNIFER Sure. Go in and help yourselves. That's $20 for the gas. And two coffees – $22, please.
DRIVER Here you are, $22 – and $1 for you.
JENNIFER Thanks. Bye.

C Later Jennifer sent an e-mail to her cousin Kelly Kline in Chicago.

There's always lots of work at our gas station. Mom and dad can't do everything themselves, so I often help them. I like to meet different people from different places. I often tell tourists about Route 66. Dad always tells me that I have to be careful when I'm working. He says, "Look after yourself" almost every day. But yesterday he hurt himself when he was checking the water in a car. He didn't laugh when I said, "You should look after yourself, Dad!" …

EXERCISE 1 ■ **At the gas station**

myself ▪ yourself ▪ himself ▪ herself ▪ yourselves ▪ themselves

1 The driver checked the oil *herself.*
2 The two tourists are enjoying …
3 "Help … to coffee," Jennifer said to them.
4 "I hurt … today," said Mr Sands.
5 He should look after …
6 And you? Did you do this exercise …?

W 13, 5

CHECKPOINT

myself, yourself, themselves, …

I hurt myself when I fell.
Jack made the cake himself.
"We can look after ourselves," the girls said.
Some drivers repair their cars themselves.

D Jennifer's youth group goes to the Grand Canyon in spring and autumn. They don't go there in summer because the temperature is much too high. They don't go there in winter because it's too cold. There's often snow in the Grand Canyon when it's a nice day in Flagstaff.

E Jennifer went to the Grand Canyon with her youth group last May.

They hiked down into the canyon on Saturday.

They stayed there on Saturday and Sunday night.

They went out on the Colorado River on Sunday afternoon.

They hiked back to the top of the canyon on Monday.

W 14, 6

Canada's Wonderland

EXERCISE 2 ■ Jennifer's cousin, Kelly, went to Toronto with her parents last year. It was her first visit to Canada.

1 to Detroit / on Friday / They travelled
They travelled to Detroit on Friday.
2 They arrived / on Saturday / in Toronto
3 to the CN Tower / They went / on Sunday
4 They watched / in the evening / a baseball game / at the Skydome
5 to Canada's Wonderland / They went / on Monday morning
6 in Chicago / on Wednesday / They arrived

✔ CHECKPOINT

Stellung von Orts- und Zeitangaben

I travel to New York every month.
Mum works in an office from Monday to Friday.
Can you meet me at the church at 8 o'clock?
Please be home before 11 pm.

F Kelly Kline usually has a week's holiday in March. This year Kelly and her mother are going to visit Jennifer and her family in Flagstaff. They're going to fly from Chicago to Amarillo and rent a car there. Then they're going to take the famous Route 66 from Amarillo to Flagstaff. They're going to stay for four nights in Flagstaff and then they're going to drive back to Amarillo on the interstate. It's much faster on the interstate.

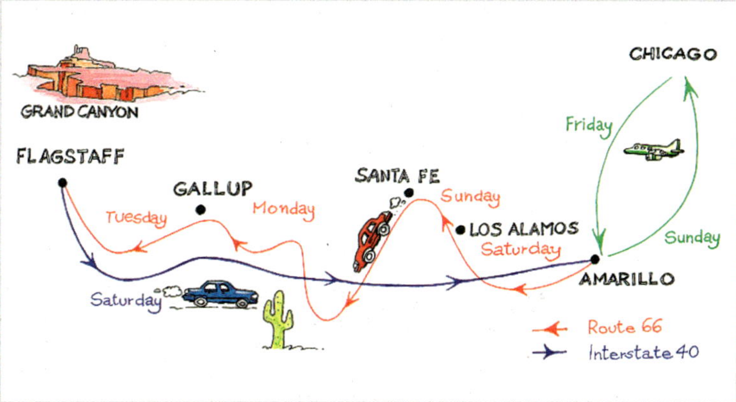

EXERCISE 3 ■ When?

1 They're going to fly to Amarillo on Friday.
2 They're going to drive to Los Alamos on …
3 …
4 …
5 …
6 They're going to drive back to Amarillo on …

G Jennifer and Mrs Sands are talking about the visit.

JENNIFER Can we go to the Grand Canyon on Thursday?
MRS SANDS Well, dad and I are going to be busy. And I don't think Aunt Helen likes hiking.
JENNIFER Oh, Mom. Kelly and I can look after ourselves.
MRS SANDS Do you think Kelly is fit enough for hiking?
JENNIFER Well, in her e-mails she says she's good at everything.
MRS SANDS OK, but you'll have to be careful. And you can only go for one day.
JENNIFER That's OK. I'm going to spend a weekend there with my youth group soon.

EXERCISE 4 ■ Mr Sands' trip to Phoenix

Mr Sands is talking to a friend about the Klines' visit.

do ▪ drive ▪ listen ▪ pay
play ▪ see ▪ visit

1 "My wife's sister and her daughter are going to *visit* us.
2 A pop group is going to … in Phoenix on Wednesday.
3 Jennifer and her cousin are going to … them.
4 My wife and I are going to … for the tickets.
5 And I'm going to … them to Phoenix."
6 – "What are you going to … when they're at the concert?"
7 "I don't know. I'm not going to … to the group. They're terrible!"

W 14, 7

What are your plans for next weekend?
I'm going to …
I'm not going to …

CHECKPOINT

Was jemand in der Zukunft (nicht) tun wird: *going to*

I'm going to visit a friend next week.
Emily isn't going to play tennis tomorrow.
Are you going to meet Adam and Tina tomorrow?
– Yes, I am. They're going to come to my house.

STORY

What should you never do in the Grand Canyon?

Leave me here!

"Don't forget. The last bus is at 8 pm. Enjoy yourselves. And be careful!" Mr Sands drove away from the car park at the Grand Canyon.

It was very early in the morning and the car park was very quiet. The two girls walked to the start of the trail. Kelly wasn't very happy about the big bottles of water in her backpack. "I don't know why each of us has to carry three bottles of water," she said. "And I think … wow! Look at the view!"
Jennifer smiled. People were always very surprised when they saw the canyon for the first time.
"Can you see the Colorado River?" asked Jennifer. "Our trail goes all the way down there. But you should never try to get to the river and back on the same day."
"OK, OK," said Kelly.
"Now, let's see," said Jennifer. "It's 6.30 now …"
"I know, I know," said Kelly.
"We'll walk downhill till we get to Cedar Ridge," said Jennifer. "That should take about 1 hour and 15 minutes. Then we'll have a break for half an hour and get back before it gets really hot."
"What! Only 1 hour and 15 minutes? We'll be back at the top much too soon."
"No," said Jennifer. "Don't forget that the uphill trip usually takes twice the time."

They started to walk down the path. It was very steep and there were lots of bends. At 7.30 they came to Cedar Ridge and ate some sandwiches.
"Listen," said Kelly. "It's so early. It only took 1 hour to get here. We could be at the Colorado River before 11.00, have a break, then walk back."
"But the uphill trip will take eight hours."
"Oh, Jennifer! We'll do it faster. We're fit."
Jennifer was quiet. But then she said, "OK, let's do it. Let's go down to the Colorado River!"

They arrived at the river at 11.00. It was very hot in the canyon.
"I told you we could do it," said Kelly.
"Don't say that till we're back at the top. It's uphill all the way," said Jennifer. "Let's go!"
They started the trip back.

After an hour they stopped. It was very hot. They drank lots of water. After 45 minutes they stopped again. Kelly looked terrible.
"Are your bottles empty?" said Jennifer. "Here, you can have some of my water."
"Thanks," said Kelly. She didn't look at Jennifer. Jennifer took Kelly's hand and helped her along the trail. Then, suddenly, Kelly stopped and fell to the ground.
"Leave me here. I'm so tired. Leave me here. Go and get help."
"No! *Please* get up!"
Jennifer tried to take her hand again, but Kelly just shouted, "Leave me here! Leave me here!"
Jennifer was really worried. "It'll be dark in five hours," she thought. "Can I get to the top and phone the rangers in time? How much water do I have to leave for Kelly? How much do I need? We don't have enough."
And then she remembered the most important rule for hiking in the Grand Canyon: "NEVER, NEVER, NEVER leave a hiker alone in the canyon."

TASK A Numbers

1 The last bus to Flagstaff leaves at … pm.
2 Each girl had … bottles of water.
3 They started at … in the morning.
4 In the Grand Canyon: two hours downhill = … hours uphill.
5 They got to Cedar Ridge at …
6 They got to the river at …
7 On the way back they stopped after an hour and then after … minutes.
8 "It'll be dark in … hours," thought Jennifer.

TASK B ■ Tell the story.

Mr Sands …
The two girls …
At 7.30 …
Kelly wanted to …
At 11.00 …
Then they started …
After an hour …
After 45 minutes …
Suddenly Kelly …
Kelly said, …
But Jennifer remembered …

TASK C ■■ Finish the story.

What do you think happened to the two girls?
You can write about:
other tourists, rangers, Mr Sands.

W 15, 8-10

ACTIONS At a gas station

On Saturday Jennifer was helping at the gas station.

Where does the driver want to go?

JENNIFER Is that all?
DRIVER Yes, thank you. Oh, how can I get to the Grand Canyon, please?
JENNIFER Turn left out of the gas station. Go straight ahead at the junction. Turn left at the lights.
DRIVER Do you mean the first lights?
JENNIFER Yes. Then turn right at the Exxon gas station. And then you're on the right road.

EXERCISE 1 ■ **Make more dialogues with a partner.**

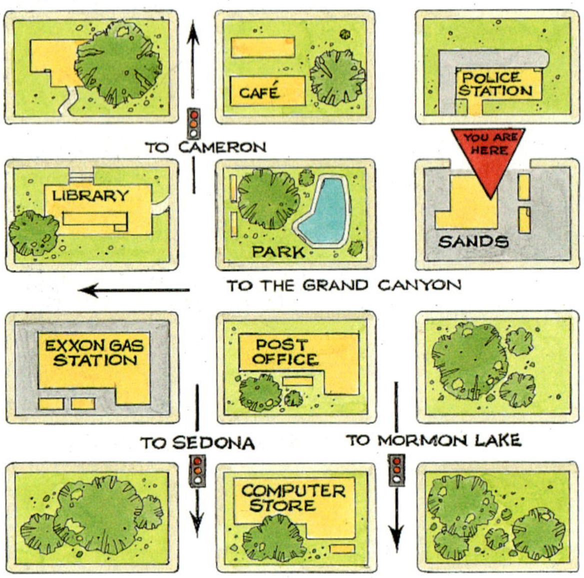

How can I get to ..., please?

Turn left out of the gas station.
Turn left/right at the ...
Go straight ahead at the junction/lights.
And then you're on the right road.

W 16, 11

GAS STATIONS: NOT JUST FOR GAS

- You buy gas in gallons in the USA. A US gallon is about 4 litres.
- Most gas stations have a shop. Some of these shops are like supermarkets. They sell so many different things. Sometimes the only shop for miles and miles is at the gas station.
- You can buy food and drinks for your trip. For example, you can often get hamburgers, hot dogs and even ice for cold drinks.
- You can almost always get coffee. Lots of people have special car coffee mugs. People take their coffee with them and drink it in their car. Americans often have to drive hundreds of miles. So they don't like to stop too often!

Later Jennifer was helping in the shop at the gas station.

What does the customer want?

CUSTOMER Do you sell sandwiches?
JENNIFER Sure. They're over there, next to the cakes.
CUSTOMER Great. And do you sell car coffee mugs?
JENNIFER Yes, we do.
CUSTOMER How much are they?
JENNIFER $2.99.

EXERCISE 2 ■ In the shop at the gas station: Make dialogues.

YOU Do you sell …?
A PARTNER Sure. It's/They're over there, next to …
YOU And do you sell …?
A PARTNER Yes, we do.
YOU How much is it / are they?
A PARTNER $ …

EXERCISE 3 □ Make a dialogue between a driver and somebody in the street.

Frage, wie du nach Winona kommst.
▼
Sage, dass er/sie an der Ampel links abbiegen muss.
▼
Frage, ob er/sie die erste Ampel meint.
▼
Sage ja. Dann muss er/sie geradeaus fahren.

Tip: The phrases are on page 36.

EXERCISE 4 ■■ In a gas station shop: Make a dialogue.

Frage, ob man … verkauft.
(Was? Das kannst du entscheiden.)
▼
Sage ja, und wo er/sie das Gesuchte findet.
(Wo? Das kannst du entscheiden.)
▼
Frage nach dem Preis.
▼
Nenne den Preis.
(Wie viel? Das kannst du entscheiden.)
▼
Frage, wie du nach … kommst.
(Wohin? Das kannst du entscheiden.)
▼
Beschreibe den Weg.
(Wie? Das kannst du entscheiden.)

* ACTIVE ENGLISH OPTIONS

* CONTEXTS Road signs

A

B

C

D

E

F

G

H

Can you find the right photo (A-H)?

1 If you want to go to Interstate 17, turn left here.
2 Flagstaff is more than 100 years old.
3 You can ride your bike safely here.
4 Don't drink alcohol if you're going to drive.
5 Drivers shouldn't stop here.
6 You can't use this road.
7 Wear your seat-belt. It can save your life.
8 Be careful. There might be animals on this road.

* SONG (Get your kicks on) Route 66

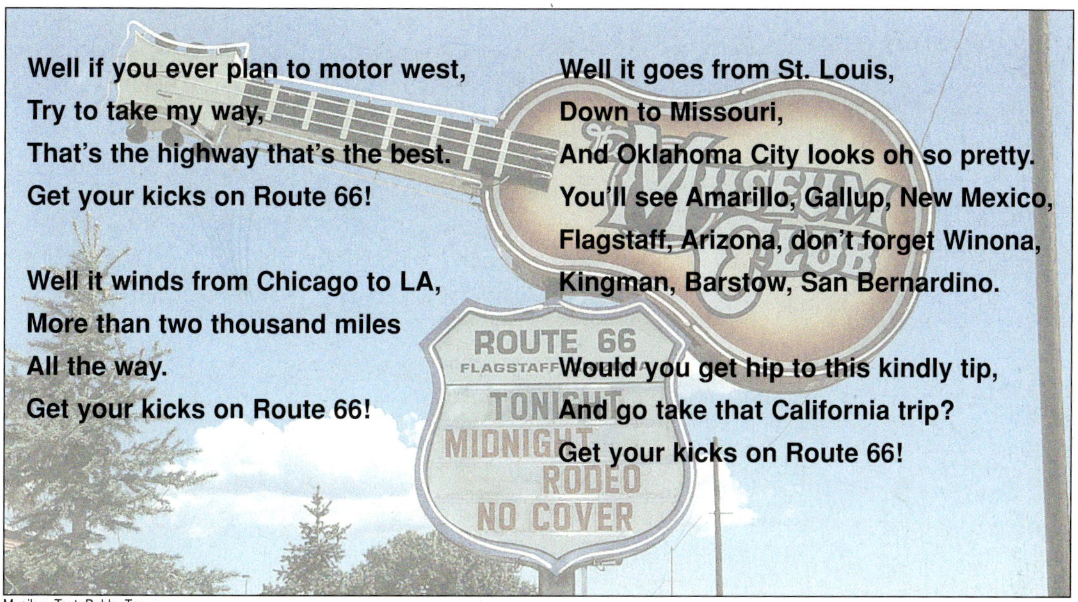

Well if you ever plan to motor west,
Try to take my way,
That's the highway that's the best.
Get your kicks on Route 66!

Well it winds from Chicago to LA,
More than two thousand miles
All the way.
Get your kicks on Route 66!

Well it goes from St. Louis,
Down to Missouri,
And Oklahoma City looks oh so pretty.
You'll see Amarillo, Gallup, New Mexico,
Flagstaff, Arizona, don't forget Winona,
Kingman, Barstow, San Bernardino.

Would you get hip to this kindly tip,
And go take that California trip?
Get your kicks on Route 66!

Musik u. Text: Bobby Troup

* CLASS PROJECT Make US-style signs for your town.

American road signs have a special style. They often say "east", "west", "north" or "south". So in the USA, you have to know which direction you want to go.

The town signs often tell you something about the town, for example, why the town is famous, or how many people live there.

Make US-style signs for German roads and towns.

* ACTION CARDS At a gas station

- Make action cards with useful words and phrases from this unit.

STRUCTURES

EXERCISE 1 ■ Jennifer's busy week

1 Jennifer met Jane outside Computer World on Monday morning.
2 She went to a concert …
3 She played …
4 She saw a film …
5 She worked …
6 She bought …
7 She visited …

EXERCISE 2 ■ Verbs with or without *herself*?

Examples:
She often listens … to CDs.
➔ She often *listens* to CDs.
She hurt … on her bike yesterday
➔ She *hurt herself* on her bike yesterday.

1 Jennifer enjoyed … at Chuck's party.
2 She met … lots of her friends there.
3 She helped … to lots of nice food.
4 Then she felt … ill.
5 So she went home and watched … a video.

EXERCISE 3 ■ A good trip

TIPS FOR HIKING IN THE GRAND CANYON
- Find out about the weather.
- Take enough food and drinks.
- Eat when you're hungry.
- Drink before you're thirsty.
- Have lots of breaks.
- Don't hike too far.

Jennifer's youth group had a good trip last spring. What did they do?

1 They found out about the weather.
2 … 3 … 4 … 5 … 6 …

EXERCISE 4 □ Problems in the canyon

fell ▪ found ▪ had ▪ hurt ▪ was ▪ went

- In 1996 a woman … to the Grand Canyon. She walked a long way but she wasn't very fit. After three hours she … and really … herself.
- In 1997 rangers … a man near the Colorado River. His temperature … very high: 42.7°C. He only … one water bottle with him.

EXERCISE 5 ■■ And you? Write about a good trip/visit/day.

Where did you go?
When did you go?
Who went with you?
What did you eat and drink?
What was the weather like?
Were there problems?
What happened?
When did you get home?

I went to the hills near Detmold last April. Two friends went with me. We had some chicken sandwiches and cans of …

SITUATIONS

Wie sagst du auf Englisch, dass …

1 … du etwas selbst überprüft hast?
2 … ihr euch gut amüsiert?
3 … jemand gut auf sich aufpassen soll?
4 … du nächste Woche eine Freundin besuchen wirst?
5 … jemand geradeaus fahren soll?
6 … jemand an der Ampel links abbiegen soll? Tip: Look again at pages 30-37.

WORDPOWER

WORDPOWER 1 ■ Find ten road words.

WORDPOWER 2 ■ What's the wrong word in the group?

1 trail, road, tourist, interstate
2 church, hotel, motel, youth hostel
3 football, hiking, basketball, baseball
4 milk, water, gas, lemonade
5 snow, ice, temperature, canyon
6 hungry, thirsty, fit, tired
7 metre, litre, gallon, gram
8 day, spring, night, evening

WORDPOWER 3 ■ Tell an American about Germany.

1 The Ruhr, the Spree and the Oder are …
2 *Autobahnen* are like American …
3 *Spezi*, *Apfelschorle* and *Sprudel* are …
4 *Mercedes*, *BMW* and *Audi* are …
5 *Stern*, *Spiegel* and *Bravo* are …
6 *Tagesschau*, *heute* and *Lindenstraße* are …
7 *Niedersachsen* and *Hessen* are like US …
8 *Krakauer*, *Thüringer* and *Knacker* are …

WORDPOWER 4 ■ AE and BE

American people usually say:

fall — movie
store — subway
mom

British people usually say:

…

WORDPOWER 5 ☒ Make a list with the right words.

I	myself
you	yourself / …
	himself
she	
	ourselves
they	

WORDPOWER 6 ■■ Make a word web.

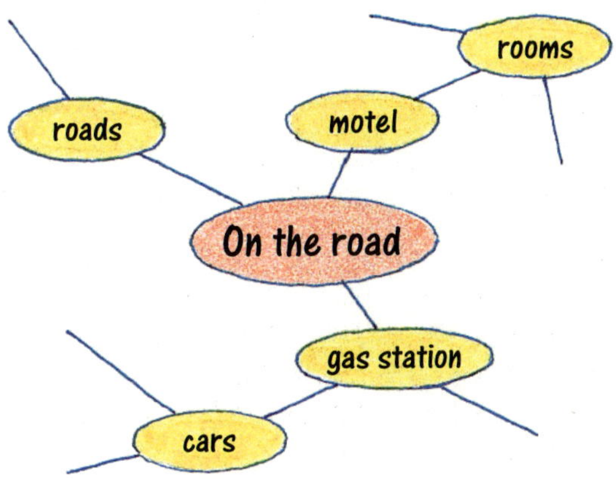

PRACTICE PAGES

READING

BEFORE YOU READ ■ Is this text from a newspaper, a hiking magazine or a tourist brochure?

Route 66

Go west through eight states on America's most famous road: Route 66 from Chicago to Los Angeles.

You can feel America's history on this road. Thousands of Americans went west this way to California. They were looking for land, gold or a new life in the sun.

In the 1950s Route 66 became too small for all the traffic, so they started to build an interstate from Chicago to LA. This was bad news for the motels and gas stations on Route 66.

In 1984, when they opened the last part of the interstate, they took down all the Route 66 signs. It looked like the end of Route 66, a road that nobody used.

But then a group of fans started a Route 66 club and people wrote books about the road. A few tourists used Route 66 and after many years, the signs came back. Now some of the old gas stations that are still open sell Route 66 souvenirs like T-shirts, mugs and posters to tourists.

Every year 10,000 cars drive along Route 66. (You think that's a lot, but it's only about 27 cars a day!) Route 66 is 2,448 miles long and you should plan at least eight days for the trip. Parts of Route 66 have gone, so sometimes you'll have to use the interstate.

But most of the time you'll be on a small, quiet road across the USA – Route 66.

Tip: You can find new words in the *Dictionary* (page 136).

EXERCISE 1 ■ Basic reading: Right or wrong?

1 Route 66 isn't a very long road.
2 Route 66 is closed now.
3 There are fans of Route 66.
4 Tourists use Route 66.

EXERCISE 2 ■ Reading for details: Put the two parts of each sentence together.

1 Route 66	at least eight days for the trip from Chicago to LA.
2 In 1984	it was the end of Route 66.
3 People thought	goes through eight states.
4 But a group of fans	a very busy road.
5 You need	they finished the interstate.
6 Today Route 66 isn't	started a Route 66 club.

EXERCISE 3 ■ Language tasks Tip: All the words are on page 42.

1 Find the opposites: a) east – …; b) everybody – …; c) they closed – …; d) start – …; e) busy – …
2 Find the words in the text for: a) *immer noch;* b) *mindestens;* c) *die meiste Zeit.*

LISTENING *Roy's*

You're going to hear a radio interview with Walt Wilson from Amboy on Route 66. Listen.

EXERCISE 1 ■ Which photo (A-E) comes first? Which photo comes next?

A

B

C

D

E

EXERCISE 2 ■■ Listen again. What's right?

1 Amboy is in (California/Arizona).
2 *Roy's* is (an old / a new) place.
3 Film companies (often/never) come to *Roy's.*
4 You (can/can't) watch TV at *Roy's.*
5 Some Santa Fe trains are (ten/two) miles long.
6 You (can/can't) buy Route 66 mugs at *Roy's.*

Weitere Fragen: W 52

SUMMARY

myself, yourself, themselves, ...

Wörter, die auf *-self*/*-selves* enden, beziehen sich auf die ausführende(n) Person(en) in einem Satz.

He can see himself.

Have you hurt yourself?

I repaired my bike myself.

I → myself	we → ourselves
you → yourself	you → yourselves
he → himself	they → themselves
she → herself	

yourself: bei *einer* Person
yourselves: bei *mehr als einer* Person

- Mit *-self*/*-selves* sagst du, dass jemand etwas für sich, mit sich, usw. tut.

I bought myself a new bike. Ich habe mir ein neues Fahrrad gekauft.
They hurt themselves when they fell. Sie verletzten sich als sie fielen.
We enjoyed ourselves at the party. Wir haben uns auf der Party amüsiert.
Bye. Look after yourselves. Tschüs. Passt gut auf euch auf.

- Mit *-self*/*-selves* kannst du auch sagen, dass jemand etwas selbst tut.

I tidied my room myself. Ich habe mein Zimmer selbst aufgeräumt.
Wendy made the model herself. Wendy hat das Modell selbst gebaut.

Stellung von Orts- und Zeitangaben

Orts- und Zeitangaben stehen oft am Ende eines Satzes.

ORT	ZEIT
at home	at 10 pm
in the park	tomorrow
to the concert	last week

Pat is helping her dad in the garden.
Pat hilft ihrem Vater im Garten.
I can meet you tomorrow.
Ich kann dich morgen treffen.

- Wenn man Ort oder Zeit betonen will, kann die Angabe am Satzanfang stehen.

In Britain you drive on the left. In Großbritannien fährt man links.
Last summer the weather was much better. Letzten Sommer war das Wetter viel besser.

- Manchmal kommen sowohl Orts- als auch Zeitangaben in einem Satz vor.

Dann kommt die **O**rtsangabe vor der **Z**eitangabe. (Im Alphabet kommt O vor Z.)

I'm meeting my friends
at the museum on Sunday.

Can we go to Flagstaff tomorrow? Können wir morgen nach Flagstaff fahren?
The bus arrives in New York at 5 am. Der Bus kommt um 5 Uhr in New York an.

Beachte die unterschiedliche Wortstellung im Deutschen.

* going to

Mit *am/is/are going to* sagst du, was in der Zukunft geschehen wird.

The girls are going to play basketball.
Mark is going to take some photos.

I'm going to meet Jo on Sunday. Ich werde Jo am Sonntag treffen.
It's going to be cold tomorrow. Morgen wird es kalt sein.
I'm not going to have a birthday party. Ich werde keine Geburtstagsparty geben.
Are you going to phone your parents tonight? Wirst du heute Abend deine Eltern anrufen?

IN DIESER UNIT HAST DU GELERNT, ...

… wie du sagst, dass du dich verletzt hast. ➡ *I've hurt myself.*

… wie du sagst, dass du etwas selbst tust. ➡ *I always repair my bike myself.*

… wie du sagst, wo und wann etwas geschah. ➡ *They arrived in Chicago on Monday.*

und wie du auf der Straße

… nach dem Weg fragst. ➡ *How can I get to Sedona?*

… Wegbeschreibungen gibst. ➡ *Turn left at the lights.*

IN DIESER UNIT HAST DU WIEDERHOLT, ...

… wie du sagst, was geschehen wird. ➡ *Troy is going to meet me at the station.*

UNIT THREE

California – the golden state

- What do you think of when you hear "California"?
- Would you like to visit California?
- What would you like to see there?

Most people think of the ocean, the beach and the sun when they hear "California".

There are lots of interesting and beautiful places in California.

Humboldt Redwoods

Mammoth Mountain

Death Valley

TV companies in California make programmes that you can see all over the world.

Fruit grows in California all year.

California has a very important computer industry.

The Spanish were the first Europeans in California. Many names are still Spanish today.

Paseo Nuevo shopping centre, Santa Barbara

In 1849 thousands of people went to California. They were all looking for gold. People still call California the "golden state".

W 22, 1

Free time USA

A Welcome to California and to number 4033 Calle Rosales in Santa Barbara. David Chan (15) and his brother Mike (16) live here. Santa Barbara is 100 miles north of Los Angeles.

Film-makers came to sunny southern California many years ago. They built studios in a place that today is part of Los Angeles – Hollywood. Lots of TV programmes come from California, too. David's favourite TV star, Sandra Heffer, lives in Santa Barbara, but he has never seen her in town. She lives in a big house in the mountains.

David and Mike love living in Santa Barbara. They often go to the beach, even in winter. Their house isn't far from the beach walk – a great place for jogging, cycling, inline-skating – or meeting friends.

? WHAT DO YOU KNOW ABOUT CALIFORNIA?

- Where's California in the USA?
  a) in the north; b) in the west; c) in the east.
- What fruit grows in California?
- The first Europeans in California were
  a) English; b) German; c) Spanish.
- In 1849 many people went to California. They were looking for
  a) sun; b) fruit; c) gold.

Find out:

- Santa Barbara is on an ocean. What's its name?
- What Hollywood films are there in your town this week?

B Here's an Internet page about Santa Barbara.

COME TO SANTA BARBARA, CALIFORNIA

Come to our beaches and go swimming, surfing, windsurfing and sailing. Or go jogging, cycling or inline-skating on our beach walk.
Visit the mountains and try mountain biking and skiing.
Sometimes you can go skiing in the mountains and swimming in the ocean – on the same day!
But there isn't just sport in California. You can visit the Hollywood studios. They aren't very far from Santa Barbara.
Or go shopping in the *Paseo Nuevo*.
The food is fantastic in Santa Barbara. Try Mexican food or have a beach barbecue.

HAVE FUN IN THE SUN!

EXERCISE 1 ■ And in your town?
Tourists can go/try …
They can't go/try …

swimming ▪ surfing ▪ windsurfing ▪ skiing
sailing ▪ inline-skating ▪ hiking ▪ mountain biking

C David sent an e-mail to a friend in San Francisco.

And you should look at the Internet page about Santa Barbara. It's great!
My brother Mike and I are interested in different things. Mike is good at inline-skating and mountain biking. He likes cycling in the mountains behind Santa Barbara. And he loves watching sports on TV. I'm not very interested in sports. Inline-skating is OK, but I'm not very good at it. Cooking is my favorite hobby and all the family like my Mexican food. This evening I'm making tacos, beans and a salad for the family. We're having ice-cream for dessert. But first I'm going to the beach. They're making a TV program on the beach walk this month with my favorite star, Sandra Heffer.

EXERCISE 2 ■ David and Mike are different.

David	is good at	inline-skating.
Mike	isn't good at	mountain biking.
	likes	cooking.
	loves	watching sports on TV.
		cycling in the mountains.

And you?
I'm good at … ▪ I'm not good at …
I like / I don't like … ▪ I love / I hate …

W 22, 2; W 23, 3-4; W 24, 5

✔ CHECKPOINT

Mit der *ing*-Form kannst du über Tätigkeiten sprechen.

Cooking is fun. | Let's go dancing.
I like mountain biking, too. | I'm not good at talking to people.

D

It's Saturday morning. Mike is at the *Paseo Nuevo* shopping centre. He has saved some money and wants to buy some new inline-skating equipment.
He often goes to the *Paseo Nuevo*. There are some good sports shops there and he likes looking at sports equipment.
Sometimes he meets his friends there. They have an ice-cream or a coffee, or they just sit on a bench and talk. And if they don't have any money, they just go window-shopping.

> **And in your town?**
> I meet my friends at/in …
> We often have a coffee/…
> I like looking at …
> I often buy …

E

Now Mike is in one of the sports shops.

MIKE Hi, I'm looking for some knee-pads.
MAN Which knee-pads would you like?
MIKE The green ones in the window look good.
MAN Here you are.
MIKE Thanks. And I'd like a helmet, too.
MAN OK. Try this one.
MIKE It's too small. Do you have a bigger one?

EXERCISE 3 ■ **Make dialogues in shops.**

1 Which shirt would you like? – The white one.
2 Which shorts would you like? – The yellow ones.
3 Which …?
4 … 5 … 6 …

W 24, 6

CHECKPOINT

one/ones

That's our house. The small one on the left.
Which helmet would you like? – The red one.
My jeans are too small. I need some new ones.
Which are your CDs? – The ones on the table.

F David is having a barbecue on his sixteenth birthday next weekend. He's at the supermarket and he's thinking about the things he needs.
All the people David knows love eating outside. So he's sure a lot of friends will be at the barbecue. He hopes a lot of girls will come, too.
The only problem is that girls are usually more interested in his brother Mike …

EXERCISE 4 ■ Barbecues

1 Steak and salad is	the drink	most people like.
2 Nachos are	the dessert	
3 Ice-cream is	the meal	
4 Coke is	the snack	

1 Steak and salad is …
2 … 3 … 4 …

W 24, 7

And in your class?

- Ask questions. *Examples:*
  What food do you like?
  What TV programmes do you watch?
  What magazines do you read?
- What did you find out? *Example:*
  Pizza is the food most people like.

G

✓ CHECKPOINT

Manchmal kann man *who* oder *that* weglassen:

Jane is the girl (who) I met at the party.
Most of the people (who) I know can't come.
Here's the helmet (that) Sarah bought yesterday.
Swimming is a sport (that) lots of people like.

STORY

What <u>isn't</u> Mike good at?

The invitations

At 2 pm Mike and David got to the beach walk. "Hi, Mike," said a girl on a mountain bike. "Hi, Kate," said Mike. "And hi, err …," said Kate. "It's always the same," thought David. "The girls always know Mike. They never know me." Mike and David started skating along the beach walk together. Mike skated with David, but every time he saw a girl he skated fast and did tricks. David was soon fed up, sat on a bench and listened to his walkman.

"Hi! What are you listening to?" A girl was suddenly standing behind David. "*The Strawberries*," he said. "I like them, too. They're great," said the girl. She sat next to David. "Are you at City High School maybe?" she asked. "Yes, I am," said David. "I'm new in Santa Barbara. I'm starting at City High next month. My name is Angela. Do you think I could borrow that cassette?" "Sure. You can take it now and give it back to me at school."

Angela started talking about her family. Her parents lived in San Diego, but she lived with her older sister in Santa Barbara. She didn't really know why she was telling David all these things. He just seemed nice. David thought Angela was nice, too. Then Mike came past. "Wow! He's good," said Angela. David said nothing. Then Mike came past again. "Hey," said Angela. "Do you know that boy over there?" "He's my brother, Mike." "He's fantastic!" said Angela. "I mean, he's very good at skating. What about you?" "I'm OK."

Then Mike stopped in front of the bench. "Hi. I've just seen the people from *Beachwatch*. They're on the beach near State Street." "Yes, I know," said Angela. "Hey, you're a good skater, Mike." "Thanks, but look at this," Mike said. "Skate and jump!" Mike skated away and then he came back. He was jumping very fast from left to right. "Wow!" said Angela. "Not again!" thought David. Mike skated nearer to Angela. "What are you doing this weekend?" Mike asked Angela. "Umm, I'm not sure," said Angela. "Well, what about a barbecue on Sunday? It's David's birthday party." "Yes, OK," said Angela. "What do you think, David?" David looked at her and smiled. "Sure," he said. "Do you like steak and salad?"

On Sunday all David's – and Mike's – friends were at the party. They had lots of fun. The music was great, the weather was great, and everybody enjoyed David's food. Angela danced a lot with Mike, but she often talked to David at the barbecue. They talked about lots of different things.

"My sister is so happy that I have some new friends in Santa Barbara," Angela said to David. "She says I can invite a friend to the house next weekend, so I wanted to ask …" (David thought, "Mike again!") "… so when would you like to come – Saturday or Sunday?"

"Are you talking to me?" asked David.

"Yes, you. And the invitation is *not* for your brother. He can skate, dance and talk – about himself. But he isn't good at listening. And he doesn't like *The Strawberries*."

David laughed. "Now, *that's* a big problem."

Angela laughed, too. "My sister is looking forward to meeting you. You might know her. She's often on TV – Sandra Heffer."

TASK A □ Find the lines that …

1 … explain why David soon sat on a bench.
2 … explain why it's no problem if Angela borrows David's cassette.
3 … show that Mike can skate and jump very well.
4 … show that Mike is interested in Angela.
5 … show that Angela likes David a lot.
6 … explain why Mike doesn't get an invitation.

- Lines 45 to 52
- Lines 79 to 82
- Lines 8 to 10
- Lines 76 to 79
- Lines 23 to 24
- Lines 55 to 58

TASK B ■ Tell the story.

A girl was there. Her name was Angela.
Angela invited David to her house.
Her sister was David's favourite TV star.
Angela told David about her family.
Mike showed Angela his "skate and jump".
Mike invited Angela to David's party.
Mike danced a lot with Angela.
David and Mike went to the beach walk.

TASK C ■■ The two sisters

Angela talked to her sister about the two brothers she met on the beach walk. Write the dialogue, then read it to the class.
Useful words: listen, talk, nice, quiet, good at.

W 25, 8-9

ACTIONS At a friend's house

Adam is staying with his friend Danny Soldano in Los Angeles for the weekend. It's his first morning there.

How can Adam help Danny's father?

MR SOLDANO What would you like for breakfast? We have ham and eggs, beans, cereal, toast.
ADAM Can I have some ham and eggs, please?
MR SOLDANO Yes, of course.
ADAM Can I help you?
MR SOLDANO Yes. Could you set the table, please?

EXERCISE 1 ■ Food and drinks for breakfast

YOU Can I have some …, please?
A PARTNER – Yes, of course.
– Sorry. We don't have any.

W 26, 10

~~ham~~

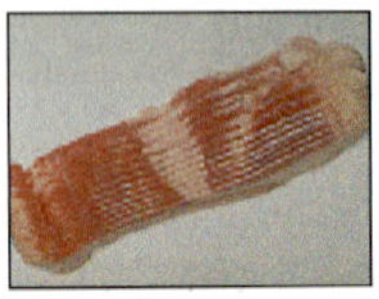
bacon

sausages

eggs

~~beans~~

tomatoes

toast

cereal

~~pancakes~~

orange juice

~~apple juice~~

milk

water

coffee

tea

i BREAKFAST IN THE USA

- A quarter of all Americans eat breakfast in their cars on their way to work. Some people stop to have breakfast at a restaurant or café.
- Most hotels and motels don't have breakfast, so the guests often have to go to a restaurant.
- Many people have a big breakfast when they go to a restaurant. It's usually cheap and you can often drink as much coffee as you want for the same price. Look for the sign "Free refills".
- At home people don't usually have a big breakfast. They often just have cereal. Did you know that the first cornflakes came from the USA?

After breakfast …

What does Adam want to use?

ADAM Can I have a shower, please?
MR SOLDANO Yes, of course. There are towels in the cupboard.
ADAM Thanks. And can I use your hair-drier, please?
MR SOLDANO No problem.

EXERCISE 2 ■ You want to use things at a friend's house. What do you say?

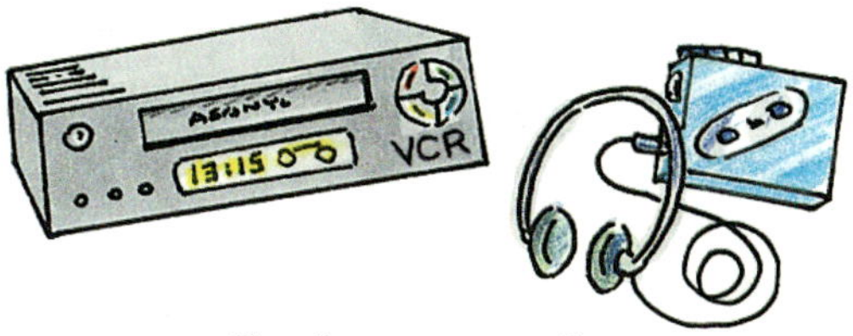

YOU Can I use your …?
A PARTNER – No problem.
– OK. In a minute.

Who's Adam going to phone?

MR SOLDANO Would you like to phone your parents and tell them you're OK?
ADAM That's a good idea. Thanks.

EXERCISE 3 ■ Make dialogues.

Would you like to …

… have a meal / some …?
… phone your parents?
… have a shower?
… watch TV/…?
… go to the beach/…?
… go to bed?

EXERCISE 4 □ Make a dialogue at a friend's house.

Frage, was er/sie zum Frühstück möchte.
▼
Frage, ob du Toast haben kannst.
▼
Sage, dass das natürlich in Ordnung ist.
▼
Frage, ob du duschen darfst.
▼
Sage ja. Es sind Handtücher im Schrank.

Tip: The phrases are on pages 54/55.

EXERCISE 5 ■■ Make a dialogue at a friend's house.

Frage, wo es Handtücher gibt.
▼
Sage, dass sie im Schrank im Badezimmer sind.
▼
Frage, ob du deine Mutter in Deutschland anrufen darfst.
▼
Sage, dass das kein Problem ist.
▼
Sage danke. Du willst ihr sagen, dass es dir gut geht.

W 26, 11

* ACTIVE ENGLISH OPTIONS

* CONTEXTS Free time in Santa Barbara

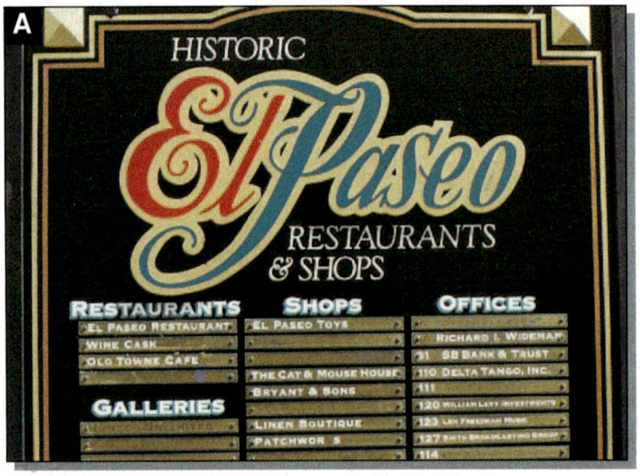

Can you find the right photos (A-G)?

1 You can have a coffee and surf the Internet here.
2 A great place if you like pop music.
3 Children don't have to pay in this museum.
4 Are you interested in natural history? This is the place for you.
5 Find out about life under water here.
6 This shopping centre has fantastic restaurants and shops.
7 What are you doing at the weekend? Would you like to see an exciting film?

* SONG California dreamin'

All the leaves are brown,
And the sky is grey.
I've been for a walk,
On a winter's day.
I'd be safe and warm,
If I was in LA.
California dreamin',
On such a winter's day.

Stopped into a church,
I passed along the way.
Got down on my knees,
And I pretend to pray.
You know the preacher likes the cold,
He knows I'm gonna stay.
California dreamin',
On such a winter's day.

Musik u. Text: J. Phillips u. M. Gillian

* CLASS PROJECT Star posters

Make posters about your favourite stars from TV, films, pop music, sports.

Each poster should have this information:
- basic information about the star,
- other information about the star.
  For example:
  - Where does he/she live?
  - How old is he/she?
  - What does he/she like doing?
  - What has the star done/won?

Don't forget a photo.

* ACTION CARDS At a friend's house

Make action cards with useful words and phrases from this unit.

PRACTICE PAGES

STRUCTURES

EXERCISE 1 ■ Parents!

one ▪ ones

1 Don't buy a big ice-cream. (small)
  Buy a small one.
2 Don't wear your red jeans. (black)
  Wear your black …
3 Don't have a cold drink. (hot)
4 Don't buy expensive trainers. (cheap)
5 Don't use those old glasses. (new)
6 Don't invite loud friends to your party. (quiet)

EXERCISE 2 ■ Make sentences about this unit.

1 Angela is the girl	Angela has invited to her sister's house.
2 Inline-skating is the sport	David likes.
3 City High is the school	all the girls know.
4 Mike is the boy	Angela goes to now.
5 David is the boy	David often watches on TV.
6 And her sister is the star	Mike enjoys.

EXERCISE 3 □ What do they like?

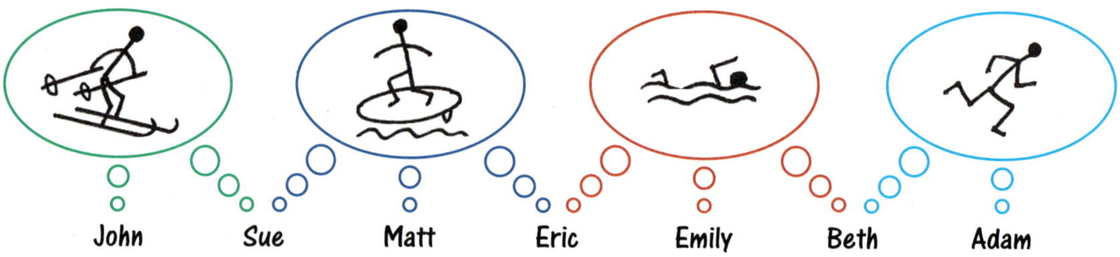

1 John likes skiing. 2 Sue likes skiing and surfing. 3 Matt likes … 4 … 5 … 6 … 7 …

EXERCISE 4 ■ Summer jobs: Mike is/isn't good at …

Example:
Mike is good at looking …

EXERCISE 5 ■■ Write about a partner's hobbies.

First ask questions.
Examples: What are you good at?
What do you enjoy doing?
What would you like to try?

Then write a report.
Examples: Daniel is good at running.
He enjoys playing football, too.
He'd like to try windsurfing.

SITUATIONS

Wie sagst du auf Englisch, dass …

1 … das Essen fantastisch ist?
2 … Kochen Spaß macht?
3 … du nicht sicher bist?

Wie fragst du auf Englisch, …

4 … welche Fernsehsendungen sich jemand anschaut?
5 … wann jemand kommen möchte?
6 … ob du duschen darfst?

Tip: Look again at pages 48-55.

WORDPOWER

WORDPOWER 1 □ What's the right word?

1 California is a big *state/star*.
2 It's in the *west/best* of the USA.
3 Film-makers moved to *silly/sunny* southern California.
4 California is famous for *beaches/benches*.
5 Wear a *headache/helmet* when you cycle.
6 Buy your sports *department/equipment* here.
7 You can meet your *fast/favourite* stars.
8 Here's an *invitation/exhibition* to my party.

WORDPOWER 2 ■ … and …

cents ▪ eggs ▪ Europeans ▪ knee-pads
salad ▪ sit ▪ south ▪ swimming
thirsty ▪ west

1 north and *south*
2 east and …
3 Americans and …
4 surfing and …
5 steak and …
6 helmet and …
7 stand and …
8 ham and …
9 dollars and …
10 hungry and …

WORDPOWER 3 ■ A German in California

In 1849 (nothing/nobody) was more important in California than gold. People sold (everything/nothing) to pay for the journey there. Life in California was very hard. But there was (somebody/something) from Germany who made things easier for people. First he tried selling tents. But (somebody/nobody) wanted them. Then he saw that there was (anything/something) different that people needed – good clothes for work. So he made jeans. Soon (nobody/everybody) wanted his jeans. Today there isn't (something/anything) that's as popular with young people as jeans. And there isn't (anybody/anything) who doesn't know the German's name – Levi Strauss. What's the name of these famous jeans?

WORDPOWER 4 □ Write the hobbies.

cook ride read
skate sing travel
walk swim hike
run dance surf

reading	ri<u>d</u>ing	swim<u>m</u>ing
…	…	…

WORDPOWER 5 ■■ Make a word web.

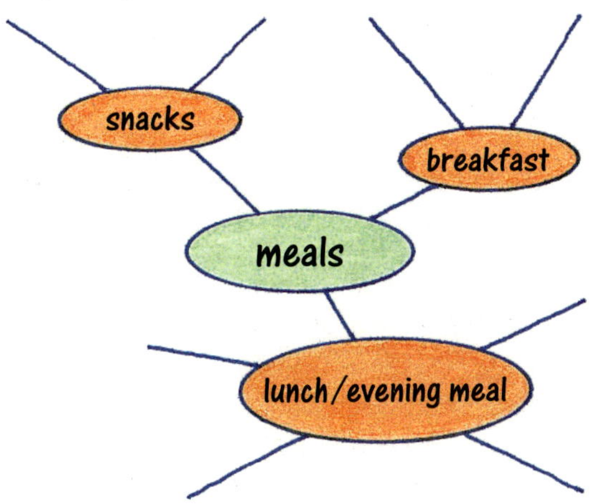

READING

BEFORE YOU READ ■ **Do you think this really happened?**

The Marathon of Hope

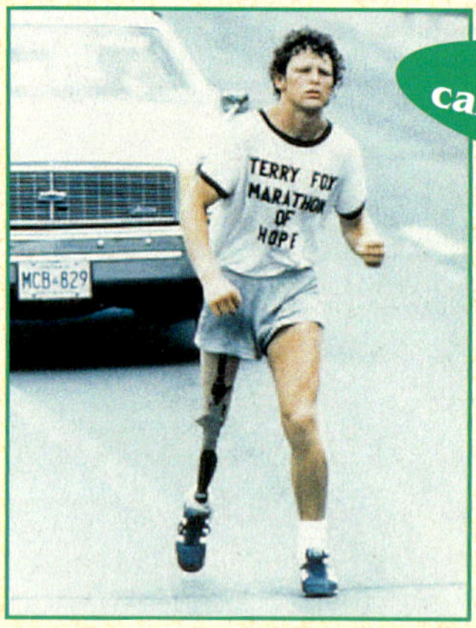

Run for cancer research!

Terry Fox was a student who really enjoyed sports. Basketball was his favourite sport and he was a really good player. Life looked great for Terry.

When he was 18 years old, he felt a pain in his right knee. First he thought he was just training too hard. But when the pain didn't stop, he visited a doctor. He found out that he had cancer. Four days later the doctors amputated his right leg.

Terry was in a hospital bed for a long time. But he didn't give up. "I can still do sports," he thought. "I still have two arms, my left leg and a false right leg." He could run a marathon and collect money for cancer research. But he didn't want to just run a 42 km marathon. He wanted to run across Canada, from the Atlantic Ocean to the Pacific Ocean. Terry called this the Marathon of Hope.

When he came out of hospital, he started to train – first in a wheelchair. Then, after two years, he ran! On April 12th, 1980 he left St. John's, a town on the Atlantic. Lots of people waited along the road to see him. And every day the TV and radio had news about where he was.

But after 143 days and 5,565 km, Terry had to stop his run in Thunder Bay. The cancer was in other parts of his body. A year later, Terry Fox died. His Marathon of Hope made 24 million dollars for cancer research.

And now, every year on the second Sunday in September, people all over the world do Terry Fox Runs (3, 5, 10 km) for cancer research.

Why don't you run with them?

Tip: You can find new words in the *Dictionary* (page 136).

EXERCISE 1 ■ Basic reading: What's right?

1 The brochure is about a famous *man/woman.*
2 Terry Fox ran in *Canada / the USA.*
3 Doctors amputated Terry's *arm/leg.*
4 After he got cancer Terry Fox *ran / never ran* again.
5 Terry *finished / didn't finish* the Marathon of Hope.
6 There *are still / aren't any* Terry Fox Runs now.

EXERCISE 2 ■ Reading for details: *Right, Wrong* or *Not in the text*?

1 Terry Fox liked basketball.
2 He felt a pain in his left knee.
3 He knew lots of people who had cancer.
4 He wanted to collect for cancer research.
5 His run made 24 million dollars.
6 Today Terry Fox Runs are 42 km long.

EXERCISE 3 ■ Language tasks Tip: All the words are on page 60.

1 Find: a) a sport; b) two oceans; c) three parts of the body.
2 Find the words for: a) *Krebsforschung;* b) *Schmerz;* c) *amputieren;* d) *Rollstuhl;* e) *Körper.*

LISTENING Technology at work

You're going to hear some interviews.
A reporter is asking people how technology has helped them in their work. Listen.

EXERCISE 1 ■ Which photo (A-E) comes first? Which photo comes next?

EXERCISE 2 ■■ Listen again. What's right?

1 Work in supermarkets (is/isn't) easier now.
2 This woman (has / doesn't have) e-mail.
3 A (dishwasher/man) washes up in this café.
4 Technology helps this man in his (car/office).
5 Computers (can/can't) fly planes all the way.

Weitere Fragen: W 53

SUMMARY

ing-Form

Mit der *ing*-Form kann man über Tätigkeiten und Hobbys sprechen.

Swimming is fun.

I like watching films.

- Die *ing*-Form steht oft am Anfang des Satzes:

Inline-skating and tennis are my hobbies. Inline-Skating und Tennis sind meine Hobbys.
Windsurfing can be very exciting. Windsurfen kann sehr spannend sein.

- Nach den Verben *like, enjoy, try* folgt oft die *ing*-Form:

I like running. Ich laufe gern.
I enjoy dancing, too. Ich habe auch Spaß am Tanzen.
You can try sailing in Santa Barbara. Man kann in Santa Barbara das Segeln ausprobieren.

- Auch nach *good at* findet man häufig die *ing*-Form:

Sally is good at singing. Sally ist gut im Singen.

one/ones

Mit *one/ones* kann man Wortwiederholungen vermeiden.

Which helmet would you like,
the red one or the green one?

These knee-pads are terrible.
I need some new ones.

- Im Deutschen verzichtet man einfach auf die Wiederholung des Substantivs. Im Englischen ersetzt man das Substantiv durch *one* (Singular) bzw. *ones* (Plural).

Which cake would you like? – The big one! Welchen Kuchen möchtest du? – Den großen!
That's our cat, the black one over there. Das ist unsere Katze, die schwarze dort drüben.
Tim collects stamps. He has lots of German ones. Tim sammelt Briefmarken. Er hat viele deutsche.
Which are Sue's books? – The ones on the table. Welche sind Sue's Bücher? – Die auf dem Tisch.

who/that

Mit *who/that* kannst du weitere Auskünfte über eine Person oder eine Sache geben.

Heike has friends who live in New York.
Jim is the boy who invited me to the party.

Kate has a camera that takes great photos.
Phil has given me a radio that doesn't work.

- Manchmal kann man *who/that* weglassen, und der Satz bleibt trotzdem verständlich.

That's the teacher (who) we all like.

Here's the sweatshirt (that) I bought last week.

Is that the girl (who) you met at the party?
Ist das das Mädchen, das du auf der Party kennen gelernt hast?
I like the people (who) we visited last year.
Ich mag die Leute, die wir letztes Jahr besucht haben.
This is the guitar (that) I got for my birthday.
Das ist die Gitarre, die ich zum Geburtstag bekommen habe.
Here's the salad (that) I made for the barbecue.
Hier ist der Salat, den ich für das Grillfest gemacht habe.

IN DIESER UNIT HAST DU GELERNT, ...

... wie du über Tätigkeiten sprichst.	➡ *Swimming is fun. I like skiing, too.*
... wie du sagst, dass du gut in etwas bist.	➡ *I'm good at running.*
... wie du Wortwiederholungen vermeidest.	➡ *Which is your computer? – The old one. The blue T-shirts are nicer than the black ones.*
... wie man (ohne *who/that*) weitere Auskünfte über eine Person oder Sache gibt.	➡ *That's the girl I met at school yesterday. Buy the same sweets you bought last week.*
wie du bei jemandem zu Hause	
... um etwas bittest.	➡ *Can I have a shower, please? Can I use your hair-drier, please?*
... etwas anbietest.	➡ *What would you like for breakfast? Would you like to phone your parents?*

UNIT FOUR

National parks in the USA

- Have you ever visited a national park?
- What can you see in a national park?
- What can you do there?

There are 49 national parks in the USA.

Everglades

Some of the parks are very big. Yellowstone is 100 km from north to south and 90 km from east to west.

National parks protect nature and are a safe home for animals.

Rocky Mountains

Big Bend

National parks are tourist places, too.

Lots of people hike, canoe and do other activities. Others only drive through the parks in their cars.

Tourists often stay at camp-sites. Some of these are in the backcountry, away from roads and traffic.

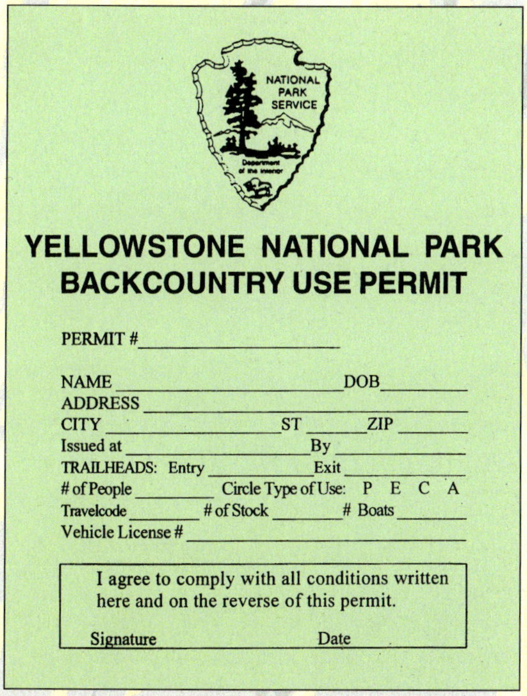

NATIONAL PARK SERVICE

YELLOWSTONE NATIONAL PARK
BACKCOUNTRY USE PERMIT

PERMIT # ____________

NAME ____________ DOB ______
ADDRESS ____________
CITY ____________ ST ______ ZIP ______
Issued at ____________ By ____________
TRAILHEADS: Entry ____________ Exit ____________
# of People ______ Circle Type of Use: P E C A
Travelcode ______ # of Stock ______ # Boats ______
Vehicle License # ____________

I agree to comply with all conditions written here and on the reverse of this permit.

Signature ____________ Date ____________

If you want to hike to a backcountry camp-site, you'll need a permit.

Rangers work in the national parks. You can get information from them at ranger stations. The rangers help to protect the animals from the people and the people from the animals.

W 32, 1

Yellowstone

A "Tents, food, camera. I think we have everything. Come on, you two. We only have till Monday."
Rachel Brown (16) and her brother Matt (14) from Miles City, Montana, got into the car with their parents. It was the Friday afternoon of a holiday weekend and they were going to Yellowstone National Park.

On Friday evening they arrived at the park entrance. They paid the ranger there and drove through the park. It was 54 miles from the entrance to Fishing Bridge camp-site.

After half an hour the Brown family stopped their car and enjoyed the nice view. They could see mountains and trees – and a river. The park was very busy. Lots of other families were there for the holiday weekend.

Rachel and Matt had their own plans. They didn't want to stay at Fishing Bridge camp-site all weekend. They wanted to hike into the backcountry and camp there for a night – away from people, roads and cars. But their parents didn't know about this idea!

WHAT DO YOU KNOW ABOUT NATIONAL PARKS?

- Do you know the names of these national parks? OAINUSNTM YKORC; GIB DENB; RDAGN NNCOYA; LEOSLTWEOYN; VGEEADLRSE.
- What states is Yellowstone National Park in?
- What do you need if you want to hike to a backcountry camp-site?
- What do you call people who work in the national parks?

Find out:

- What are the names of some other national parks in the USA?
- What are the names of three animals you can find there?

B It's Saturday morning. The Browns have spent their first night in Yellowstone National Park. Mr Brown has just come back from the ranger station.

RACHEL Dad! Matt and I have an idea.
MR BROWN What idea?
RACHEL Well, you've often told us about the backcountry …
MR BROWN Yes?
MATT … and we've never been to the backcountry, so …
MR BROWN You want to go there.
OK. We'll leave this afternoon.
RACHEL What?
MR BROWN I've just been to the ranger station. Here are our permits – for four people and two tents.
MATT Hey, that's great!

EXERCISE 1 ■ What has Mr Brown done this morning?

1 been / to the ranger station / has / He
He has been to the ranger station.
2 talked / He / to a ranger / has
3 has / backcountry permits / organised / He
4 He / some brochures / read / has
5 bought / He / some hiking maps / has
6 He / about / animals in the park / found out / has

C

MATT Have you ever seen a grizzly bear, Dad?
DAD Yes, I have. When I was a teenager, I often came to Yellowstone.
RACHEL Yes, but have you ever been really near a bear?
DAD Well, no. But don't worry. I've read lots of brochures about bears.

EXERCISE 2 ■ A poster about Yellowstone

camped ▪ canoed ▪ hiked
seen ▪ tried ▪ visited

Come to Yellowstone National Park

- See grizzly bears.
- Camp in the backcountry.
- Canoe on Yellowstone Lake.
- Hike along a trail.
- Try mountain biking.
- Visit the park in winter.

You're Rachel. Ask your father questions.
1 Have you ever seen grizzly bears?
2 Have you ever …?
3 … 4 … 5 … 6 …

Ask a partner.
Have you ever seen a bear / hiked 20 km / …?
– Yes, I have. / No, I haven't.

W 32, 2; W 33, 3

CHECKPOINT

Was (soeben, schon einmal, oft, noch nicht) geschehen ist:
I've often been to the backcountry.
Mr Brown has just asked the ranger for a permit.
I haven't read this brochure about bears.
Have you ever been to the USA?

D Rachel and Matt are talking to Daniel and Susan Dobson, two teenagers who are staying at Fishing Bridge camp-site, too.

RACHEL Hi! Where are you from?
DANIEL Oh, we're from Cody – it's about an hour from here.
MATT Well, we're from Chicago, but we live in Miles City now. We've lived there since last December.
SUSAN We've lived in Cody for 15 years …
Have you seen the backcountry?
MATT No, but we're going to hike there today.
SUSAN Oh, we've often been there.
RACHEL Have you ever seen a bear?
SUSAN Of course.

EXERCISE 3 ■ *For* and *since*

1 Sam, New York, twelve years
Sam has lived in New York *for* twelve years.
So he has lived there *since* …
2 Pat, Chicago, three years
3 Al, San Francisco, seven years
4 Sarah, Dallas, three years
5 Jim, Washington, two years
6 Diana, Boston, five years

EXERCISE 4 ■ *For* or *since*?

1 I've known Jim for 50 years.
2 These jeans have been famous … 1850.
3 Joe Fox has played for the *Bears* … five years.
4 Alan has had a cold … Tuesday.
5 Karen has lived in San Francisco … ten years.
6 Yellowstone has been a national park … 1872. W 34, 4

And you?
I'm from …
Our family has lived in … since …
I've lived in … for … years.

CHECKPOINT

For **(= Wie lange?):**
I've lived in Germany for three years.
She has known Frank for seven months.

Since **(= Seit wann?):**
I've worked in this shop since January.
He has been here since two o'clock.

 since last December; for 15 years

E After seven hours in the backcountry the Browns arrived at the camp-site. Rachel and Matt were very tired.

MR BROWN Haven't you two pitched your tent yet? We've pitched ours. I'll help you with yours now.
RACHEL It's OK, Dad. We're just tired. We're going to pitch ours later.
MATT And my feet hurt, Dad.
MR BROWN Well, mine hurt, too, Matt. Come on. This trip was your idea.
MATT Not just mine. It was your surprise. Remember?

EXERCISE 5 ■ Find words in the dialogue that mean …

1 … your tent – *yours*.
2 … our tent – …
3 … my feet – …
4 … my idea – …

F Rachel and Matt pitched their tent. It didn't look as good as their parents' tent. Theirs looked much better. Matt wasn't very happy. His feet still hurt and he was very tired. There were other problems, too. His penknife was still at the first camp-site. Mr Brown said he could use his, but Matt still wasn't happy.
And Rachel wanted to borrow Matt's walkman all the time. Hers was broken. But the biggest problem was that Matt didn't think the backcountry was very exciting – lots of boring walking, and no bears!

EXERCISE 6 ■ At the backcountry camp-site

mine ▪ yours ▪ his ▪ hers ▪ ours ▪ theirs

1 "Look. Some more people are here. Those bags under the trees must be …"
2 "My walkman is broken. Can I borrow …, Matt?"
3 "Can I use this penknife?" – "I don't know. Ask dad. It's …"
4 "No penknife? Of course you can use …," said Mr Brown.
5 "Rachel has borrowed my walkman again. … is broken."
6 "Look at your tent, Rachel and Matt! … looks much better," said Mrs Brown. W 34, 5

CHECKPOINT

mine, yours, …

This walkman is mine. It isn't yours.
Your tent is new. Ours is very old.
These aren't Mike's knee-pads. His are new.
Our parents' tent? The blue one is theirs.

STORY

Black bears and grizzly bears – how are they different?

Nobody knows everything

Everything was quiet at the backcountry camp-site, but Rachel was still awake. She was reading a brochure about bears.

"Matt! Matt!" she said.

"What's the matter? I was almost asleep."

"Where did you put the food?"

"It's here, in my backpack."

"Oh, Matt! Mom put a rope between the two trees behind the tents. We have to hang the food from it."

"Why?"

"Bears will come to the tent if they know that they can find food here – and then we'll have a problem."

"OK, OK," Matt said. "I'll do it now. But I don't know why. There are no bears in the boring backcountry. I think the rangers only tell people about bears so that tourists will come to the park."

Matt left the tent and hung his backpack from the rope. When he got back, his sister was already asleep.

"Now I'm awake," he thought. "And my feet still hurt. What a terrible day!"

In the morning the family started to hike back. Rachel was talking to her mother and father. Matt was walking slowly behind them. He was reading the brochure about bears.

"I don't know why Matt is so quiet," Rachel said. "He isn't even looking at the view."

Mr Brown looked at her and smiled.

"I think I know why he isn't happy. He doesn't think this trip is exciting. All he has are feet that hurt. Poor Matt!"

Then they saw it – and it saw them. A very big bear!

"Matt! Stay where you are! There's a grizzly in front of us," said Mrs Brown.

"We have to be very quiet," Mr Brown said.

"I know," said Rachel. "And we have to walk backwards very slowly."

They started to move backwards. The bear watched them very carefully.

"Ouch!" It was Matt. Mr Brown was standing on his foot. "What are you doing there, Matt? Why didn't you move backwards with us?"

"I wanted to look at the bear," said Matt.

"We aren't in a zoo," said Mrs Brown. "Now, come on."

At that moment the bear got up on its hind legs.

"What's it doing?" said Rachel.

"It's trying to find out who or what we are," said Matt. "We have to talk quietly to it."

"Nice bear, nice bear." But the bear didn't want to be nice. It started to walk towards the family.

"It's going to attack," said Rachel.

"Yes," said Mr Brown. "It's big, so it must be a grizzly. All we can do now is play dead. We have to roll ourselves up into a ball."

The bear was getting very near.

"It isn't a grizzly," said Matt. "It's big. But look at its back. It doesn't have a hump. So it must be a black bear."

"Hey, you're right," said Rachel. "Give me that rock next to you, Matt."

Matt gave Rachel the rock and she threw it. The bear ran away.

"We were very lucky," said Mr Brown. "What you did was very dangerous, Rachel. You shouldn't throw anything at a bear. If it attacks, you should play dead."

"Only if it's a grizzly bear," said Rachel. "Matt saw that the bear was a black bear. If a black bear attacks, you should try to frighten it."

"Sorry," said Mr Brown. "You know more about bears than me."

"That's OK, Dad," laughed Matt. "Nobody knows everything – not even you!"

"Now we can tell Daniel and Susan that we've seen a bear, too," said Rachel.

"Do you mean the brother and sister from Cody?" asked Mrs Brown. "Their mother told me that they've never been to the backcountry. And they've never seen a bear, except from the car."

TASK A □ What's wrong with the sentences?

1 Only Rachel and Matt went to the backcountry.
2 Mrs Brown put a rope between the two tents.
3 Matt was reading a brochure about camping.
4 Matt threw a rock at the bear.
5 Mr Brown knew it was a black bear.
6 Daniel and Susan have often been to the backcountry.

TASK B ■ Find the five most important things in the story.

1 The Browns were in the backcountry.
2 Matt hung his backpack from the rope.
3 Rachel spoke to her parents.
4 The family saw a bear.
5 It was a *black* bear.
6 Matt was standing on his father's foot.
7 Rachel threw a rock at the bear.
8 The bear ran away.
9 Mr Brown said, "Sorry."

TASK C ■■ What did the bear tell its family? Tell the bear's story.

These words can help you: backcountry, look for food, nothing, see family, attack, girl, rock, run away.

W 35, 6-8

ACTIONS In a national park

Why is Dave at a ranger station?

DAVE I'd like to book a camp-site, please.
RANGER For how long?
DAVE Two nights. From tonight to Sunday.
RANGER How many people?
DAVE Three.
RANGER And how many tents?
DAVE One.
RANGER You're very lucky. You usually have to book before you come. But you can stay at the Fishing Village camp-site.

EXERCISE 1 ■ Make dialogues: Book camp-sites.

YOU I'd like to book a camp-site, please.
RANGER For how long?
YOU … nights. From … to …
RANGER How many people?
YOU …
RANGER How many tents?
YOU …

W 36, 9

i SOME WARNINGS IN YELLOWSTONE

Buffaloes
Don't go near a buffalo. Buffaloes are very big. They can run very fast.

Hot water
The water in some pools is really hot. Don't put even a finger in the water!

Falling trees
Dead trees can fall without warning. So always be careful!

Is it going to be warm?

MEIKE I'd like some information about fishing in the park.
RANGER Here's a brochure.
MEIKE Thanks. What's the weather forecast?
RANGER It's going to be sunny – 81 degrees.
MEIKE What's that in Celsius, please?
RANGER 27 degrees.

F Fahrenheit	C Celsius
32	0
50	10
59	15
61	16
68	20
77	25
81	27
86	30

EXERCISE 2 ■ Make more dialogues.

YOU I'd like some information about … in the park.
A PARTNER Here's a brochure.
YOU Thanks. What's the weather forecast?
A PARTNER It's going to be … – … degrees.
YOU What's that in Celsius, please?
A PARTNER … degrees.

camping
cloudy: 59°F

boat trips
sunny: 68°F

hiking
rainy: 61°F

cycling
hot: 86°F

canoeing
cold: 50°F

EXERCISE 3 □ Make a dialogue at a ranger station.

Sage, dass du einen Zeltplatz reservieren möchtest.
▼
Frage, für wie lange.
▼
Sage, für eine Nacht, von Montag auf Dienstag.
▼
Frage nach der Anzahl der Personen.
▼
Ihr seid zu viert.

Tip: The phrases are on page 72.

EXERCISE 4 ■■ Phoning a ranger station: Make a dialogue.

Sage, dass du gerne Informationen übers Zelten im „Hinterland" hättest.
▼
Sage, dass es viele Zeltplätze gibt, aber man sollte buchen.
▼
Frage, ob du eine Genehmigung brauchst.
▼
Sage ja und dass man sie hier bekommen kann.
▼
Frage nach der Wettervorhersage.
▼
Sage, wie das Wetter sein wird.
(Wie? Das kannst du entscheiden.)

W 36, 10

* ACTIVE ENGLISH OPTIONS

* CONTEXTS Signs in a national park

A

B

C

D

E

F

Can you find the right signs (A-F)?

1 Smokey says, "Be careful. There might be a forest fire today."
2 Be especially careful on this road for the next 15 miles.
3 You can camp or make camp-fires only at camp-sites.
4 You can go skiing here, but not all year.
5 Don't forget to put out your camp-fire.
6 Wild animals aren't pets. Don't give them any food.

* POEMS Bears

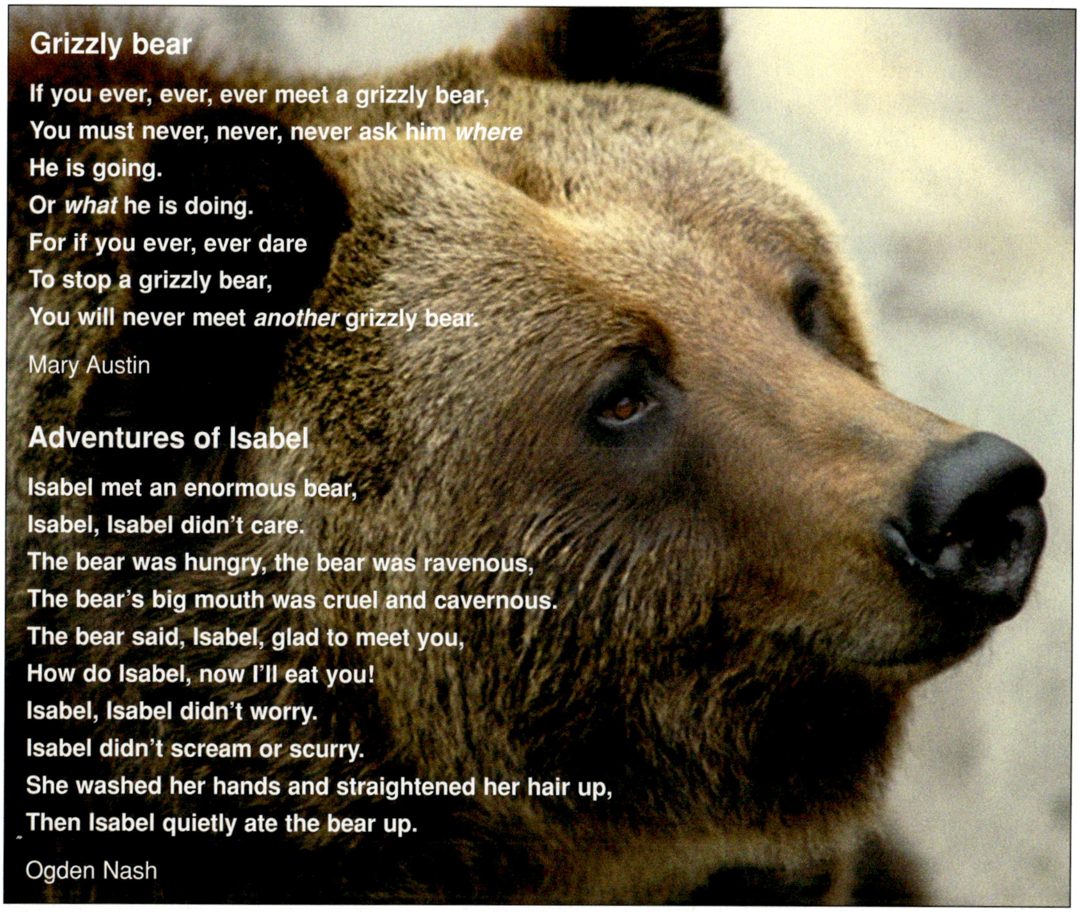

Grizzly bear

If you ever, ever, ever meet a grizzly bear,
You must never, never, never ask him *where*
He is going.
Or *what* he is doing.
For if you ever, ever dare
To stop a grizzly bear,
You will never meet *another* grizzly bear.

Mary Austin

Adventures of Isabel

Isabel met an enormous bear,
Isabel, Isabel didn't care.
The bear was hungry, the bear was ravenous,
The bear's big mouth was cruel and cavernous.
The bear said, Isabel, glad to meet you,
How do Isabel, now I'll eat you!
Isabel, Isabel didn't worry.
Isabel didn't scream or scurry.
She washed her hands and straightened her hair up,
Then Isabel quietly ate the bear up.

Ogden Nash

* CLASS PROJECT Write a poem

Here are two "rhyme boxes":

zoo	do	blue
you	two	view

bear	there	hair
fair	stare	chair

And here's a poem from the "rhyme boxes":

**If you don't know what to do,
Visit the animals in the zoo.
Say "Hallo, buffalo", "Morning, bear",
"What's the weather like in there?"**

- Write a short poem (4 lines).

The first two lines and the last two lines should rhyme.
These "rhyme boxes" will help you to get some ideas.

dead	bed
Fred	said

go	slow
disco	hallo

like	Mike
bike	hike

pop	shop
stop	top

hear	near
year	idea

knee	tree
me	free

* ACTION CARDS In a national park

- Make action cards with useful words and phrases from this unit.

PRACTICE PAGES

STRUCTURES

EXERCISE 1 ■ An interview with a TV star

for ▪ since

1 I've lived in LA … six months.
2 I've been in the *Beachwatch* programme … last year.
3 I've known David Kesselkopf … 1994.
4 And I've worked with him … three years.
5 But I've been a fan of the programme … 1990.
6 Sorry. I've had a headache … an hour. I have to leave now. Goodbye!

EXERCISE 2 ■ What are they saying?

mine ▪ his ▪ hers ▪ ours ▪ theirs ▪ yours

1 This isn't my sock.
– Is it …?

2 Can I borrow your pen?
I've forgotten …

3 Is that the Smiths' tent?
– No, … is blue.

4 Do you have some ketchup?
We've left … at home.

5 Jim's inline-skates aren't as good as Sue's. … are better.

6 Check Mr Dunn's car, please.
– OK. Which one is …?

EXERCISE 3 □ No problems with bears?

been ▪ camped ▪ cooked
hiked ▪ pitched ▪ visited

1 I've often *visited* a national park.
2 I've often … to the backcountry.
3 I've often … 20 miles.
4 … a meal in the backcountry.
5 … a tent.
6 … in a national park.
– And I've never had problems with bears.

EXERCISE 4 ■■ New in the USA

Julia Lammertz has just arrived in California. Lots of things are new for her.

1 (eat tacos) She has never eaten tacos.
2 (visit a national park)
3 (see a film in English)
4 (play baseball)
5 (travel on an interstate)
6 (wear a T-shirt and shorts in December)

EXERCISE 5 ■■ New in Germany

You're from the USA. You've just arrived in Germany.
What things are new? (Write about 6 things.)
I've never eaten/seen/played/…

SITUATIONS

Wie sagst du auf Englisch, dass …

1 … du seit drei Jahren in Deutschland lebst?
2 … du fast geschlafen hast?
3 … ihr viel Glück hattet?

Wie fragst du auf Englisch, …

4 … ob jemand schon einmal in den USA gewesen ist?
5 … was los ist?
6 … wie die Wettervorhersage ist?

Tip: Look again at pages 66-73.

WORDPOWER

WORDPOWER 1 ■ What's the right word?

1 You need a *permit/project* for the backcountry.
2 You must never go near a *dead/date* bear.
3 Let's hike along this *trail/train*.
4 I've walked for 8 hours. My feet *hike/hurt*.
5 A bear! We have to walk *slowly/snowy*.
6 Have you *picked/pitched* your tent yet?
7 We have to leave the camp-site in an hour. Are you *awake/away*, Matt?

WORDPOWER 2 ■ What's the wrong word in the group?

1 remember, teacher, driver, ranger
2 barbecue, snack, meal, table
3 walk, swim, hike, run
4 bear, dog, permit, buffalo
5 his, ours, she, yours
6 temperature, sunny, Celsius, brochure
7 awake, asleep, hungry, rainy

WORDPOWER 3 ■ What's the right word?

Jim Vandermolen works (at/by) Yellowstone National Park. He has been a ranger (for/since) 5 years. He's very interested (at/in) his job. Sometimes he gets very angry (after/with) tourists. They go into the backcountry (outside/without) a permit. They go near the bears or they aren't careful (for/with) their barbecues. Jim is very busy (at/over) the ranger station today. It's the first day (of/up) a long weekend and everybody wants to find out (about/over) the weather, good places for a barbecue, and hundreds (of/from) other things. Jim has been at work (for/since) 9 am today and he'll be there (by/till) 6 pm. Then he can go home and watch TV with his daughter. Her favourite programme is (in/on) TV tonight – *Yogi Bear in Jellystone Park*!

WORDPOWER 4 □ "Ranger bear"? No! Put the right words together.

ranger	bear
grizzly	forecast
national	legs
backcountry	park
hind	station
weather	entrance
park	permit

ranger station, grizzly …

WORDPOWER 5 ■■ Make a word web.

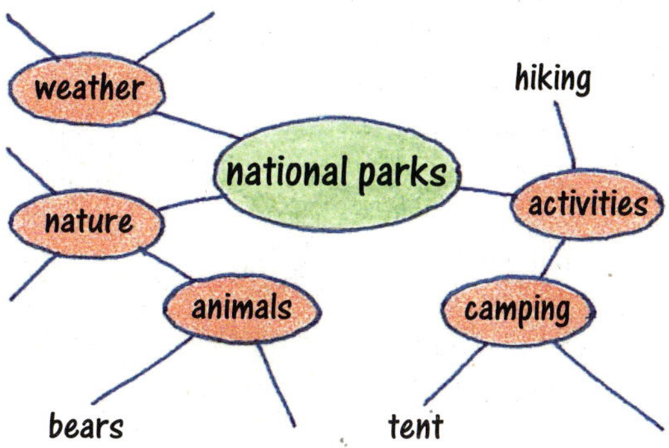

PRACTICE PAGES

READING

BEFORE YOU READ ■ **Is this a brochure for rangers, tourists – or bears?**

You are in BEAR country

Bears are always hungry.

Don't leave food in your tent. For example, you can hang it on a rope between two trees, but it should be 12 feet from the ground. Take your garbage with you. Don't leave it at the camp-site. Bears love garbage.

Bears have a good sense of smell.

Cook away from your tent. Don't use deodorants or perfumes in the backcountry.

Bears don't like surprises.

Most bears will leave if they know you're there. So:
- whistle, talk, sing or have a bell or a can of rocks with you;
- be careful in forests, near loud, fast water or when you're walking into the wind. Bears might not hear or smell you;
- carry a flashlight at night.

If you meet a bear ...

Don't panic, speak quietly to the bear and walk slowly backwards. Never run! Bears can run very fast. Climb a tree if there's one near to you. Put your backpack on the ground. Bears find backpacks interesting.

If the bear attacks ...

Grizzlies: Play dead. Roll yourself up into a ball. Don't move. Don't throw anything.

Black bears: They aren't as dangerous as grizzlies. **Don't** play dead. Frighten the bear – shout or throw something.

Be careful, enjoy your vacation – and good luck!

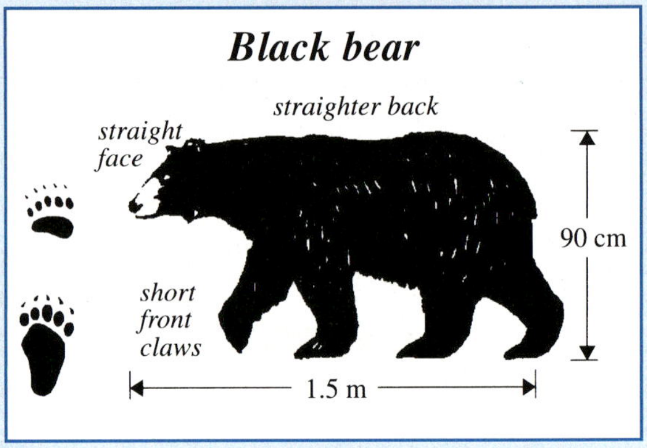

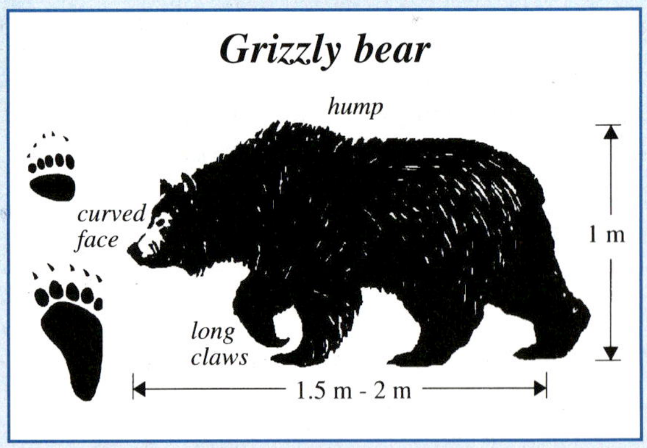

Tip: You can find new words in the *Dictionary* (page 136).

EXERCISE 1 ■ Basic reading: The text is about …

1 … differences between bears.
2 … good places for a holiday in the backcountry.
3 … a TV programme about bears.
4 … what you shouldn't do if you see a bear.
5 … bears in a zoo.
6 … a friendly bear in Yellowstone.

EXERCISE 2 ■ Reading for details: *Yes, No* or *Not in the text*?

1 Bears often attack cars.
2 People should leave garbage at the camp-site.
3 It's good if a bear can hear you.
4 Fast water can be a problem.
5 If you see a grizzly bear, you should throw something.
6 Black bears don't like grizzlies.

EXERCISE 3 ■ Language tasks Tip: All the words are on page 78.

1 Find: a) two things that smell nice; b) the American English words for *torch, rubbish;* c) three things you can do so that bears know you're there.
2 Look at the two last pictures. Find the words for: a) *gerade;* b) *kurz;* c) *Vorder-;* d) *Gesicht;* e) *Krallen.*

LISTENING Radio Yellowstone

Here's Radio Yellowstone. Listen.

EXERCISE 1 ■ Which photo (A-E) comes first? Which photo comes next?

A

B

C

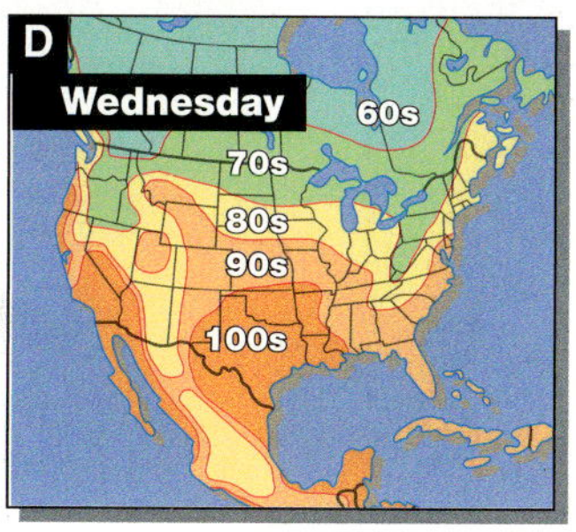

D

E

EXERCISE 2 ■■ Listen again. What's wrong in each sentence?

1 There was a big lake here in 1988.
2 Cold water comes out of Old Faithful.
3 The lake is very warm.
4 A bear came very near a ranger station.
5 It's going to get warmer next week.

Weitere Fragen: W 53

SUMMARY

* Vollendete Gegenwart

Mit dieser Zeitform *(present perfect form)* sagst du, dass jemand etwas getan hat.

Bob has walked ten miles.

I've often been to the USA.

▪ Manchmal willst du betonen, dass etwas *soeben* geschehen ist:
Hi! We've just arrived in Yellowstone. Hallo! Wir sind gerade in Yellowstone angekommen.

▪ Oder du willst sagen, dass jemand etwas schon einmal, oft oder noch nicht getan hat:
I've often hiked in national parks. Ich bin schon oft in Nationalparks gewandert.
I haven't seen a bear yet. Ich habe noch keinen Bären gesehen.

▪ Fragen stellst du mit *have/has*:
Have you ever pitched a tent? Hast du schon einmal ein Zelt aufgestellt?
Has dad organised a permit? Hat Papa schon eine Genehmigung organisiert?

for/since

Mit *for/since* und der *present perfect*-Form sagst du, wie lange *(for)* oder seit wann *(since)* etwas andauert.

You've worked here for 25 years.

Sally has been at the station since 10.00.

▪ *For* verwendest du, wenn es um einen Zeitraum (z.B. *ten minutes*) geht.
I've had this backpack for two months. Ich habe diesen Rucksack seit zwei Monaten.
Jill has played basketball for three years. Jill spielt seit drei Jahren Basketball.

▪ *Since* verwendest du, wenn es um einen bestimmten Zeitpunkt (z.B. *last Friday*) geht.
I've known Amy since 1998. Ich kenne Amy seit 1998.
Jack has been ill since last Tuesday. Jack ist seit letztem Dienstag krank.

mine, yours, ...

Mit *mine, yours* usw. kannst du sagen, wem etwas gehört, ohne das Substantiv zu wiederholen.

Don't wear those old jeans. You can borrow mine.

Is this your ball? – No, it's his.

This sweatshirt isn't mine. It's yours. Dieses Sweatshirt ist nicht meins. Es ist deins.
That isn't Sue's room. This is hers. Das ist nicht Sues Zimmer. Dies ist ihres.
Is your camera broken? You can use ours. Ist eure Kamera kaputt? Ihr könnt unsere benutzen.

Vergleiche:

It's	my your his/her our your their	house.

My, your usw. verwendet man in Verbindung mit einem Substantiv.

It's	mine. yours. his/hers. ours. yours. theirs.

Mine, yours usw. verwendet man hingegen, wenn man das Substantiv nicht wiederholen will.

IN DIESER UNIT HAST DU GELERNT, ...

... wie du sagst, wie lange etwas andauert. ➡ *Kate has lived here for ten years.*

... wie du sagst, seit wann etwas andauert. ➡ *I've worked here since 1998.*

... wie du sagst, wem etwas gehört. ➡ *This isn't yours. It's mine.*

wie du in einem Nationalpark

... einen Zeltplatz reservierst. ➡ *I'd like to book a camp-site, please.*

... um Informationen bittest. ➡ *I'd like some information about hiking.*

... nach der Wettervorhersage fragst. ➡ *What's the weather forecast?*

IN DIESER UNIT HAST DU WIEDERHOLT, ...

... wie du sagst, dass etwas (soeben) geschehen ist. ➡ *They've arrived at the camp-site. I've just seen a bear.*

... wie du fragst, ob etwas (schon einmal) geschehen ist. ➡ *Have you ever hiked 20 miles?*

UNIT FIVE
Texas

- Where is Texas in the USA?
- What do you know about Texas?
- Would you like to visit Texas?

Texas is famous for its cattle ... ... its cowboys ...

... its oil ...

... and its food.

San Antonio is the most popular tourist town in Texas. One million people live there.

Texas was part of Mexico till 1845.

About a hundred years ago many Germans moved to Texas. Some towns in Texas have German names.

Many Hispanics – Spanish-speaking people – live in Texas.

Brownsville is near Mexico.

Here are some students at Simon Rivera High School in Brownsville, Texas.

W 42, 1

High school highlights

A Rick Alvarez finished his breakfast and ran out of the house. He was late for school – again! He got into his car. It was only a small one, but it was better than the school bus!

Rick is 16 and goes to Rivera High School in Brownsville, Texas. He's in the 10th grade. Rick enjoys school. Lessons aren't always fun, of course, but there are so many interesting activities. In the afternoons there are sports – baseball, (American) football, soccer and basketball – and lots of school clubs.

In the evenings, students and teachers sometimes organise dances in the school hall. One of the students is the DJ for the evening. Student bands often play, too.

Rick does lots of different sports at school. And when Rivera High plays football against other schools Rick is usually in the team. He's one of the best football players in the 10th grade.

WHAT DO YOU KNOW ABOUT SCHOOL IN THE USA?

- What can you do at school
  a) in the afternoons? b) in the evenings?
- What's special about American football (a, b or c)?
  a) Players wear helmets.
  b) Players never play outside.
  c) Players don't throw the ball.

Find the words Americans use for:

- … a school for older students.
- … (European) football.
- … Year 10.

W 42, 2

B Now Rick is driving to school. What's he thinking?

C The traffic on the way to school was terrible. So Rick was very late when he drove into the car park. He saw a grey car. Somebody was getting out of it. It was Sylvia!

RICK Hi, Sylvia!
SYLVIA Hi, Rick. So you're late, too.
RICK Yeah. Late again.
SYLVIA It's too bad that school starts so early. I mean, 7.25 is terrible.
RICK Right. And I sometimes have breakfast in the school cafeteria. So then I'm here at 6.30. – Hey, is this *your* car?
SYLVIA Yes, it was a birthday present.
RICK It's great – much nicer than my old car.
SYLVIA Thanks. Come on. The teachers will give us tardy slips again.
RICK And that means detention.
SYLVIA No long lunch break today.
RICK Yeah. Well, at least we can do our homework.

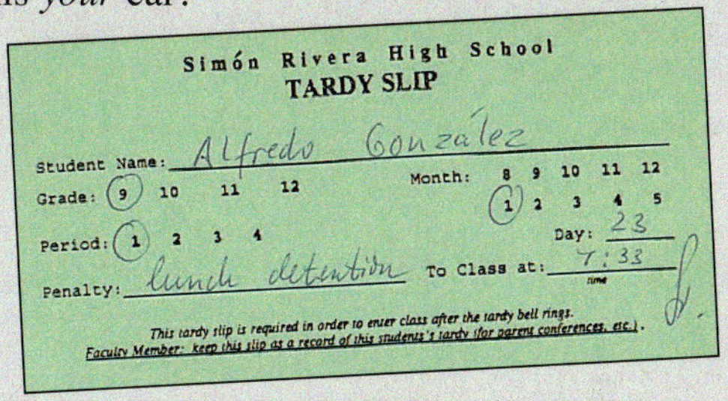
Simón Rivera High School
TARDY SLIP
Student Name: Alfredo González
Grade: (9) 10 11 12
Month: 8 9 10 11 12 (1) 2 3 4 5
Period: (1) 2 3 4
Day: 23
Penalty: lunch detention
To Class at: 7:33 (time)
This tardy slip is required in order to enter class after the tardy bell rings.
Faculty Member: keep this slip as a record of this students's tardy (for parent conferences, etc.).

EXERCISE 1 ■ At Rivera High School

1 If you're 16,	you're late.
2 If you have a car,	you can do your homework in the lunch break.
3 If you don't have breakfast at home,	you can park it in the school car park.
4 If you arrive at school after 7.25,	you can have it in the school cafeteria.
5 If you get a tardy slip,	you can drive a car to school.
6 If you have detention,	you have to go to detention in the lunch break.

1 If you're 16, you can drive a car to school.

And at your school?
If we're early/late/hungry/ill/..., we can/can't/have to ...

W 43, 3-4

CHECKPOINT

***If*-Sätze:**
If Sylvia is in the cafeteria, Tony will talk to her.
If I'm late again, my teacher will be angry.
If our team wins, we'll all be very happy.
If you go to Texas, you must visit San Antonio.

D

Students at Rivera High come from many different places. Rick's parents were born in Mexico, but Rick was born in the USA. Tina Hernandez – she's sitting next to Rick in the photo – is Hispanic, too. Melissa Ryan – she's on the left – is Irish-American. Her family has been in the USA for a long time. Sylvia Lehman's great-great grandparents came to Texas from Germany over a hundred years ago. Sylvia is standing behind Tina.

EXERCISE 2 ■ Where were they born? Tip: Look at Units 1-5.

Brooklyn ▪ Chicago ▪ Flagstaff ▪ Santa Barbara ▪ Mexico

1 Michelle and Steve Wilson were born in …
2 Jennifer Sands was born in …
3 Mr and Mrs Alvarez …
4 David and Mike Chan …
5 Rachel and Matt Watts …

Where were you born?
I was born in Germany/… ▪ I'm German/…
My parents were born in …
Tip: Look at the list on page 155.

E

The students are in the journalism lesson. They're working on the school newspaper. Rick is sitting next to Sylvia. He wants to invite her to the dance. There's just one problem. How should he ask her?

RICK Umm, that's a nice ring, Sylvia.
SYLVIA Yes. It was my grandmother's. It was made in Germany.
RICK Oh really? That's interesting. I like your shoes, too. Er, where were they made?
SYLVIA What? I don't know. Is it important? I'm working on my article, Rick. Let's talk later.

And your things?
My bike/pen/bag/… was made in …
My shoes/jeans/… were made in …

EXERCISE 3 ■ When were they made?

1 The first toaster was made in *1909/1809*.
2 The first CDs were made in *1949/1979*.
3 The first inline-skates … *1960/1990*.
4 The first telephone … in *1876/1976*.
5 The first mountain bike … in *1973/1989*.
6 The first cornflakes … in *1898/1960*.

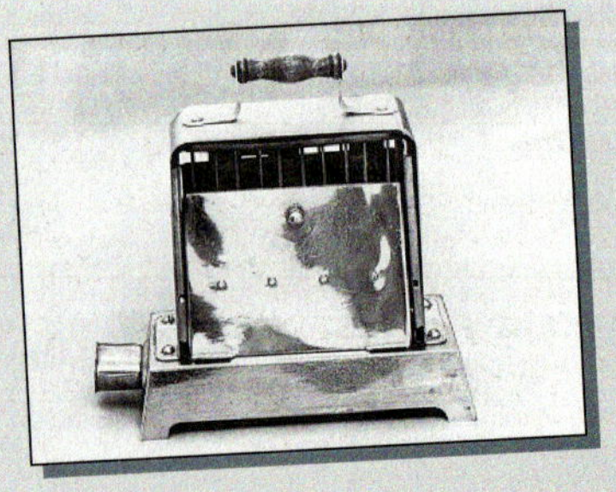

W 44, 5

CHECKPOINT

Wo jemand geboren wurde:
I was born in Berlin.
My parents were born in Izmir.

Wo etwas hergestellt wurde:
My camera was made in Japan.
My trainers were made in Germany.

F There's a great cafeteria at Rivera High. Students can get lots of different food there: full meals and salads, even hamburgers, tacos and fries. Students enjoy the long lunch breaks. They can talk to friends in the cafeteria and get all the news. Somebody always has some interesting gossip.

STELLA You're very quiet today, Tina. Do you have some news for us?
TINA Yeah, Bob Breuer was picked for the football team last night!
BRAD Vince Garcia isn't very happy. He was told the news this morning.
STELLA No, I'm sure he's very unhappy – like poor Tom.
TINA Do you mean Tom Dooley, Haley's boyfriend?
STELLA Haley's *ex*-boyfriend. Haley was seen with Frank Connell at the stadium yesterday, but I'm not going to say who saw them.
KAY Listen. Have you heard the news? Sylvia and Tony split up yesterday. So now Sylvia is looking for another partner for the dance.
TINA No, she isn't. She was invited to the dance ten minutes ago. Do you want to know who invited her? – Rick Alvarez.
STELLA Oh, Tina. I'm so sorry. I know you like Rick.

EXERCISE 4 ■ Find the sentences in the text that mean …

1 … somebody invited Sylvia to the dance ten minutes ago.
2 … a teacher picked Bob for the football team.
3 … somebody saw Haley at the stadium.
4 … somebody told Vince the news.

EXERCISE 5 ■ Things that happened to students

asked ▪ given ▪ picked ▪ seen ▪ taken ▪ told

1 Bob was *told* the good news.
2 Freddy was … to hospital after a football game.
3 Ben and Jerry were … a tardy slip.
4 Tina wasn't … for the team.
5 Ted was … lots of questions in the Spanish lesson.
6 Sylvia and Dawn were … at the shops in school time.

What happened to you last week? – I was/wasn't …
asked difficult questions in the … lesson ▪ given lots of … homework
invited to a party ▪ picked for the … team ▪ taken to the cinema/…

W 44, 6

CHECKPOINT

Aktiv: Was jemand tat	**Passiv: Was mit jemandem geschah**
The teacher asked me lots of questions.	I was asked lots of questions.
The girls invited the boys to the party.	The boys were invited to the party.

STORY

How many messages were there at the gas station? Who were they for?

Would you like to dance?

"Hi, Sylvia. You look fantastic."
"Thanks," said Sylvia. "Let's go now, or we'll be late."
Rick got into Sylvia's car. The two young people looked really good. Sylvia's dress was a present from her parents. And Rick's suit came from a shop in town that hired clothes.
Rick was looking forward to the dance. He knew that Sylvia really wanted to go with Tony. But he was happy that she was his partner for the evening – and maybe for other evenings, too.

"That's nice. Look at that message," Sylvia said. There was a sign outside the Texaco gas station. It said, "Happy birthday, Pam Kelly – the best mom in town."
Rick thought it was silly. People paid the gas station, and their messages were shown for a day or two. "Why don't they just send birthday cards?" he thought.

Sylvia and Rick arrived at Rivera High and went into the school hall with lots of other students. "Hi, Rick. You look nice tonight." It was Tina Hernandez.
"Thanks, Tina," said Rick. "You look good, too. What a cool dress!"
There were great decorations – made by the students, a super buffet – organised by the teachers, and music from three different student bands and "DJ Stella", Stella Arthur from Rick's grade.
Rick was a fantastic dancer. Sylvia was very happy that he was her partner. They danced together for a long time.

And then Rick saw him – Tony. He was standing near the door and watching them. Every time that they danced near Tony, Sylvia looked at him. Rick wasn't very pleased.
Then there was a break. Sylvia and Rick went to their table. Rick went to get some food for himself and Sylvia.

When he came back to the table, Tony was sitting next to Sylvia. "Hey, it's Ricky-boy," said Tony. "I'm dancing with Sylvia from now on. Why don't you go for a walk? Goodbye, Alvarez!" He pushed Rick away.
"Stop it," said Sylvia. "Rick has been really nice to me this evening."
But Rick saw that Sylvia wanted her old boyfriend back. It was silly to start a fight with Tony. And Tony was older and bigger than Rick. Rick left the hall.

In the cafeteria on Monday everybody was talking about the dance. Rick was very quiet. "Cheer up, Rick," said Stella. "We all know what happened. I think Sylvia is making a big mistake. Tony is just playing with her. He isn't the nicest Rivera High student."

"No," said Tina Hernandez. "You're right. There are much nicer students at this school." She looked at Rick, but he didn't see her.

"It's too bad that you didn't stay longer on Saturday, Rick," said Tina. "You're a fantastic dancer! My partner for the evening had two left feet."

Rick laughed. Tina was great fun. She sat next to him in the cafeteria every day that week.

On Friday morning Rick drove past the Texaco gas station. There was a new message outside. Rick read it:

Would you like to dance with me, Rick?

TASK A ☐ **What's missing?**

1. Rick was looking forward to the …
2. Rick and Sylvia saw a … at the gas station.
3. Rick was a fantastic …
4. Rick didn't want to start a … with Tony.
5. Rick was quiet in the … on Monday.
6. Tony isn't the school's nicest …
7. When Rick drove past the gas station, he saw a new …

TASK B ■ **Put the people and the messages together.**

1 Sylvia to Tony: 3 Rick to Sylvia:
2 Tony to Sylvia: 4 Tina to Rick:

- Would you like to dance?
- Stay with him!
- You're the boy for me.
- You're still my girl.

TASK C ■■ **Make more gas station messages.**

Tony to Rick; Sylvia to Rick; Stella to Sylvia; Sylvia to Stella; Rick to Tina.

W 45, 7-10

ACTIVE ENGLISH

ACTIONS Going out

When are Rick and Tina going to meet?

RICK Would you like to go to the next dance with me?
TINA Great idea!
RICK When should we meet?
TINA What about 7.30?
RICK No, that's too late. The dance starts at 7.30. Let's say 7.15.
TINA OK. See you at 7.15 then.

EXERCISE 1 ■ When should you meet for the football game? Make dialogues.

YOU When should we meet?
A PARTNER What about …?
YOU No, that's too late/early. Let's say …
A PARTNER OK. See you at … then.

Brownsville School Football
Porter High against Rivera High
Game starts: 7 pm
Stadium opens: 5 pm

Where does Tina want to meet Rick?

TINA Where should we meet?
RICK What about outside the cafeteria? That's the best place.
TINA Good idea. I'm really looking forward to the dance.
RICK Me, too.

EXERCISE 2 ■ Where should you meet? Make dialogues.

YOU Where should we meet?
A PARTNER What about outside the …? That's the best place.
YOU Good idea. I'm really looking forward to the …
A PARTNER Me, too.

cinema – film
restaurant – meal
stadium – game
disco – music
bus station – trip

i GOING OUT IN THE USA

- In the USA school is an important place for meeting other young people. Students often live miles apart, but school brings them together.
- Students who do sports and go to clubs in the afternoon can go home on school buses.
- Churches often organise youth groups and discos for young people.
- In many US cities young people have to be home before 10 pm.
- In most US states you can't buy alcohol till you're 21.

Why can't Tony go out on Saturday?

SYLVIA Let's go to the concert on Friday evening, Tony.
TONY Sorry. I can't.
SYLVIA That's too bad. Why not?
TONY Er, I have to help my mom at home.
SYLVIA What about Saturday afternoon?
TONY Sorry, I'm playing football on Saturday afternoon.

EXERCISE 3 ■ Make dialogues. Your partner can't go out with you.

YOU Let's go to … on …
A PARTNER Sorry. I can't.
YOU That's too bad. Why not?
A PARTNER I have to …

the cinema ▪ the disco ▪ the football game
the CD shop ▪ the park ▪ the youth club ▪ …

help at home ▪ work in/at … ▪ visit my …
buy … ▪ look after … ▪ finish my …
go to the …

EXERCISE 4 □ Make a dialogue about going out.

Frage, wann ihr euch treffen sollt.
▼
Schlage 7.15 Uhr vor.
▼
Sage, dass das in Ordnung ist. Frage, wo ihr euch treffen sollt.
▼
Schlage vor, dass ihr euch vor dem Restaurant trefft.

Tip: The phrases are on page 90.

EXERCISE 5 ■■ Make a dialogue about going out.

Schlage vor, dass ihr heute Nachmittag ausgeht. *(Wohin? Das kannst du entscheiden.)*
▼
Du kannst nicht. Du musst …
(Was musst du machen?)
▼
Schlage vor, dass ihr heute Abend ausgeht.
(Wohin?)
▼
Sage, dass du … musst.
(Was musst du machen?)
▼
Sage, dass das schade ist. Schlage vor, dass ihr am Wochenende ausgeht.
▼
Reagiere darauf.

W 46, 11-12

* ACTIVE ENGLISH OPTIONS

* CONTEXTS Signs at an American high school

A

B

C

D

E

F

Can you find the right photos (A-F)?

1 In the cafeteria: You can get a meal for one dollar.
2 Outside the school: Don't bring drugs into this school.
3 In the library: Please don't eat or drink here.
4 On the road: Car drivers, be careful! You might have to stop for children.
5 In the classroom: Please follow the classroom rules.
6 Outside the school: Cars can't stop here.

* SONG Deep in the heart of Texas

The stars at night are big and bright,
Deep in the heart of Texas.

The prairie sky is wide and high,
Deep in the heart of Texas.

The sage in bloom is like perfume,
Deep in the heart of Texas.

Reminds me of the one I love,
Deep in the heart of Texas.

Musik: Don Swander, Text: June Hershey

* CLASS PROJECT Dedications

In many American high schools, students make a school yearbook – with news about the school, its students and teachers, about sports and all the other activities.
There are dedications, too – messages from students to other students, to parents and to teachers. And there are messages from parents to students.

Congratulations
L
A
U
R
A
You have brought so much happiness! We love you and are very proud of you.
Mom, Dad, Mariza, Ricardo, & Eduardo
Laura Boone

Make dedications for a "Class Dedications Page". Then copy the page and send it to parents, teachers and friends.

* ACTION CARDS Going out

- Make action cards with useful words and phrases from this unit.

PRACTICE PAGES

STRUCTURES

EXERCISE 1 ■ Going out: What are they thinking?

invite her to the concert ▪ ask her to dance ▪ say "no"
dance ▪ say "yes" ▪ know it's from me

1 If I ask Sylvia, she'll …

2 If Rick asks me, I'll …

3 If I play this song, everybody will …

4 If Stella is at home, I'll …

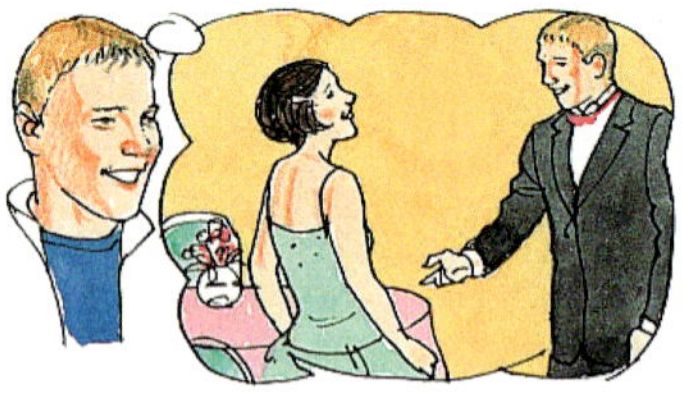

5 If Sylvia is there, I'll …

6 If Rick sees the sign, he'll …

EXERCISE 2 ■■ Parents!

Parents all over the world say the same things. Finish these sentences.

1 If you go to bed late, …
2 If you don't do your homework, …
3 If you don't eat good food, …
4 If you have a cold, …
5 If you eat too much chocolate, …
6 If you watch TV all the time, …
7 If you don't tidy your room, …
8 If you play loud music, …

EXERCISE 3 ■ Here's Beth Fujito.

was born ▪ were born ▪ was made ▪ were made

1 It's my birthday today. I … 15 years ago.
2 My brothers are much younger. They … last year.
3 I got lots of presents. These shoes … in Japan.
4 This new camera … in the USA.
5 It's from my grandparents. They … in Japan. They came to the USA 40 years ago.
6 My parents … here. So they're American.

EXERCISE 4 □ A bad day

1 John wasn't invited	for his work.
2 Paul wasn't picked	for a walk.
3 Sadie wasn't given	to the party.
4 Dave wasn't paid	her pocket-money.
5 Lassie wasn't taken	for the team.

1 John wasn't invited to the party.

EXERCISE 5 ■■ A good day

1 Pete (tell) about his present – a car.
Pete was told about his present – a car.
2 Mo and Jo (send) tickets for a live TV show.
3 Tim's dog (find) in a garage.
4 Gail's story (print) in the newspaper.
5 *The Gumbos'* first song (play) on MTV.
6 The students (give) an easy exercise.

SITUATIONS

Wie sagst du jemandem auf Englisch, dass …

1 … er/sie heute sehr still ist?
2 … er/sie fantastisch aussieht?
3 … er/sie (mit etwas) aufhören soll?

Wie fragst du auf Englisch, …

4 … wo jemand geboren ist?
5 … ob jemand mit dir tanzen möchte?
6 … wo ihr euch treffen sollt?

Tip: Look again at pages 84-91.

WORDPOWER

WORDPOWER 1 ■ What's the word for …

1 … a place where you can watch sports?
2 … the grandparents of your grandparents?
3 … something you wear on a foot?
4 … something you wear on a finger?
5 … something that's wrong?
6 … news about other people (but sometimes it isn't true)?

WORDPOWER 2 ■ Find 5 school words.

G	R	T	U	C	L
↑	A	S	D	T	A
N	D	E	E	N	S
O	T	E	E	T	S
I	E	D	R	E	C
T	N	A	I	F	A

WORDPOWER 3 ■ Gas station signs: One word is wrong. What's the right word?

1
BUY PARTY DETENTIONS AT SAL'S STORE

2
HAVE A VERY HAPPY BURGER, AUNT JANE!

3
HELP! BOY (16) NEEDS A PARTY FOR THE SCHOOL DANCE

4
CLAIRE'S ON 2ND ST HAS BEAUTIFUL EVENING CLASSES

5
PART-TIME JOBS: BE A WATER AT MCBURGER

6
SEND A MISTAKE FROM THIS GAS STATION

1 ~~detentions~~ – decorations

WORDPOWER 4 □ An article for the school newspaper: What's the right word?

Last *month/lunch* was Valentine's Day, February 14th. Students brought *pets/presents* to school. Lots of girls wore red *clothes/gossip* to school and lots of people brought *flowers/fights*. There was a special Valentine's *meal/mile* in the cafeteria. Teachers read *tourists/stories* about boyfriends and girlfriends to students. Everybody enjoyed the *dance/gas* in the evening. Now we're all looking *backwards/forward* to next February!

WORDPOWER 5 ■■ Find the missing words.

Country	… people
…	American
…	Mexican
…	Japanese
Britain	…
Germany	…
…	Irish
…	Scottish
Wales	…
England	…

PRACTICE PAGES

READING

BEFORE YOU READ ■ **Is this a brochure about a school, an invitation to a school dance or a page from a school newspaper?**

PORTER HIGH NEWS

A very special night

It's the end of the season for the Porter High football team. The end-of-season dance was a very special night for many Porter students. Over 300 students came.
King and Queen of the dance were Ron Perez and Sandra Murphy. Thanks to the school band and "DJ Maria", Maria Lopez, for the fantastic music.

A fantastic future

A mixed start to the season for the girls' basketball team. The Porter High team won their first game. Then the girls were unlucky, and lost the next two games. The good news is that they won the fourth game last week. "We have some very good players this year," says Coach Sachse.
"Jill Frommer, Rita Gonzalez and Mary Devine have a fantastic basketball future in front of them."

Don't forget the Christmas dance.

We rent out tuxedos from $59.95.

Mr Tux,
1018 Hill Street

$400 for the school library

There was a Book Fair in the Porter library from November 9th to November 21st. The fair's aim was to make money to buy more books for the library. And it made a lot of money: $400! Students bought and sold old books and comics. What books were the most popular? – Horror stories!

To Amy,
Thank you. You're my girlfriend and my best friend, too.
I love you.
Adam

Special person of the month

Can you imagine getting to school at 5.45 every morning? Mr Jim Tara in the school copy room does this every day.
He makes all the photocopies our teachers need. He copies tests, too.
Mr Tara is very nice. But don't ask him – he won't show you any tests!

Tip: You can find new words in the *Dictionary* (page 136).

EXERCISE 1 ■ Basic reading: Which five of these things can you find in the text?
a) a photo of a woman who works at the school b) a photo of a school dance c) an article about baseball d) an article about basketball e) a message f) two jokes g) an article about a sports shop h) an article about a dance i) an article about a book fair j) a photo of three boys

EXERCISE 2 ■ Reading for details: *Yes, No* or *Not in the text*?
1 The dance is only for the football team.
2 The basketball team has won every game.
3 Mr Tux has dresses, too.
4 Teachers organised the book fair.
5 Three girls are very good basketball players.
6 Somebody makes photocopies for teachers.

EXERCISE 3 ■ Language tasks Tip: All the words are on page 96.
1 Find the partners:
a) bought and …; b) king and …; c) books and …; d) won and …; e) hate and …
2 Find the words for:
a) *Saison;* b) *Zukunft;* c) *Weihnachten;* d) *Ziel;* e) *gemischt.*
3 Find the phrases for:
a) *Vielen Dank an;* b) *Geld erzielen;* c) *Kannst du dir vorstellen, …?*

LISTENING A very different school activity

Richard Craig from England is visiting his cousin Marvin Ortega in Brownsville, Texas. They're talking about school. Listen.

EXERCISE 1 ■ *Yes* or *No*?
1 Students were at school all night for the activity.
2 The activity was for all students at the school.
3 The students had a lot of fun.
4 There was no food.
5 There were films.
6 Teachers were there, too.

EXERCISE 2 ■■ Look at the pictures. Now listen again. Which poster is right (A or B)?

A

B

Weitere Fragen: W 54

SUMMARY

* *If*-Sätze

Mit *if*-Sätzen wird gesagt, was unter bestimmten Bedingungen geschehen wird, kann usw.

If Tom gets a letter from Jill, he'll be happy.

If she doesn't run faster, she'll miss the bus.

If I'm late, I won't get any lunch.
Wenn ich zu spät komme, werde ich kein Mittagessen bekommen.
If I invite Sally, she might say "no".
Wenn ich Sally einlade, sagt sie vielleicht „nein".
If you come to Berlin, you must go to the zoo.
Wenn du nach Berlin kommst, musst du in den Zoo gehen.

Das Passiv

Mit dem Passiv kann gesagt werden, was mit einer Person oder einer Sache geschah.

Alan was taken to hospital last week.

These skyscrapers were built before 1950.

Brad was picked for the baseball team. Brad wurde für das Baseballteam ausgesucht.
Tina was seen in town in the lunch break. Tina wurde in der Mittagspause in der Stadt gesehen.
The parents were invited to the party. Die Eltern wurden zur Party eingeladen.
The bikes were checked before the trip. Die Fahrräder wurden vor der Fahrt überprüft.

- Beachte diese häufig gebrauchten Ausdrücke: **was/were made ▪ was/were born**

This book was made in Germany.
Dieses Buch wurde in Deutschland hergestellt.
My parents were born in Bielefeld.
Meine Eltern wurden in Bielefeld geboren.

- Das Passiv in der Vergangenheit wird mit *was/were* und dem Partizip Perfekt des Verbs gebildet.

Das Partizip Perfekt kennst du bereits von der vollendeten Gegenwart *(present perfect form)*.
Das Partizip Perfekt kann regelmäßig oder unregelmäßig sein.

was/were +

Regelmäßig
z.B.

asked	cooked	repaired
checked	helped	washed

Unregelmäßig
z.B.

bought	made	taken
built	seen	told

Tipp: Das Partizip Perfekt unregelmäßiger Verben findest du in der dritten Spalte in der Liste auf den Seiten 158-159.

IN DIESER UNIT HAST DU GELERNT, ...

... wie du sagst, wo jemand geboren wurde. ➡ *I was born in Detmold.*

... wie du sagst, wo etwas hergestellt wurde. ➡ *These CDs were made in Germany.*

... wie du sagst, was mit einer Person oder einer Sache geschah. ➡ *Jill was hurt in the hockey game.*
They were seen at the disco.
The school was built in 1998.

wie du bei der Planung eines Treffens

... eine Uhrzeit vereinbarst. ➡ *When should we meet?*
– Let's say 7.30 pm.

... einen Treffpunkt vereinbarst. ➡ *Where should we meet?*
– What about outside the restaurant?

... erklärst, warum du nicht mitkommen kannst. ➡ *Sorry. I can't. I have to help at home.*

IN DIESER UNIT HAST DU WIEDERHOLT, ...

... wie du sagst, dass etwas unter bestimmten Bedingungen geschehen wird. ➡ *If I miss the bus, I'll walk.*
If you're careful, you won't hurt yourself.

A FROM ALL PARTS OF THE WORLD

New York is the biggest and most exciting city in the USA. The people of New York have come from all parts of the world. For example there are more 'Irish' people in New York than in Dublin, more 'Italians' than in Pisa and more Jewish people than in Tel Aviv. There are more people of German origin than in Stuttgart or Dortmund.

Here are some New York teenagers. They're talking about their origins and what they hope for the future.

Steuben Day Parade – a 'German' day in New York

Hi! My name is Lisa Rackowsky. I like sport and my favourite one is basketball. I hope I can go to college next year. Later I'd like to be a nurse and work with young children. My family name is Polish. My dad's family came to America about 100 years ago. They wanted a better life and that's what they got.

I'm Ali Khan. My dad came to New York eight years ago. He has a food store. I came here from Pakistan with my mother and my sisters two years ago. When I finish high school, I want to go to college and then get a good job. America is very different from Pakistan. In New York you see boys and girls kissing on the street.

My name is Sarah Chang. Yes, that's Chinese. My grandfather and grandmother came here from China a long time ago. I've never been to China. I've lived in New York all my life and I'm one hundred per cent American. When I finish school, I'd like to be a reporter and work for a TV company.

EXERCISE 1 ■ Write about your family – and what you hope for the future.

Hi! My name is … My family is from … I've lived … When I leave school, I …

EXERCISE 2 ■ A friend from a different country: Write about him/her.

Example:
I have a friend. Her name is Shyrette Pepaj. Her family is from Albania. They came to Germany two years ago. Shyrette's mum works in a shop. Shyrette wants to get a good job when she leaves school. She'd like …

Some useful words:

Albania	Italy
Bosnia	Russia
Croatia	Turkey
Greece	Portugal

W 55, 1

B NEW YORK AND MANHATTAN

There are five parts of New York. They're Manhattan, the Bronx, Queens, Brooklyn and Staten Island. Most of the famous sights are in Manhattan. In Manhattan, like in many other American cities, there are streets and avenues. Most of them have numbers, not names. In Manhattan the streets go from east to west, and the avenues go from north to south. Fifth Avenue divides the streets into west and east. From one street or avenue to the next is a block.

EXERCISE 3 ■ You're at Grand Central Station. Tell people the way to:

1 The Empire State Building
2 Rockefeller Center
3 The Public Library
4 Macy's department store
5 The Museum of Modern Art
6 Times Square

1 How do I get to the Empire State Building?
– Go along East 42nd Street for two blocks and then turn left at 5th Avenue. It's on West 34th Street. You'll see it on the right.
2 How do I get to …?
– Go …
3 … 4 … 5 … 6 …

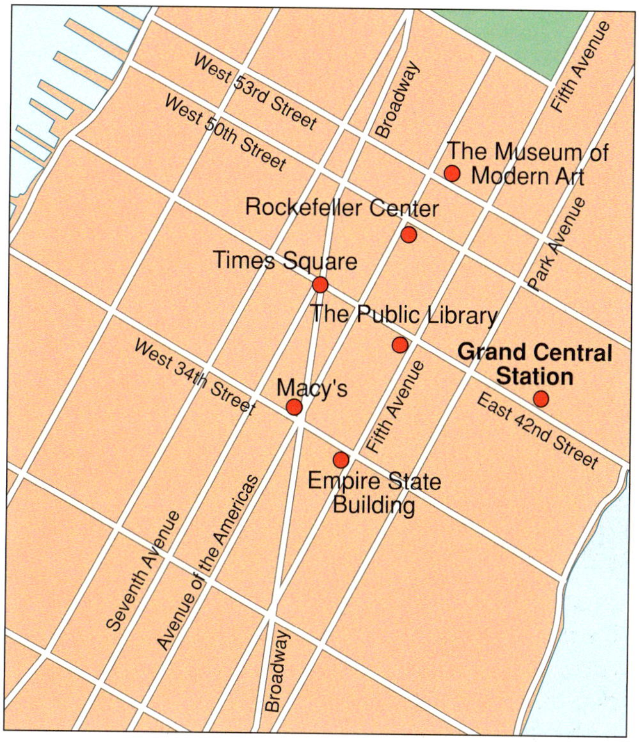

EXERCISE 4 ■ People from New York: Who are they? Where did their families come from?

	1	2	3	4	5
Name:	Eileen Burns	Costa Tanios	James Vu	Tatyana Malkin	Jade Grant
Lives:	The Bronx	Queens	Staten Island	Brooklyn	Manhattan
Family from:	Ireland	Greece	Vietnam	Russia	Africa
When?	150 years ago	30 years ago	20 years ago	5 years ago	300 years ago

1 This is Eileen Burns. She lives in the Bronx in New York. Her family came from Ireland 150 years ago.
2 This is … 3 … 4 … 5 …

C RAP – SONGS ABOUT LIFE

My name is Ashley Clifford and I love rap. It's black music and it's about life. One day, while reading our church magazine, I saw something about a rap group at the church. "I'll go there and see what happens," I thought. Knowing that rap sometimes has bad words, I was surprised that the rap group was at the *church*.

On the first evening there were five boys and me. The teacher was a man called Michael Brennan. He had a cassette with rap music. Each of us had to rap in front of the group. We used our own words. That was OK because I had a few of my own songs. But I felt nervous in front of the boys.
After listening to our songs, Michael said, "While singing, you all looked down. You shouldn't do that. Rappers have to talk to the audience. And you have to look at them."
In the next weeks we all worked at our rap styles.

'My life isn't bad and I don't feel sad.
But listen to me because I want to be free.
Use your brain, that's the name of the game,
If you like my style, then start to smile.'

On the last evening Michael told us about his plans for a show. We all felt nervous about a big audience. "Don't worry," said Michael, trying to help. "You have to believe you can do it."
I rapped every night in the week before the show. I sang the words and I moved to the music. Not being a rap fan, my mom wasn't very happy about this. She didn't like the loud music.

The Fugees

On the evening of the show, I left home very early to go to the church. I felt nervous.
The audience started to arrive. Some of my friends were there. I wanted to run away.
One of the boys started and he was great. Then I sang. When I started, the music didn't feel right. But then I remembered Michael's words. Looking at the audience, I tried to *talk* to them. I wasn't nervous then.

After the show I felt tired, but happy. "You were great, Ashley," Michael told me. He was pleased. "You really showed us what you can do," he said, smiling.

EXERCISE 5 ■ Put the two parts of each sentence together.

1 Ashley read about the rap group	to the audience.
2 Rap doesn't really	at their rap styles.
3 There were six people	in the church magazine.
4 The rappers had to talk	in the rap group.
5 All the young people worked	about the music at home.
6 Ashley's mother wasn't happy	belong in church.

W 56, 2

EXERCISE 6 ■ Phrases in the text: What do they mean?

1 "... while reading our church magazine ..." (lines 2-3)
   a) I was reading the magazine. b) I often read the magazine.
2 "Knowing that rap sometimes has bad words ..." (line 5)
   a) I didn't know that rap sometimes has bad words.
   b) I knew that rap sometimes has bad words.
3 "While singing, you all looked down ..." (line 13)
   a) When you were singing ... b) Because you were singing ...
4 " ... said Michael, trying to help." (line 22)
   a) Michael wanted to help us. b) We wanted to help Michael.
5 "Not being a rap fan, my mom ..." (lines 25-26)
   a) I'm not a rap fan. b) My mom isn't a rap fan.
6 "Looking at the audience, I tried ..." (lines 34-35)
   a) The audience looked at me. b) I looked at the audience.

W 56, 2-3

D BLACK KATT – A RAPPER

EXERCISE 7 ■ Listen to the rap.

1 What "colour" is the rap about?
2 How do you think the man feels?

The rap "You think I don't know": Black Katt and Dream Warriors

EXERCISE 8 ■ Now listen to the interview on the radio show.

1 Who's the interviewer, Janet or David?
2 Is David black or white?
3 Is David angry?
4 David and Janet talked about phrases with the word "black". Can you remember some of them?

EXERCISE 9 ■ First read these sentences. Then listen to the interview again and finish the sentences.

1 A black ... is a terrible day.
2 You give somebody a ... look if you are angry with him or her.
3 Nobody wants to be the ... of the family.
4 People wear ... when somebody has died.
5 Lots of people think if you meet a ..., you'll be unlucky.

W 57, 4

E FAST FOOD IN NEW YORK

People are often in a hurry in New York and so fast food is very popular. Lots of people buy a coffee and a doughnut in the street. Then they eat and drink on the way to work. But fast food is a big problem for the environment. Hamburgers and pizzas come in boxes. Many fast food places use plastic cups, knives, forks and spoons. And you can get fast food all day.

All this is part of Manhattan's garbage problem. The garbage goes by boat every day from Manhattan to the Fresh Kills dump on Staten Island.
Tourists can visit the dump. Then they can see what a big problem garbage is. It's a very smelly problem, too. If you visit the dump, you'll smell it before you see it!

EXERCISE 10 ■ Finish the text about *Ray's Pizza*.

all ▪ best ▪ bike ▪ buy ▪ here
pizzas ▪ restaurant ▪ till

Ray's Pizza is a famous … in New York. You can get good … there. Some people say that they're the … pizzas in town. You can get pizzas … day. You can get drinks, too. Tourists often come …, but New Yorkers eat at the restaurant, too. They often come by … You can eat the pizzas in the restaurant or you can … a take-away pizza. *Ray's Pizza* is open from 6 am … 12 pm.

EXERCISE 11 ■ Now write about this restaurant.

Big Nick's Burger Joint is a famous restaurant in New York. You can …

And in your town?
Write about a restaurant or fast food place that you like.

W 57, 5

F MANHATTAN – CITY OF SKYSCRAPERS

EXERCISE 12 ■ **Which photo (A-E) comes first? Which photo comes next?**
You're going to hear a guide at the Skyscraper Museum in New York. Listen.

Empire State Building

Flatiron Building

Chrysler Building

United Nations

Rockefeller Center

W 57, 6

G AMERICAN ENGLISH

Emily lives in Manhattan. When her English cousin Nicola visited her, they went to Macy's. They wanted to go shopping. Nicola wanted to buy a T-shirt, and Emily needed a book for her mother. "I'll meet you on the first floor in ten minutes. I'll be at the elevator," said Emily. Nicola bought a T-shirt and went up to the first floor. She knew that 'elevator' was the American English word for 'lift'. But she still had to wait a long time for Emily. Do you know why?

H ONE LAST THING

Here's a story. (Maybe it's just a story, but maybe it's true.) Many years ago immigrants to the USA sometimes got new "American" names when they arrived in New York.

And from that moment he was … Shaun Ferguson.

* EXTRA UNIT TWO

A AMERICAN INDIANS

What do you know about American Indians? Look at the photo of the Indian chief, Big Foot. What do you think happened to him?

THE SIOUX

Before white people came to America, Indian tribes like the Sioux crossed the country and hunted buffaloes for clothes and food. The white people wanted the land. The army put the Indian tribes in reservations. But for the Indians the reservations were like prison.

WOUNDED KNEE

On a cold December day in 1890 the Sioux chief, Big Foot, and 350 of his people left their reservation. They wanted to go back to their old land.
But they didn't have much food, and some of them were ill. Soon the army came and found them. The soldiers took them to Wounded Knee. The Sioux were cold and frightened.
On the next morning they had to stand in groups with the soldiers around them. The Sioux had to put their guns down. But one man didn't put his gun down.
Suddenly there was a shot. Then there were many more shots. Big Foot and about 300 Sioux men, women and children died. The soldiers left the dead Indians in the snow.

EXERCISE 1 ■ Write a sentence for each of the pictures. Use the text "American Indians".

1 The Sioux hunted …

2 The army put …

3 Big Foot …

4 The Sioux were …

5 …

6 …

EXERCISE 2 ■ Finish the sentences.

1 Big Foot was …
2 The Sioux are an Indian …
3 The white people wanted …
4 Big Foot and his people wanted to go back to ...
5 On the way the Sioux had problems. They …
6 … died at Wounded Knee.

W 58, 1

*B

WESTERNS

Do you like westerns? What westerns have you seen?
Have you ever seen the famous western *High Noon*?

Will Kane and Amy Fowler fell in love and got married. Will was marshal of Hadleyville. Amy and Will wanted to start a new life together. But then they heard that Frank Miller was free. Will had sent Miller to prison five years earlier. Now Miller was coming on the train to Hadleyville to kill Will. Will and Amy left Hadleyville. But outside town Will suddenly stopped and turned around. "I have to fight Miller," he said.
They went back to Hadleyville. Amy said goodbye to Will. She didn't want to see the gunfight. Will looked for his friends. But they had left town. And Miller's friends had already arrived …

EXERCISE 3 ■ How does the film finish?

arrived ▪ bought ▪ said ▪ shot ▪ started

After Amy had … goodbye to Will, she bought a train ticket. After she had … her ticket, Miller arrived. After Miller had …, Amy got on the train. Then the train started to move, but Amy got off again. Miller met his friends in the town. They waited for Will on Main Street. Then Will arrived, and Miller and his friends started to shoot at him. After they had … to shoot, Amy arrived. She wanted to help Will. Will shot two of Miller's men. Then Amy shot the third man. After she had … him, Will shot the last man. Amy and Will left town.

EXERCISE 4 ■ Sue's "western" day. Write the sentences with the right form of the verb.

After Sue had watched a western, she didn't want to think about cowboys. But then her dad came home …

1 After her dad (come) home, he made beans on toast.
2 After Sue (eat) her beans, her sister phoned from Arizona.
3 After she (speak) to her sister, she went to a jeans shop.
4 After she (buy) some jeans, she bought a magazine.
5 After she (open) the magazine, she saw an article about cowboys.

W 58, 2

CHECKPOINT

Mit der *past perfect*-Form (Vorvergangenheit) drückt man aus, welches von zwei Ereignissen in der Vergangenheit weiter zurückliegt.
Amy and Will went back to Hadleyville. Amy said goodbye to Will.
After Amy and Will had gone back to Hadleyville, Amy said goodbye to Will.

Das *past perfect* bildest du mit *had* und dem Partizip Perfekt des Verbs.

* Diese Seite behandelt die Zeitform *past perfect* und gehört nicht zum Pflichtpensum für Nordrhein-Westfalen.

C MYTH AND REALITY

In westerns cowboys shoot each other and fight Indians all the time.
What was life really like in the American West?

Cowboys ...
Cowboys moved cattle hundreds of miles to railway stations. It was a hard, dangerous job. For 3 months of the year they worked 15 hours a day, 7 days a week. They didn't get much money. 10 to 12 men could move 1,500 cattle, so there weren't many cowboys. It's true that there were a lot of guns. But there wasn't a gunfight every day. Cowboys spent most of their time at work. So who fought the Indians? It was the army, not the cowboys. Later people built railways nearer to the cattle. So the cowboys didn't have to move the cattle so far. The life of a cowboy changed forever. But the myth of the cowboy with his gun hasn't changed.

EXERCISE 5 ■ Is it true or is it a myth?

1 The cowboys took the cattle a long way to the railway stations.
2 Cowboys worked 15 hours a day all year.
3 Cowboys made a lot of money.
4 One cowboy could move 1,500 cattle.
5 Cowboys fought the Indians.

... and Indians
Tradition is still an important part of Indian life. But Indians are interested in modern life, too. Lots of the tribes' money comes from gas, oil and coal under their reservations. Some tribes even have casinos on their reservations. Indians are as proud as other Americans on Independence Day. And many of them love popular games like football and baseball.

EXERCISE 6 ■ These sentences about Indians are wrong. What's right?

1 Tradition isn't important for Indians today.
2 Lots of the tribes' money comes from gold under their reservations.
3 There are never casinos on reservations.
4 Indians don't like Independence Day.
5 They never go to football games.

W 59, 3-4

D AN INTERVIEW WITH A NAVAJO TEENAGER

Listen to this interview with Sandra Russell, a 16-year-old Navajo.

EXERCISE 7 ■ Which are the right words?

1 Sandra lives on the (biggest/smallest) reservation in the USA.
2 The Navajo reservation is in (beautiful/boring) country.
3 Window Rock (is/isn't) like other American towns.
4 Sandra (goes / doesn't go) to school.
5 Many Navajo (speak / don't speak) the Navajo language.
6 A hogan is a Navajo (village/house).

EXERCISE 8 ■ Write Sandra's e-mail to a friend in New York.

reservation – 148,000 – mountains, lakes, … – Window Rock – school – Navajo language – visit friends – listen to music – houses and hogans

W 59, 5

E SPECIAL DAYS IN THE USA

Look at the photos. Do you know these special days?
Read texts 1-5. Put the photos and the texts together.

1 The Fourth of July is **Independence Day**. It's a public holiday. It celebrates America's independence from Britain. People often go to the park and watch the fireworks. There are American flags everywhere.

2 **Valentine's Day** (February 14th) is a day for people who are in love. People often send a Valentine's card to the man or woman they like. But they don't put their name on the card! People give each other flowers, too. They often go out for a special meal together.

3 **Mardi Gras** is on a Tuesday in February or March. It's very important in New Orleans, with costumes, music, parades – and lots of colour. People throw beads, and everybody tries to get them.

4 **Thanksgiving** is always the fourth Thursday in November. It's a public holiday. Families spend the day together and usually have a turkey dinner.

5 Children in the USA really enjoy themselves at **Halloween** (October 31st). They disguise themselves as ghosts, witches or monsters. Then they go from house to house and get sweets from the people there.

EXERCISE 9 ■ What day is it?

On which special days could you say these things? Look at page 109 again if you need help.

1 "That's a good monster's costume."
2 "Throw me something, please!"
3 "This turkey is fantastic."
4 "Did you send me this card?"
5 "Can you help me with the flag, please?"

EXERCISE 10 ■ Write about a special day in Germany.

Here are some ideas:

- … is/isn't a public holiday.
- … is a special day in our village/town/part of Germany.
- People go/buy/wear/watch/play …
- They eat/drink …

Karneval	carnival
Ostern	Easter
Himmelfahrt	Ascension Day
Pfingsten	Whitsun
Weihnachten	Christmas
Silvester	New Year's Eve

EXERCISE 11 ■ Write the words with *-self/-selves*.

Dear Robert,
It was Halloween yesterday. I really enjoyed … Sandra and I met at my house and we disguised … as monsters. We made the costumes … They were great! I put some ketchup on my clothes, and looked at … in the mirror. Sandra looked at … in the mirror, too and then we laughed a lot.
Later we went to Mr Brown's house. He saw the ketchup on my costume and asked me, "Hi! Did you hurt …?"

W 60, 6-7

✓ CHECKPOINT

Sowohl *themselves* als auch *each other* bedeuten „sich". Aber *each other* wird nur verwendet, wenn „einander" gemeint ist.

The boys looked at themselves in the mirrors.

Kane and Miller looked at each other angrily.

EXERCISE 12 ■ Which is right: *each other* or *themselves*?

Sue and Martin met *each other* on Independence Day. They liked … a lot, so they went to a concert together. They enjoyed … at the concert. Then they saw … every day. Very soon they fell in love with … They got married. But they couldn't find a house that they liked. So they built a house … That was ten years ago. And they still love … today.

F AMERICAN ENGLISH

Adam from Britain is at school in the USA for a month. He's talking to Erica, a girl in his class. He's showing her some photos.

ADAM Look. Here's my dad, outside our flat.
ERICA What? Oh, your apartment.
What does your dad do, Adam?
ADAM He drives a lorry.
ERICA A what?
ADAM A lorry. You know, like that thing over there.
ERICA Oh, you mean a truck.
ADAM Yes. We sometimes say 'truck', too.
What about your parents, Erica?
What work do they do?
ERICA My dad is a mailman ...
ADAM We say 'postman'.
ERICA ... and my mom works in a sports store.
She sells sports equipment and sports shoes.
ADAM Oh, trainers.
ERICA What?
ADAM Trainers. You know, shoes you wear for sport, or sometimes with jeans.
ERICA Trainers – I've never heard that word before.
You know, sometimes I think we speak different languages.

EXERCISE 13 ■ Read the dialogue and make two lists.

American English	British English
apartment	flat
…	…

EXERCISE 14 ■ What are these words in British English?

1 elevator
2 trailer
3 garbage
4 flashlight
5 vacation

W 60, 8

G ONE LAST THING

In the days before the railway it was a long, slow trip over the mountains and across the desert to California.
People who didn't have enough water often saw the funniest things …

The US army used camels in the Indian wars.

* EXTRA UNIT THREE

A ON THE INTERNET

Have you ever used the Internet? Can you visit web sites at your school?
Westbrook High School in Texas has a web site. Here's the news page from their web site.

NEWS FROM WESTBROOK HIGH

Homepage
News
Student life
Sports
Clubs
E-mail

A great night
300 people came to our Father-Daughter Dance last week. Everybody danced to music from the 1960s. It was great! Thanks for all your help. If you want to come to the Mother-Son Dance next month, you can buy tickets now. If you don't hurry, you won't get any tickets.

Parking problems?
Do you think the parking lot is too small? Well, we have good news! There are 50 new parking spaces. If you buy a ticket for 50 cents, you can win a parking space!

Cheerleaders
If you want to become a cheerleader, join us now. But if you become a cheerleader, you'll have to practise regularly. And you'll have to buy a uniform.

German Club
We're going to Braun's German restaurant on Friday evening at 7.00 pm. If you speak German all evening, the German Club will buy you a German dessert. Bis dann!

Baseball
Westbrook boys' baseball team beat Springsville at the last game. "If we win the next three games, we'll be in the play-offs," said Coach Joe Morales.

EXERCISE 1 ■ **Pick 5 photos for the news page.**

A

B

C

D

E

F

G

H

EXERCISE 2 ■ **The sentences are wrong. But what's right?**

1 At the Winter Dance 200 people danced to music from the 1990s.
2 The Father-Daughter Dance wasn't very good because nobody came and nobody helped.
3 If you buy a ticket for a dollar, you can win a car.
4 Cheerleaders never have to practise and they don't need a uniform.
5 If you speak French, the German Club will pay for all food and drinks.
6 If the basketball team wins two more games, they'll be in the play-offs.

EXERCISE 3 ■ Finish the sentences.

1 If you want to come to the Mother-Son Dance,
   a) … you won't get any tickets.
   b) … you'll have to buy tickets soon.
   c) … you'll have to wait till next year.

2 If you want to drive to school,
   a) … you'll have to park in a car park far from the school.
   b) … you can always park in the school car park.
   c) … you can try to win a parking space.

3 If you don't have a cheerleader's uniform,
   a) … you'll have to buy one.
   b) … you won't have to buy one.
   c) … you should wear jeans and a T-shirt.

4 If you come to Braun's next Friday,
   a) … the German Club will buy you a frankfurter.
   b) … you can watch a German film.
   c) … you'll meet students from the German Club.

5 Westbrook baseball team will be in the play-offs
   a) … if they win tomorrow.
   b) … if they lose another game.
   c) … if they win the next three games.

EXERCISE 4 ■ From the Westbrook High news page

1
PHOTO CLUB
– learn all about cameras

2
1980s music
– bring CDs
MUSIC CLUB
Tonight!

3
Go hiking!
The Hill Country
– join the
Hiking Club

4
Inline-Skating Club
– meeting:
Thursday 6 pm

1 If you come to the photography club, you'll learn all about cameras.
2 If you like 1980s music, you should …
3 If you want to …
4 If you like …

EXERCISE 5 ■ What clubs and activities are there at your school?

you can … ▪ you'll have to … ▪ you won't … ▪ you should …

1 If you're interested in …,
2 If you like …,
3 If you want to learn all about …,
4 If you're good at …,
5 If you want to …,
6 If you want to learn …,

Some ideas:
books, computers, music, sport,
(go) canoeing, (go) hiking, (go) swimming,
English, French, Turkish

W 61, 1

CHECKPOINT

Mit *if*-Sätzen wird gesagt, was unter bestimmten Bedingungen geschehen wird oder kann.
If you're interested in computers, you'll learn a lot at the computer club.
If you like inline-skating, you can come to our club.
You'll become a good cheerleader if you practise every day.

B SHAQUILLE O'NEAL

Do you sometimes watch or play basketball?
Do you know Shaquille O'Neal?
How tall do you think he is?
a) 1m 96; b) 2m 06; c) 2m 16.

Not just a basketball star

Shaquille O'Neal is one of America's most famous basketball stars. He's loved by thousands of fans. He plays for the Los Angeles Lakers. Shaq is 2m 16 and has a lot of talent! But Shaq wasn't always a star. He was born March 6th, 1972 in New Jersey.
At 16 Shaq was just an ordinary high school student – with a lot of problems. His father was in the army, and the family lived in lots of different places. At first Shaq didn't work hard at school. But he was taught to do the right thing by his parents. When he came home with a bad report, he was told, "No more basketball!".

So Shaq started to work harder at school and at basketball. Things got better. He went to college and at 20 he became one of the most famous sportsmen in the world. But Shaq isn't just a basketball star. He has written a book, has been in a movie and has made rap CDs. He has already made millions of dollars.

Now he wants to help teenagers. He talks to them about drugs and about the future.
"You can't do it. It's too dangerous," he says. "You'll probably die or go to prison. You need a dream, and then you have to work hard for it."
When he was younger, he was laughed at because he was so tall. But his mother said, "Be proud of yourself. You are who you are."
Today Shaq says, "Do you know what? My mother was right!"

EXERCISE 6 ■ Tell the story.

After college Shaq became a famous basketball player.
→ At school Shaq didn't work hard enough.
He has made a film and some rap CDs, too.
Today Shaq tries to help teenagers.
So then Shaq worked hard and went to college.
When he had a bad report, his parents said, "No more basketball!"

EXERCISE 7 ■ Language tasks

1 Find the word for:
   a) a very famous man or woman;
   b) something good that you hope will happen.
2 Find the missing words:
   a) If you can do something very well, you have …
   b) A soldier works in the …
   c) If you take drugs, you'll probably …

Tip: All the words are in the text.

W 62, 2

EXERCISE 8 ■ A baseball star

born ▪ made ▪ laughed ▪ loved ▪ taught ▪ told

Tim Davey was … in New York. At first he didn't like school. He was … at because he was so small. When he was 11, he was … baseball. He was …, "You must practise if you want to be famous." So he worked hard. Today he's … by thousands of baseball fans. Last year a film was … about his life.

EXERCISE 9 ■ Your favourite sports star

Find information about your favourite sports star.
You can use sports magazines or maybe the Internet.

Example:
Name: *Martina Hingis*
Born: *September 30, 1980*
Where: *Kosice, Slovakia*
Job: *tennis player*
Home: *Switzerland and the Czech Republic*
Interests and hobbies: *her pets – 3 horses and a dog*

W 62

C AT A BASKETBALL GAME

Tom Lewis from Britain is at a basketball game in Los Angeles with his uncle. Listen.

EXERCISE 10 ■ Which photos (a or b) are right?

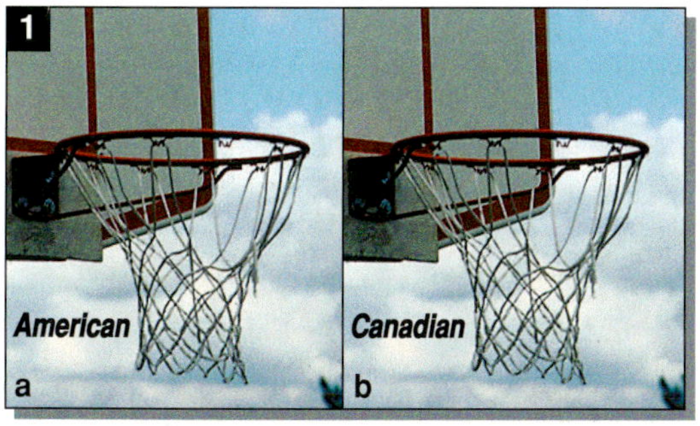

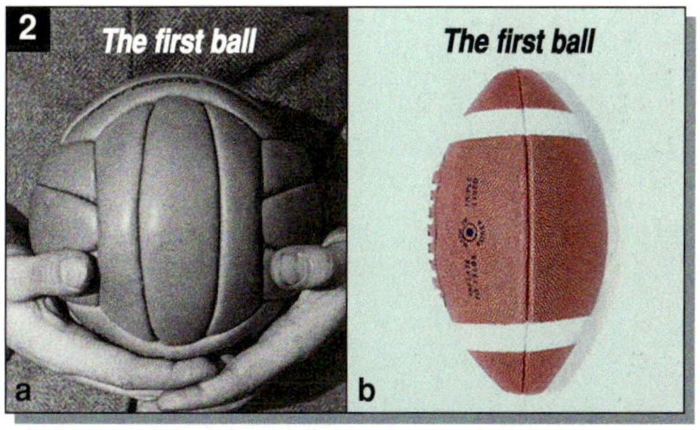

W 62, 4

D SPORT IN THE USA

Sport is very important in the USA. People watch sport in stadiums, at school and at college. And lots of Americans watch sport on TV, of course. People often go to sports bars to watch sport. These bars often have ten or more TVs that show different sports at the same time.

Look at the photos. Do you know these sports? Have you ever played or watched them?

Baseball is a very popular sport in the USA. The American president even throws the first ball to start the baseball season in spring. Baseball is played everywhere, in parks, at school and at college.

People like to play basketball at all times of the year. Just look at how many houses in the USA have a basketball net above the garage door. The Harlem Globetrotters from New York are a famous basketball team.

American football is played at school, college and as a professional game. Football is played in the autumn. Players carry the ball more often than they kick it. It's a rough game, so players wear special clothing and helmets. There are lots of breaks in the game.

Ice hockey is a fast, exciting and often rough game. Ice hockey players have to be very good skaters. Most ice hockey games are played on ice-rinks indoors. Ice hockey is played professionally and at college.

W 63, 5

EXERCISE 11 ■ **What sports are these things used for?**

1

2

3

4

5

1 This is used for American football.
2 This is used for …
3 …
4 …
5 …

EXERCISE 12 ■ **What are these inventions used for? Finish the sentences.**

answering the phone ▪ cooking food ▪ drying hair ▪ toasting bread
sending e-mails and surfing the Internet ▪ sending faxes ▪ washing clothes ▪ washing dishes

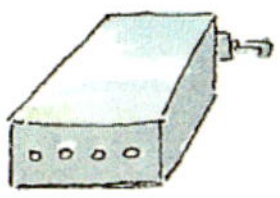
1 a modem

2 a toaster

3 a microwave

4 a fax machine

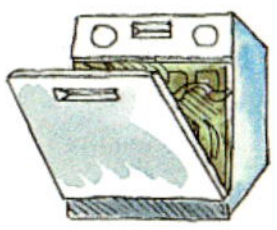
5 a dishwasher

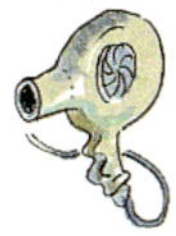
6 a hair-drier

7 a washing-machine

8 an answerphone

1 A modem is used for sending e-mails and surfing the Internet.
2 A toaster is used for …
3 A microwave …
4 … 5 … 6 … 7 … 8 …

EXERCISE 13 ■ **More helpful inventions: Answer the questions.**

1 What's used for recording TV programmes? – *A video-recorder.*
2 What's used for playing CDs? – …
3 What's used for taking photos? – …
4 What's used for telling the time? – …
5 What's used for phoning people? – …

W 63, 6

✔ **CHECKPOINT**

Was mit etwas gemacht wird:
A net is used for basketball.
Many computers are made in Japan.

Was mit etwas gemacht wurde:
This ball was made in the USA.
These photos were taken at a football game.

Vocabulary

Dieses Wörterverzeichnis enthält alle neuen Wörter des Buches in der Reihenfolge, in der sie im Buch zum ersten Mal vorkommen.

In der eckigen Klammer steht, wie die Wörter ausgesprochen werden.

Der Pfeil bedeutet: Schau in die rechte Spalte.

Hier sind Wörter in Gruppen zusammengefasst. Das macht das Lernen leichter.

Die ganz schwarz gedruckten Wörter sind besonders wichtig.

Normal gedruckte Wörter sind wichtig für das Kapitel, in dem sie vorkommen.

(AE) bedeutet *American English*.

Diese Zahl gibt die Seite an, auf der die Wörter zum ersten Mal vorkommen.

Ein Sternchen heißt: Die drei Formen dieses unregelmäßigen Verbs findest du in dem grauen Kasten auf der rechten Seite.

Dieses Zeichen bedeutet „Aufgepasst!".

Schräg gestellte Wörter kommen z.B. in Liedern und *activities* vor.

In diesem Abschnitt kannst du selbst überprüfen, ob du Wörter richtig verstanden hast.

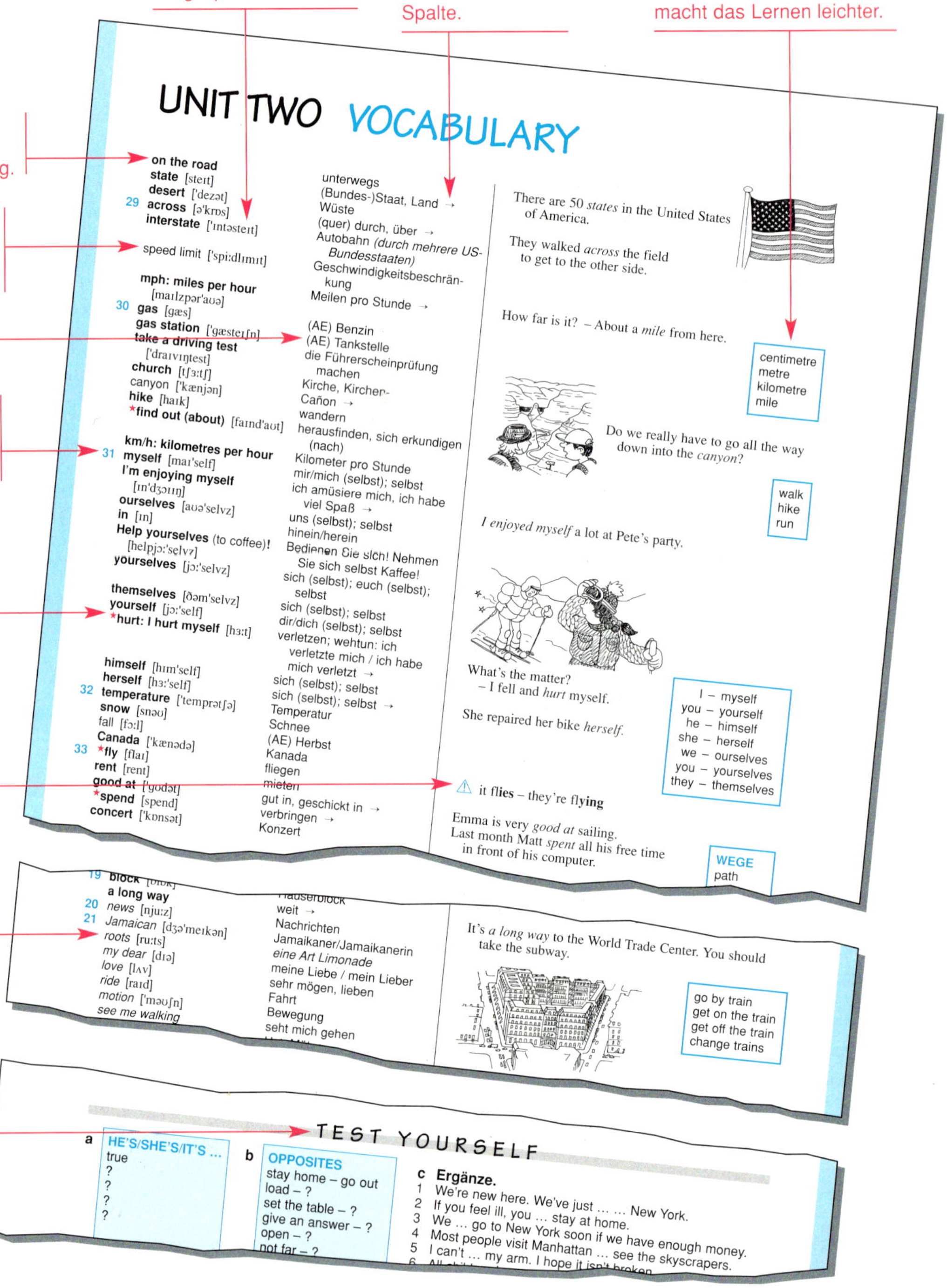

UNIT TWO VOCABULARY

on the road	unterwegs	
state [steɪt]	(Bundes-)Staat, Land →	There are 50 *states* in the United States of America.
desert ['dezət]	Wüste	
29 **across** [ə'krɒs]	(quer) durch, über →	They walked *across* the field to get to the other side.
interstate ['ɪntəsteɪt]	Autobahn *(durch mehrere US-Bundesstaaten)*	
speed limit ['spi:dlɪmɪt]	Geschwindigkeitsbeschränkung	
mph: miles per hour [maɪlzpər'aʊə]	Meilen pro Stunde →	How far is it? – About a *mile* from here. (centimetre, metre, kilometre, mile)
30 **gas** [gæs]	(AE) Benzin	
gas station ['gæsteɪʃn]	(AE) Tankstelle	
take a driving test ['draɪvɪŋtest]	die Führerscheinprüfung machen	
church [tʃɜ:tʃ]	Kirche, Kirchen-	
canyon ['kænjən]	Cañon →	Do we really have to go all the way down into the *canyon*?
hike [haɪk]	wandern	(walk, hike, run)
***find out (about)** [faɪnd'aʊt]	herausfinden, sich erkundigen (nach)	
31 **km/h: kilometres per hour**	Kilometer pro Stunde	
myself [maɪ'self]	mir/mich (selbst); selbst	
I'm enjoying myself [ɪn'dʒɔɪɪŋ]	ich amüsiere mich, ich habe viel Spaß →	*I enjoyed myself* a lot at Pete's party.
ourselves [aʊə'selvz]	uns (selbst); selbst	
in [ɪn]	hinein/herein	
Help yourselves (to coffee)! [helpjɔ:'selvz]	Bedienen Sie sich! Nehmen Sie sich selbst Kaffee!	
yourselves [jɔ:'selvz]	sich (selbst); euch (selbst); selbst	
themselves [ðəm'selvz]	sich (selbst); selbst	
yourself [jɔ:'self]	dir/dich (selbst); selbst	
***hurt: I hurt myself** [hɜ:t]	verletzen; wehtun: ich verletzte mich / ich habe mich verletzt →	What's the matter? – I fell and *hurt* myself.
himself [hɪm'self]	sich (selbst); selbst	
herself [hɜ:'self]	sich (selbst); selbst →	She repaired her bike *herself*. (I – myself, you – yourself, he – himself, she – herself, we – ourselves, you – yourselves, they – themselves)
32 **temperature** ['temprətʃə]	Temperatur	
snow [snəʊ]	Schnee	
fall [fɔ:l]	(AE) Herbst	
Canada ['kænədə]	Kanada	
33 ***fly** [flaɪ]	fliegen	⚠ it flies – they're flying
rent [rent]	mieten	
good at ['gʊdət]	gut in, geschickt in →	Emma is very *good at* sailing.
***spend** [spend]	verbringen →	Last month Matt *spent* all his free time in front of his computer.
concert ['kɒnsət]	Konzert	(WEGE: path)

19 **block**	Häuserblock	
a long way	weit →	It's *a long way* to the World Trade Center. You should take the subway.
20 *news* [nju:z]	Nachrichten	
21 *Jamaican* [dʒə'meɪkən]	Jamaikaner/Jamaikanerin	
roots [ru:ts]	*eine Art Limonade*	
my dear [dɪə]	meine Liebe / mein Lieber	
love [lʌv]	sehr mögen, lieben	
ride [raɪd]	Fahrt	
motion ['məʊʃn]	Bewegung	(go by train, get on the train, get off the train, change trains)
see me walking	seht mich gehen	

TEST YOURSELF

a HE'S/SHE'S/IT'S …
true
?
?
?
?

b OPPOSITES
stay home – go out
load – ?
set the table – ?
give an answer – ?
open – ?
not far – ?

c Ergänze.
1 We're new here. We've just … … New York.
2 If you feel ill, you … stay at home.
3 We … go to New York soon if we have enough money.
4 Most people visit Manhattan … see the skyscrapers.
5 I can't … my arm. I hope it isn't broken.

WELCOME … VOCABULARY

6	**life, lives** [laɪf, laɪvz]	Leben
	national park ['næʃnəl'pɑːk]	Nationalpark
	go camping ['kæmpɪŋ]	zelten gehen
	Mexico ['meksɪkəʊ]	Mexiko
7	**California** [kælɪ'fɔːniə]	Kalifornien
8	**United States of America** [ju'naɪtɪd'steɪtsəvə'merɪkə]	Vereinigte Staaten von Amerika
	time [taɪm]	Mal →
9	**spell** [spel]	buchstabieren →

I've been to the United States three *times*.
Can you *spell* "Mexico"? – M-E-X-I-C-O.

AMERICAN ENGLISH VOCABULARY

AE (AMERICAN ENGLISH)	BE (BRITISH ENGLISH)	
apartment [ə'pɑːtmənt]	flat	Wohnung
downtown [daʊn'taʊn]	town centre	Stadtmitte
fall [fɔːl]	autumn	Herbst
flashlight ['flæʃlaɪt]	torch	Taschenlampe
garbage ['gɑːbɪdʒ]	rubbish	Abfall, Müll
grade: 9th grade [greɪd]	Year 9	Klasse(nstufe), Jahrgang
line [laɪn]	queue	(Warte-)Schlange
mom [mɒm]	mum	Mama, Mutti
movie ['muːvi]	film	Film
parking lot ['pɑːkɪŋlɒt]	car park	(großer) Parkplatz
store [stɔː]	shop	Laden, Geschäft
subway ['sʌbweɪ]	underground	U-Bahn
trailer ['treɪlə]	caravan	Wohnwagen
vacation: go on vacation [və'keɪʃn]	go on holiday	in Urlaub fahren

UNIT ONE VOCABULARY

	English	German	Example
10	Ground Zero [graʊnd'zɪərəʊ]	*Ort, an dem das World Trade Center stand*	
	top [tɒp]	Spitze, oberes Ende →	We often ride our bikes to the *top* of the hill. It's fun to come down again.
	Statue of Liberty ['stætʃu:əv'lɪbəti]	Freiheitsstatue	
	skyscraper ['skaɪskreɪpə]	Wolkenkratzer, Hochhaus	
11	**Little Italy** [lɪtl'ɪtəli]	„Klein-Italien"	
	***go shopping** ['ʃɒpɪŋ]	einkaufen gehen →	In the afternoon Kate and Danny *went shopping*.
	World Trade Center [wɜ:ld'treɪdsentə]	Welthandelszentrum	
	***stand: I stood** [stænd, stʊd]	stehen: ich stand / ich habe gestanden	
	terrorist ['terərɪst]	Terrorist/Terroristin	
	destroy [dɪ'strɔɪ]	zerstören	
12	**mom** [mɒm]	(AE) Mama, Mutti	
	it's his turn [tɜ:n]	er ist dran, er ist an der Reihe	
	just [dʒʌst]	nur →	Don't get angry! It was *just* a joke.
	move (to) [mu:v]	umziehen (nach), ziehen (nach) →	The Walkers sold their house in Atlanta and *moved to* New York.
	still [stɪl]	(immer) noch →	Alice is feeling better, but she's *still* in hospital.
13	**movie** ['mu:vi]	(AE) Film	
	true [tru:]	wahr	
	dance [dɑ:ns]	Tanz; Tanzveranstaltung, Ball	
	go out [gəʊ'aʊt]	ausgehen, weggehen →	Paula and I are *going out* on Saturday evening. Do you want to come, too?
	load [ləʊd]	einräumen, (be)laden	
	empty ['empti]	ausräumen, leeren	⚠ she emp**ties** – she's emp**tying** – she emp**tied**
	dishwasher ['dɪʃwɒʃə]	Geschirrspülmaschine	
	***set the table** [set]	den Tisch decken	
	clear the table ['klɪə]	den Tisch abräumen	
14	**you should** [ʃʊd, ʃəd]	du solltest, du müsstest →	Nick feels ill today. I think he *should* stay in bed. – You're right. He *shouldn't* go to school today.
	Natural History Museum [nætʃrəl'hɪstrimju'zi:əm]	Naturgeschichtliches Museum	
	around Manhattan [ə'raʊnd]	um Manhattan herum	
15	**I might** ask her … [maɪt]	Vielleicht bitte ich sie, … →	Hannah *might* come to the party too if she isn't too busy.
	pleased [pli:zd]	zufrieden; erfreut	
	she owes me a favour [əʊ, 'feɪvə]	sie schuldet mir einen Gefallen	

taxi
bus
tram
train
underground (BE)
subway (AE)

STORY

	English	German	Example
16	**disaster** [dɪ'zɑ:stə]	Katastrophe	
	subway ['sʌbweɪ]	(AE) U-Bahn	
	act [ækt]	sich benehmen, sich verhalten →	Don't *act* like a child, Carlos.
	cool [ku:l]	ruhig, überlegen; kühl	
	stare at [steə]	anstarren	
	ask a question	eine Frage stellen →	When my teacher *asks* me *a question*, I often know the answer.
	backpack ['bækpæk]	Rucksack	
	maybe ['meɪbi]	vielleicht →	Is this a true story? – *Maybe*, I'm not sure.
	she was worried (about) ['wʌrid]	sie machte sich Sorgen (um)	
	lift [lɪft]	Aufzug	
	to go	um zu fahren →	Most tourists visit New York *to* see Manhattan.
	storey ['stɔ:ri]	Stockwerk	
	go window-shopping ['wɪndəʊʃɒpɪŋ]	einen Schaufensterbummel machen	
	exhibition ['eksɪ'bɪʃn]	Ausstellung	
	store [stɔ:]	(AE) Laden, Geschäft	
17	**closed** [kləʊzd]	geschlossen, zu	
	guide [gaɪd]	(Fremden-)Führer/Führerin	
	frankfurter ['fræŋkfɜ:tə]	(Frankfurter) Würstchen	
	coke [kəʊk]	Cola	

VIELLEICHT
perhaps it's true
maybe it's true
it could be true
it might be true

TRAVELLING
tourist
travel agency
ticket
guide
go on a journey
see the sights

move [muːv]	(sich) bewegen →	Can you *move* it? – No, I can't. I think it's broken.
meter ['miːtə]	Fahrpreisanzeiger	
dollar ($) ['dɒlə]	Dollar *(amerik. Geld)*	⚠ one dollar – two dollars
cent (¢) [sent]	Cent *(amerik. Geld)*	

MONEY	
British:	American:
£ pound	$ dollar
p pence	¢ cent

ACTIVE ENGLISH

18	**subway token** ['təʊkən]	U-Bahn-Münze, -Marke	
	change (trains/…) [tʃeɪndʒ]	umsteigen; (den Zug/…) wechseln →	Mr Smith always has to *change trains* at Grand Central Station.
	especially [ɪ'speʃəli]	besonders →	All tourists love New York, *especially* Manhattan.
19	**block** [blɒk]	Häuserblock	
	a long way	weit →	It's *a long way* to Chinatown. You should take the subway.
20	*news* [njuːz]	Nachrichten	
21	*Jamaican* [dʒə'meɪkən]	Jamaikaner/Jamaikanerin	
	roots [ruːts]	*eine Art Limonade*	
	my dear [dɪə]	meine Liebe / mein Lieber	
	love [lʌv]	sehr mögen, lieben	
	ride [raɪd]	Fahrt	
	motion ['məʊʃn]	Bewegung	
	see me walking	seht mich gehen	
	hat [hæt]	Hut, Mütze	
	lean [liːn]	sich neigen	
	alien ['eɪliən]	Ausländer/Ausländerin	
	legal ['liːgl]	legal, rechtlich zugelassen	
	English-speaking	englischsprachig	
	area ['eəriə]	Gegend	
	commentary ['kɒməntri]	Kommentar	
	tip [tɪp]	Trinkgeld	

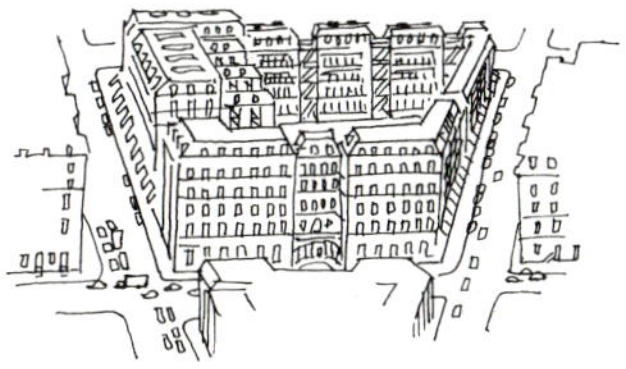

a block

go by train
get on the train
get off the train
change trains

*IRREGULAR VERBS

INFINITIVE FORM	SIMPLE PAST FORM	PRESENT PERFECT FORM
go [gəʊ]	I went [went]	I've gone [gɒn]
stand [stænd]	I stood [stʊd]	I've stood [stʊd]
set [set]	I set [set]	I've set [set]

AMERICAN ENGLISH VOCABULARY

AE (AMERICAN ENGLISH)	BE (BRITISH ENGLISH)	
mom [mɒm]	mum	Mama, Mutti
movie ['muːvi]	film	Film
store [stɔː]	shop	Laden, Geschäft
subway ['sʌbweɪ]	underground	U-Bahn

TEST YOURSELF

a HE'S/SHE'S/IT'S …

true
?
?
?
?

b OPPOSITES

stay home – go out
load – ?
set the table – ?
give an answer – ?
open – ?
not far – ?

c Ergänze.

1 We're new here. We've just … … New York.
2 If you feel ill, you … stay at home.
3 We … go to New York soon if we have enough money.
4 Most people visit Manhattan … see the skyscrapers.
5 I can't … my arm. I hope it isn't broken.
6 All children love animals, … dogs.

UNIT TWO VOCABULARY

28	**on the road**	unterwegs
	state [steɪt]	(Bundes-)Staat, Land →
	desert ['dezət]	Wüste
29	**across** [ə'krɒs]	(quer) durch, über →
	interstate ['ɪntəsteɪt]	Autobahn *(durch mehrere US-Bundesstaaten)*
	speed limit ['spi:dlɪmɪt]	Geschwindigkeitsbeschränkung
	mph: miles per hour [maɪlzpər'aʊə]	Meilen pro Stunde →
30	**gas** [gæs]	(AE) Benzin
	gas station ['gæsteɪʃn]	(AE) Tankstelle
	take a driving test ['draɪvɪŋtest]	die Führerscheinprüfung machen
	church [tʃɜ:tʃ]	Kirche, Kirchen-
	canyon ['kænjən]	Cañon →
	hike [haɪk]	wandern
	***find out (about)** [faɪnd'aʊt]	herausfinden, sich erkundigen (nach)
	km/h: kilometres per hour	Kilometer pro Stunde
31	**myself** [maɪ'self]	mir/mich (selbst); selbst
	I'm enjoying myself [ɪn'dʒɔɪɪŋ]	ich amüsiere mich, ich habe viel Spaß →
	ourselves [aʊə'selvz]	uns (selbst); selbst
	in [ɪn]	hinein/herein
	Help yourselves (to coffee)! [helpjɔ:'selvz]	Bedienen Sie sich! Nehmen Sie sich selbst Kaffee!
	yourselves [jɔ:'selvz]	sich (selbst); euch (selbst); selbst
	themselves [ðəm'selvz]	sich (selbst); selbst
	yourself [jɔ:'self]	dir/dich (selbst); selbst
	***hurt: I hurt myself** [hɜ:t]	verletzen; wehtun: ich verletzte mich / ich habe mich verletzt →
	himself [hɪm'self]	sich (selbst); selbst
	herself [hɜ:'self]	sich (selbst); selbst →
32	**temperature** ['temprətʃə]	Temperatur
	snow [snəʊ]	Schnee
	fall [fɔ:l]	(AE) Herbst
	Canada ['kænədə]	Kanada
33	***fly** [flaɪ]	fliegen
	rent [rent]	mieten
	good at ['gʊdət]	gut in, geschickt in →
	***spend** [spend]	verbringen →
	concert ['kɒnsət]	Konzert

STORY

34	**start** [stɑ:t]	Anfang
	trail [treɪl]	Wanderweg; Pfad
	view [vju:]	Aussicht, Sicht
	for the first time	zum ersten Mal
	have a break [breɪk]	(eine) Pause machen
	for half an hour	eine halbe Stunde lang
	uphill [ʌp'hɪl]	bergauf →
	twice the time [twaɪs]	doppelt so lange
	bend [bend]	Kurve
	hot [hɒt]	heiß
35	**ground** [graʊnd]	(Erd-)Boden →
	ranger ['reɪndʒə]	Aufseher/in (in Nationalparks)
	hiker ['haɪkə]	Wanderer/Wanderin
	alone [ə'ləʊn]	allein →

There are 50 *states* in the United States of America.

They walked *across* the field to get to the other side.

How far is it? – About a *mile* from here.

centimetre
metre
kilometre
mile

Do we really have to go all the way down into the *canyon*?

walk
hike
run

I enjoyed myself a lot at Pete's party.

What's the matter?
– I fell and *hurt* myself.

She repaired her bike *herself*.

I	myself
you	yourself
he	himself
she	herself
we	ourselves
you	yourselves
they	themselves

⚠ it fl**ies** – they're fl**ying**

Emma is very *good at* sailing.
Last month Matt *spent* all his free time in front of his computer.

WEGE
path
trail
road
street
interstate

uphill

downhill

cold
warm
hot

There weren't enough chairs, so the children sat on the *ground*.

I can't go out *alone* at night, my parents say that it isn't safe.

ACTIVE ENGLISH

36	**straight ahead** [streɪtə'hed]	geradeaus →
	junction ['dʒʌŋkʃn]	Kreuzung
	lights [laɪts]	Ampel
	gallon ['gælən]	Gallone *(in den USA = 3,8 l)*
	litre ['li:tə]	Liter
	the only	der/die/das einzige →
	for miles and miles	meilenweit
	ice [aɪs]	Eis *(gefrorenes Wasser)*
	mug [mʌg]	Becher, große Tasse →
38	*alcohol* ['ælkəhɒl]	Alkohol
	seat-belt ['si:tbelt]	Sicherheitsgurt
	save your life [seɪv]	dein Leben retten
39	*get your kicks* [kɪks]	hol dir deinen Spaß
	motor ['məʊtə]	mit dem Auto fahren
	highway ['haɪweɪ]	Fernstraße
	wind [waɪnd]	sich schlängeln
	pretty ['prɪti]	hübsch
	Would you get hip to …? [get'hɪp]	Möchtest du eingeweiht werden in …?
	kindly ['kaɪndli]	freundlich
	Go take the trip.	Geh auf die Reise.
	US-style signs ['ju:'es'staɪl]	Schilder im amerikan. Stil
	direction [də'rekʃn]	Richtung

If you look *straight ahead*, you'll see it.

This is *the only* yellow T-shirt that I have.

a *mug*

TRAFFIC
- driver
- car
- start
- drive
- road
- junction
- lights
- stop
- gas station (AE)
- gas (AE)
- park

* IRREGULAR VERBS

INFINITIVE FORM	SIMPLE PAST FORM	PRESENT PERFECT FORM
find [faɪnd]	I found [faʊnd]	I've found [faʊnd]
fly [flaɪ]	I flew [flu:]	I've flown [fləʊn]
hurt [hɜ:t]	I hurt [hɜ:t]	I've hurt [hɜ:t]
spend [spend]	I spent [spent]	I've spent [spent]

AMERICAN ENGLISH VOCABULARY

AE (AMERICAN ENGLISH)	BE (BRITISH ENGLISH)	
fall [fɔ:l]	autumn	Herbst
gas [gæs]	petrol ['petrəl]	Benzin
gas station ['gæsteɪʃn]	petrol station ['petrəlsteɪʃn]	Tankstelle

TIPS

Wörter zum Selbermachen (1)

In der englischen Sprache kann es ganz einfach sein, ein neues Wort zu bilden. So wird manchmal mit der Endung **-er** aus einem Tätigkeitswort (z. B. *read*) ein Wort für die Person, die diese Tätigkeit ausübt (z. B. *reader*).

Wenn du solche Wörter selbst bildest, gib Acht: Wie bei der *ing*-Form musst du

- manche Endkonsonanten verdoppeln, z. B. *swim (swimming) – swimm**er***,
- manchmal ein -e am Ende des Verbs weglassen, z. B. *hike (hiking) – hik**er***.

Versuche nun selbst, aus den Verben rechts neue Wörter zu bilden.

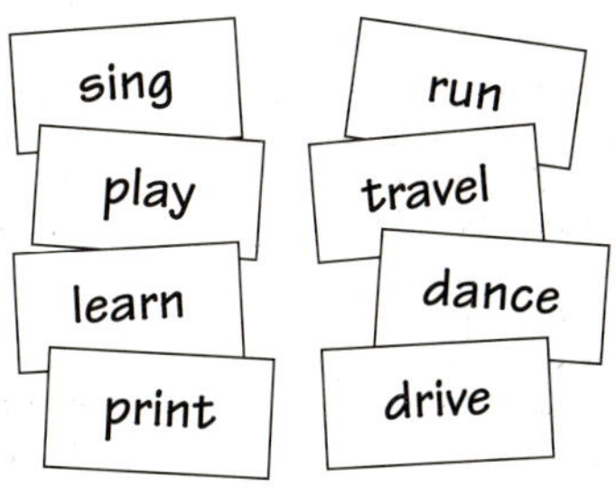

UNIT THREE VOCABULARY

46	golden ['gəʊldən]	golden
	***What do you think of …?** ['θɪŋkəv]	Woran denkst du …? →
	ocean ['əʊʃn]	Ozean; Meer
	sun [sʌn]	Sonne
47	**all over** ['ɔ:l'əʊvə]	überall (in/auf) →
	***grow** [grəʊ]	wachsen
	all year [ɔ:l'jɪə]	das ganze Jahr (lang) →
	Spanish ['spænɪʃ]	spanisch; Spanisch; Spanier/Spanierin
	European [jʊərə'pi:ən]	europäisch; Europäer/in
	look for ['lʊkfɔ:]	suchen →
	gold [gəʊld]	Gold
48	**southern** ['sʌðən]	Süd-, südlich
	they love living …	sie leben sehr gern …
	beach walk ['bi:tʃwɔ:k]	*(asphaltierter)* Strandweg
	cycling ['saɪklɪŋ]	Radfahren
	for meeting friends	um Freunde zu treffen
49	**Go swimming.**	Geh schwimmen.
	surf [sɜ:f]	surfen →
	ski [ski:]	Ski fahren
	fantastic [fæn'tæstɪk]	fantastisch
	Mexican ['meksɪkən]	mexikanisch; Mexikaner/in
	barbecue ['bɑ:bɪkju:]	Grill; Grillfest
	interested in ['ɪntrəstɪd'ɪn]	interessiert an →
	taco ['tɑ:kəʊ]	Taco *(knuspriger, gefüllter Teigfladen)*
	dessert [dɪ'zɜ:t]	Nachtisch, Nachspeise
50	**save** [seɪv]	sparen
	equipment [ɪ'kwɪpmənt]	Ausrüstung
	bench [bentʃ]	(Garten-, Park-)Bank
	just [dʒʌst]	einfach →
	knee-pad ['ni:pæd]	Knieschoner →
	the (green) **one** [wʌn]	der/die/das (grüne) →
	helmet ['helmɪt]	Helm
51	nachos ['nɑ:tʃəʊz]	Nachos *(Tortillachips mit geschmolzenem Käse)*
	skate [skeɪt]	Inline Skates (Rollschuh/Schlittschuh) laufen

STORY

52	**invitation** [ɪnvɪ'teɪʃn]	Einladung
	he was fed up [fed'ʌp]	er hatte die Nase voll
	borrow ['bɒrəʊ]	(sich) borgen, (sich) ausleihen →
	he seemed nice [si:md]	er schien nett zu sein →
53	**enjoy** [ɪn'dʒɔɪ]	genießen, Spaß haben an, gern haben/tun →
	invite [ɪn'vaɪt]	einladen
	She's looking forward to meeting you. ['fɔ:wəd]	Sie freut sich darauf, dich kennen zu lernen. →
	line [laɪn]	Zeile

ACTIVE ENGLISH

54	**ham** [hæm]	Schinken
	cereal ['sɪəriəl]	Getreide-, Frühstücksflocken
	tomato, tomatoes [tə'mɑ:təʊ, tə'mɑ:təʊz]	Tomate, Tomaten
	pancake ['pænkeɪk]	*(kleiner)* Pfannkuchen

I always *think of* skyscrapers when I hear "Manhattan".

sun – sunny
rain – rainy
snow – snowy

All over the USA the fans were watching the game on TV.

It rained *all* day.

all morning
all day
all night
all week
all month
all year

What are you *looking for*?
– I can't find my money.

⚠ south [saʊθ] – southern ['sʌðən]

south – southern
north – northern
east – eastern
west – western

Surfing is a very popular sport in California.

⚠ she ski**s** – they're ski**ing** – she ski**ed**

My brother is very *interested in* films. He loves going to the cinema.

nice
good
great
super
fantastic

⚠ favo**rite** (AE) – favo**urite** (BE)
progra**m** (AE) – progra**mme** (BE)

Our holiday in California was *just* fantastic.
Because she wasn't wearing *knee-pads*, she hurt her knee.
Is your bike *the red one*? – My bike is *the one* over there.

⚠ desert ['dezət] (= Wüste)
dessert [dɪ'zɜ:t] (= Nachtisch)

⚠ **kn**ee [ni:]

stand
sit
lie

Can I *borrow* your helmet?
– I'm sorry, I need it myself.
What's the problem? – This doesn't *seem* right.

Rebecca *enjoys* playing tennis a lot.

We're really *looking forward to* seeing you again.

she's interested in
she likes
she enjoys
she loves
she's good at

ING-FORM OHNE -E-
skate – ska**ting**
invite – invi**ting**
use – us**ing**
phone – phon**ing**
smile – smi**ling**

PLURAL MIT -ES
bench – bench**es**
church – church**es**
tomato – tomato**es**
potato – potato**es**

guest [gest]	Gast
refill ['ri:fɪl]	„Nachfüllung" *(eine weitere Portion)*
55 **have a shower** ['ʃaʊə]	duschen
towel ['taʊəl]	Handtuch
hair-drier ['heədraɪə]	Föhn
I'm OK.	Mir geht's gut. →
56 *natural history* [''nætʃrəl'hɪstri]	Naturgeschichte
57 *dream* [dri:m]	träumen
sky [skaɪ]	Himmel
grey [greɪ]	grau
I've been for a walk	ich bin auf einem Spaziergang gewesen
I'd be ...	ich würde ... sein
if I was ...	wenn ich ... wäre
such [sʌtʃ]	so
(I) stopped into ...	(ich) hielt an und ging ... hinein
pass [pɑ:s]	vorbeikommen
(I) got down on my knees	(ich) fiel auf die Knie
pretend [prɪ'tend]	so tun, als ob
pray [preɪ]	beten
preacher ['pri:tʃə]	Prediger/Predigerin
cold [kəʊld]	Kälte
gonna ['gɒnə]	*(= going to)*
basic information ['beɪsɪk]	die wichtigsten Informationen

Are you OK? – Yes, thanks. I don't think I'm hurt.

HAVE

have a shower	(= duschen)
have a wash	(= sich waschen)
have a break	(= Pause machen)
have breakfast	(= frühstücken)

*IRREGULAR VERBS

INFINITIVE FORM	SIMPLE PAST FORM	PRESENT PERFECT FORM
grow [grəʊ]	I grew [gru:]	I've grown [grəʊn]
think [θɪŋk]	I thought [θɔ:t]	I've thought [θɔ:t]

TEST YOURSELF

a FOOD
taco
?
?
?
?
?

b "EA" OR "UE"?
oc??n – ocean
Europ??n
barbec??
cer??l
g??st

c YOU CAN GO...
cycling
s????ing
s???ing
s??ing
s???ing

d Ergänze.
1 When I hear "Arizona", I ... ... the desert.
2 The weather wasn't very good. It snowed ... week.
3 My sister is very ... ... sports. She loves skiing.
4 Which is your car? – ... ... in front of the house.
5 Rebecca doesn't ... watching TV. She hates it.
6 I'm really ... ... meeting your friend.

TIPS

„Stumme" Buchstaben (1)

Im *Vocabulary* und im *Dictionary* zeigt die Lautschrift in der eckigen Klammer hinter dem englischen Wort, wie es ausgesprochen wird. Das ist wichtig, weil einige Wörter anders geschrieben als gesprochen werden. Manche Buchstaben dürfen gar nicht gesprochen werden, z. B. bleibt bei *know* das k- stumm: [nəʊ].

Suche in den Wörtern rechts den „stummen" Buchstaben. Das *Dictionary* (ab S. 136) kann dir helfen.

EXERCISE ■ Welcher Buchstabe bleibt stumm – h, k, l, t, u oder w?

answer ▪ castle ▪ guest
guide ▪ half ▪ hour ▪ knee
listen ▪ should ▪ walk
what ▪ who ▪ write

UNIT FOUR VOCABULARY

64	**protect (from)** [prə'tekt]	schützen, beschützen (vor) →	Inline-skaters should *protect* their heads with a helmet.
	nature ['neɪtʃə]	Natur	
65	**camp-site** ['kæmpsaɪt]	Campingplatz; Zeltplatz	
	backcountry ['bækʌntri]	„Hinterland“ *(unerschlossenes Gelände)*	
	permit ['pɜ:mɪt]	Genehmigung(sschein), (schriftliche) Erlaubnis	
	ranger station ['reɪndʒə'steɪʃn]	Wache der Parkaufsicht	
66	**entrance** ['entrəns]	Eingang →	I'll meet you at the *entrance* to the park.
	camp [kæmp]	zelten	
67	**grizzly bear** ['grɪzlibeə]	Grislibär	
68	**since** last December [sɪns]	seit letztem Dezember →	We've known the Daltons *since* last summer.
	for 15 years	seit fünfzehn Jahren →	They've been in Germany *for* two weeks but …
69	**pitch a tent** [pɪtʃ]	ein Zelt aufstellen	
	not … yet [jet]	noch nicht →	… they have*n't* visited us *yet*.
	ours ['aʊəz]	unsere/unserer/unseres	
	yours [jɔ:z]	deine/r/s, eure/r/s, Ihre/r/s	
	foot, feet [fʊt, fi:t]	Fuß, Füße	
	mine [maɪn]	meine/meiner/meines	
	theirs [ðeəz]	ihre/ihrer/ihres	
	penknife, penknives ['pennaɪf, 'pennaɪvz]	Taschenmesser →	a *penknife* / some knives
	his [hɪz]	seine/seiner/seines →	What's the matter? – That ball is mine, not *his*!
	hers [hɜ:z]	ihre/ihrer/ihres	

NATURE

animals	rocks
trees	caves
flowers	hills
rivers	mountains
oceans	deserts

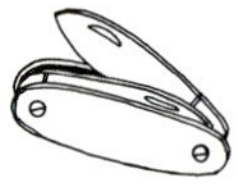

a *penknife*

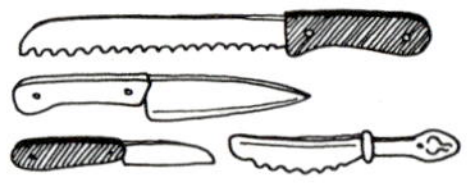

some knives

⚠ one **foot** – two **feet**
one kni**fe** – two kni**ves**

⚠ **knife** [naɪf]

STORY

70	**black bear** ['blækbeə]	Schwarzbär	
	she was awake [ə'weɪk]	sie war wach	
	I was asleep [ə'sli:p]	ich schlief / ich habe geschlafen →	Be quiet. Grandfather *is asleep*.
	rope [rəʊp]	Seil	
	***hang (from)** [hæŋ]	aufhängen (an), hängen (an)	
	so that [səʊ'ðæt]	damit →	My French teacher always speaks *slowly*, *so that* everybody can understand her.
	slow [sləʊ]	langsam →	
	poor [pʊə]	arm	
	backwards ['bækwədz]	rückwärts; nach hinten	
	hind leg [haɪnd'leg]	Hinterbein →	The *hind legs* of an animal are usually very strong legs.
	towards [tə'wɔ:dz]	auf … zu, in Richtung →	When the teacher came *towards* them, they all ran away.
71	**attack** [ə'tæk]	angreifen	
	play dead	sich tot stellen	
	roll up [rəʊl'ʌp]	zusammenrollen	
	back [bæk]	Rücken	
	hump [hʌmp]	Höcker, Buckel →	a *hump*
	***throw (at): I threw** [θrəʊ, θru:]	werfen (nach): ich warf / ich habe geworfen	
	frighten ['fraɪtn]	erschrecken →	Don't shout! You'll *frighten* the baby.
	more **than me**	mehr als ich →	My sister is older *than me*. She's 20 and I'm 16.

mine
yours
his
hers
ours
theirs
yours

⚠ ['bakwədz] backwards
[tə'wɔ:dz] towards

finger
hand
arm
foot
knee
leg
back

ACTIVE ENGLISH

72	**warning** ['wɔ:nɪŋ]	Warnung, Vorwarnung →	The bear attacked without *warning*.
	buffalo, buffaloes ['bʌfələʊ, 'bʌfələʊz]	Büffel	
	pool [pu:l]	Becken, Teich	
73	**fish** [fɪʃ]	fischen, angeln →	He usually *goes fishing* at the weekend.
	What's the weather forecast? ['weðəfɔ:kɑ:st]	Wie ist die Wettervorhersage?	
	degree [dɪ'gri:]	Grad →	I don't like warm weather. I hate it when the temperature is over 30 *degrees*.
74	*forest fire* ['fɒrɪstfaɪə]	Waldbrand	
	camp-fire ['kæmpfaɪə]	Lagerfeuer	⚠ one degree – two degrees

river
pool
lake
ocean

	put out a fire [pʊt'aʊt]	ein Feuer löschen
	wild [waɪld]	wild
75	*you must never …*	du darfst niemals …
	for [fɔː]	denn
	dare [deə]	wagen
	adventure [əd'ventʃə]	Abenteuer
	enormous [ɪ'nɔːməs]	riesig
	she didn't care [keə]	ihr war es egal
	ravenous ['rævənəs]	ausgehungert
	mouth [maʊθ]	Maul
	cruel ['kruːəl]	grausam
	cavernous ['kævənəs]	tief
	(I'm) Glad to meet you. [glæd]	(Ich) Freue mich, dich kennen zu lernen.
	How do … ['haʊduː]	Wie geht's …
	scream [skriːm]	schreien
	scurry ['skʌri]	hasten
	wash [wɒʃ]	waschen
	she straightened her hair up ['streɪtnd, heə]	sie glättete ihr Haar
	eat up [iːt'ʌp]	aufessen
	poem ['pəʊɪm]	Gedicht
	rhyme [raɪm]	Reim; (sich) reimen
	hair [heə]	Haar, Haare
	short [ʃɔːt]	kurz
	disco ['dɪskəʊ]	Disko(thek)

★ IRREGULAR VERBS

INFINITIVE FORM	SIMPLE PAST FORM	PRESENT PERFECT FORM
hang [hæŋ]	I hung [hʌŋ]	I've hung [hʌŋ]
throw [θrəʊ]	I threw [θruː]	I've thrown [θrəʊn]

TEST YOURSELF

a **OPPOSITES**

already – not … yet
awake – ?
fast – ?
happy – ?

b **FINDE DEN REIM**

meet [miːt] – feet
line [laɪn] – ?
grow [grəʊ] – ?
black [blæk] – ?
cool [kuːl] – ?

c **Ergänze.**

1 Nick has lived in California … 1997.
2 Ruby has been in hospital … three days.
3 Can you speak …, please? I don't understand you.
4 My brother is younger … … He's only 10, I'm 16.
5 The temperature will be over 30 … all week.

TIPS

Wörter zum Selbermachen (2)

In der deutschen Sprache muss man manchmal nur eine neue Silbe vor ein Wort stellen, damit es den gegenteiligen Sinn erhält. So wird aus „glücklich" ganz schnell „unglücklich". Im Englischen funktioniert das oft genauso: *happy – unhappy* [ʌn'hæpi].

Versuche, aus den Adjektiven rechts mit *un-* neue Wörter zu bilden. Was bedeuten sie?

fair · tidy · exciting · safe · friendly · important · true · popular · interested

UNIT FIVE VOCABULARY

82	**cattle** ['kætl]	Vieh, Rinder →	In summer the *cattle* are in the fields all day.
83	**Hispanic** [hɪ'spænɪk]	Hispano-Amerikaner/in; hispanisch; spanischsprachig	
	Spanish-speaking ['spænɪʃ'spi:kɪŋ]	spanischsprachig	
84	**high school** ['haɪsku:l]	Oberschule *(in den USA)*	
	highlight ['haɪlaɪt]	Höhepunkt	
	grade [greɪd]	(AE) Klasse, Klassenstufe	
	soccer ['sɒkə]	Fußball →	
	school hall ['sku:lhɔ:l]	Aula	
	DJ (= disc jockey) ['dɪskdʒɒki]	Diskjockey	
	against [ə'genst]	gegen →	Lots of people are *against* the new airport.
85	**cafeteria** [kæfə'tɪəriə]	Cafeteria, Selbstbedienungsrestaurant	
	too bad ['tu:'bæd]	schade →	Phil can't come to the party tonight. – That's *too bad.*
	go out (together)	miteinander gehen	
	probably ['prɒbəbli]	wahrscheinlich →	Is Helen coming with us? – *Probably* not. She isn't feeling very well.
	tardy slip ['tɑ:dislɪp]	Strafzettel fürs Zuspätkommen *(in den USA)*	
	detention [dɪ'tenʃn]	Nachsitzen	
	at least [ət'li:st]	zumindest; mindestens →	A bike like that will cost *at least* $200.
86	**they were born ...** [bɔ:n]	sie wurden ... geboren →	Chris *was born* in London.
	great-great grandparents ['grænpeərənts]	Ururgroßeltern	
	journalism ['dʒɜ:nəlɪzəm]	Journalismus	
	ring [rɪŋ]	Ring →	
	it was made in ... ['meɪdɪn]	es wurde in ... hergestellt →	These cars were *made in* Mexico.
	shoe [ʃu:]	Schuh	
87	**news** [nju:z]	Nachricht(en); Neuigkeit(en) →	I found a job! – That's good *news.*
	gossip ['gɒsɪp]	Klatsch, Tratsch	
	he was picked	er wurde ausgesucht →	*They were picked* because they're very good players.
	stadium ['steɪdiəm]	Stadion	
	*****split up: they split up** [splɪt'ʌp]	sich trennen: sie trennten sich / haben sich getrennt	

soccer (football)

American football

café
cafeteria
chip shop
pub
restaurant

some *rings*

NIE MIT "A/AN"
~~an~~ accommodation
~~a~~ cattle
~~an~~ equipment
~~an~~ information
~~a~~ news
~~a~~ work

STORY

88	**dress** [dres]	Kleid	
	suit [su:t]	Anzug; Kostüm	
	hire ['haɪə]	vermieten; mieten →	Where can I *hire* a car for a day?
	decoration [dekə'reɪʃn]	Dekoration, Verzierung	
	by [baɪ]	von, durch →	The story is from a book *by* Stephen King.
	buffet ['bʊfeɪ]	Büffet	
	for a long time	lange →	They were quiet *for a long time.*
	push [pʊʃ]	stoßen, schieben; drücken	
	Stop it. ['stɒpɪt]	Lass das; Hör auf (damit).	
	fight [faɪt]	Schlägerei; Kampf	
89	**Cheer up!** [tʃɪə'ʌp]	Kopf hoch! →	*Cheer up,* Mandy! Things will look better tomorrow.
	mistake [mɪ'steɪk]	Fehler	

CLOTHES
dress
suit
shirt
T-shirt
sweatshirt
pullover
jeans
shorts
socks
trainers
shoes

ACTIVE ENGLISH

90	**When should we ...?**	Wann sollen wir ...?	
	Me, too. [mi:]	Ich auch. →	I'm soo hungry! – *Me, too.*
	miles apart [ə'pɑ:t]	meilenweit voneinander entfernt	
	do sports	Sport treiben →	I like *doing sports,* but I'm not very good at running.
	disco ['dɪskəʊ]	Disko(thek)	
	alcohol ['ælkəhɒl]	Alkohol	

MIETEN & LEIHEN
rent a flat
hire a car
borrow a CD

93 *deep* [diːp]	tief
heart [hɑːt]	Herz
star [stɑː]	Stern
bright [braɪt]	hell, strahlend
prairie sky ['preəriskaɪ]	Präriehimmel
wide [waɪd]	weit
the sage in bloom ['seɪdʒ, bluːm]	der blühende Salbei
perfume ['pɜːfjuːm]	Parfüm
remind [rɪ'maɪnd]	erinnern
love [lʌv]	sehr mögen, lieben
dedication [dedɪ'keɪʃn]	Widmung
copy ['kɒpi]	kopieren

*IRREGULAR VERBS

INFINITIVE FORM	SIMPLE PAST FORM	PRESENT PERFECT FORM
split up [splɪt'ʌp]	they split up [splɪt'ʌp]	they've split up [splɪt'ʌp]

AMERICAN ENGLISH VOCABULARY

AE (AMERICAN ENGLISH)	BE (BRITISH ENGLISH)	
9th grade [greɪd]	Year 9	Klasse(nstufe), Jahrgang

TEST YOURSELF

a **PLACES**
high school
?
?
?
?

b **FINDE DEN REIM**
made [meɪd] – grade
drawn [drɔːn] – ?
sing [sɪŋ] – ?
true [truː] – ?
fruit [fruːt] – ?
fire ['faɪə] – ?

c **Ergänze.**
1 Will the *Raiders* win tonight? – … not. They aren't very good at the moment.
2 A new dress for the dance will cost … … $50.
3 I have some good … for you: We can all go on holiday.
4 I don't have a suit. Where can I … one?
5 The song is from a new CD … *Alissa.*

TIPS

„Stumme" Buchstaben (2)

Es sind nicht nur einzelne Buchstaben, die manchmal „stumm" bleiben, sondern auch Buchstabenkombinationen. Schau immer genau hin: Manchmal werden sie gesprochen, manchmal nicht – und manchmal anders, als du denkst.

Zum Beispiel die Buchstaben **gh**. Oft werden sie nicht ausgesprochen, z. B. bei *fight* [faɪt], manchmal aber spricht man sie wie ein "f", z. B. bei *laugh* [lɑːf].

Schau dir die Wörter rechts an und sortiere sie in zwei Listen:
1. **gh** nicht gesprochen, 2. **gh** gesprochen.
Zur Überprüfung schlage die Wörter im *Dictionary* (ab S. 136) nach. Hattest du Recht?

EXERCISE ■ Make two lists.

bought ▪ cough ▪ enough
frighten ▪ high ▪ highlight
light ▪ lights ▪ might
neighbour ▪ night ▪ right
straight ▪ thought ▪ through
tough

EXTRA UNIT ONE VOCABULARY

100	**Italian** [ɪ'tæliən]	italienisch; Italienisch; Italiener/Italienerin
	Jewish ['dʒu:ɪʃ]	jüdisch
	origin ['ɒrɪdʒɪn]	Ursprung, Herkunft; Abstammung →
	(sport:) my favourite one	mein Lieblingssport
	college ['kɒlɪdʒ]	Hochschule *(in den USA)*
	Polish ['pəʊlɪʃ]	polnisch; Polnisch; Pole/Polin
	high school ['haɪsku:l]	Oberschule *(in den USA)*
	kiss [kɪs]	(sich) küssen →
	Chinese [tʃaɪ'ni:z]	chinesisch; Chinesisch; Chinese/Chinesin
	Albania [æl'beɪniə]	Albanien
	Bosnia ['bɒzniə]	Bosnien
	Croatia [krəʊ'eɪʃə]	Kroatien
	Greece [gri:s]	Griechenland
	Russia ['rʌʃə]	Russland
	Turkey ['tɜ:ki]	Türkei
101	**avenue** ['ævənju:]	Straße *(in einer Stadt)*
	divide [dɪ'vaɪd]	teilen →
	The Public Library [pʌblɪk'laɪbrəri]	Öffentliche Bibliothek *(von New York)*
	Africa ['æfrɪkə]	Afrika
102	**love** [lʌv]	lieben, sehr mögen
	while [waɪl]	während →
	church [tʃɜ:tʃ]	Kirche, Kirchen-
	five boys and **me**	fünf Jungen und ich
	a man **called …** [kɔ:ld]	ein Mann, der … heißt
	rap [ræp]	rappen
	nervous ['nɜ:vəs]	ängstlich, nervös
	after ['ɑ:ftə]	nachdem →
	audience ['ɔ:diəns]	Publikum
	style [staɪl]	Stil
	brain [breɪn]	Gehirn
103	**line** [laɪn]	Zeile
	give somebody a look	jemandem einen Blick zuwerfen →
104	**in a hurry** ['hʌri]	in (großer) Eile
	doughnut ['dəʊnʌt]	Doughnut *(eine Art Krapfen oder Berliner)* →
	they come in boxes	sie sind in Schachteln erhältlich
	knife, knives [naɪf, naɪvz]	Messer
	fork [fɔ:k]	Gabel
	spoon [spu:n]	Löffel
	all day [ɔ:l'deɪ]	den ganzen Tag (lang) →
	garbage ['gɑ:bɪdʒ]	(AE) Abfall, Müll
	dump [dʌmp]	Müllkippe
	smelly ['smeli]	stinkend
	smell [smel]	riechen →
	New Yorker [nju:'jɔ:kə]	New Yorker / New Yorkerin
	take-away pizza ['teɪkəweɪ]	Pizza zum Mitnehmen
105	**Flatiron Building** ['flætaɪənbɪldɪŋ]	„Bügeleisengebäude" →
	United Nations [ju'naɪtɪd'neɪʃənz]	Vereinte Nationen
	on the … floor [flɔ:]	im … Stock(werk) →
	elevator ['elɪveɪtə]	(AE) Aufzug
	a long time	lange →
	immigrant ['ɪmɪgrənt]	Immigrant/Immigrantin, Einwanderer/Einwanderin

People in New York are of many different *origins*.

I saw Tina and Mick in front of the school last night – and they were *kissing*!

Let's *divide* the class into two teams for this game.

Africa	African
Albania	Albanian
Bosnia	Bosnian
China	Chinese
Croatia	Croatian
Greece	Greek
Italy	Italian
Poland	Polish
Russia	Russian
Turkey	Turkish

While Dave was writing a letter, the children were playing outside.

like
love
hate

After finishing my homework, I went to bed.

Before we …
While we …
After we …

The man in the car *gave* the officer *an* angry *look*.

different *doughnuts*

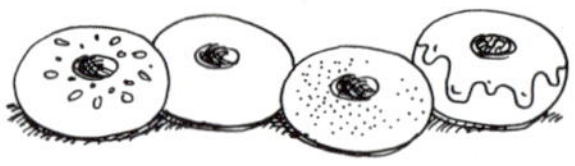

⚠ one kni**fe** – two kni**ves**
knife [naɪf]

Mary is really ill. She's been in bed *all* week.

knife
fork
spoon
plate
cup
glass

Lunch *smells* good today!

an *iron*

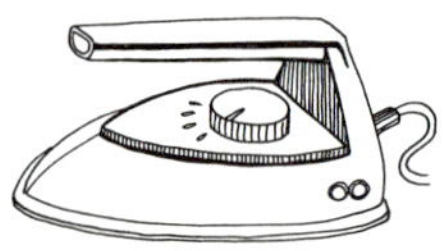

knife	kni<u>ves</u>
life	li<u>ves</u>
wife	wi<u>ves</u>
leaf	lea<u>ves</u>

Our flat is *on the* third *floor*, but there's a lift in the house.

It might take *a long time* to build this model.

EXTRA UNIT ONE

AMERICAN ENGLISH VOCABULARY

AE (AMERICAN ENGLISH)	BE (BRITISH ENGLISH)	
elevator ['elɪveɪtə]	lift	Aufzug
garbage ['gɑ:bɪdʒ]	rubbish	Abfall, Müll

TEST YOURSELF

a **-OO- OR -OU- ?**

fav??rite
high sch??l
nerv??s
d??ghnuts
sp??n
fl??r

b **-F-, -V- OR -W- ?**

Je?ish
a?enue
di?ide
lo?e
kni?e
?ork

c **Ergänze.**

1 Rosa and Hans are Americans, but they're of different …
2 … Lisa was reading a book, Richard was watching TV upstairs.
3 The weather was terrible. It rained … week.
4 What are you cooking? It … fantastic!
5 Can you see the window … … fourth …? That's my room.
6 You usually have to wait … … … before you get an answer.

USING A DICTIONARY

In einem Wörterbuch wird auch die Aussprache eines Wortes angegeben.
Sie steht immer in der eckigen Klammer hinter dem Wort.

DICTIONARY 1 ■ Can you say these words?

buffalo	['bʌfələʊ]	Büffel	language	['læŋgwɪdʒ]	Sprache
chief	[tʃi:f]	Häuptling	regular	['regjələ]	regelmäßig
disguise	[dɪs'gaɪz]	verkleiden	rough	[rʌf]	hart, rauh
fight	[faɪt]	bekämpfen	talent	['tælənt]	Talent

DICTIONARY 2 ■ Find the missing words.

1 My friend went to ['kɒlɪdʒ] in New York.
2 She met lots of people from different ['ɒrɪdʒɪnz].
3 Her best friend came from ['rʌʃə].
4 They liked the food there – especially ['dəʊnʌts].
5 But the best place for a meal was the [ɪ'tæliən] restaurant.
6 They always had a special "Manhattan ['aɪlənd]" pizza there.

EXTRA UNIT TWO VOCABULARY

	English	German	Example
106	**(American) Indian** [ə'merɪkən'ɪndiən]	(amerikanische/r) Indianer/in; indianisch	
	chief [tʃi:f]	Häuptling	
	tribe [traɪb]	Stamm →	Before the white people came, the Indian *tribes* were independent and free.
	hunt [hʌnt]	jagen	
	buffalo, buffaloes ['bʌfələʊ, 'bʌfələʊz]	Büffel	
	land [lænd]	Land →	They bought some *land* outside town and built a small house on it.
	army ['ɑ:mi]	Armee, Heer	
	reservation [rezə'veɪʃn]	(Indianer-)Reservation, Reservat	
	prison ['prɪzn]	Gefängnis	
	soldier ['səʊldʒə]	Soldat/Soldatin	
	★put down [pʊt'daʊn]	niederlegen	
	gun [gʌn]	Gewehr; Schußwaffe	
	shot [ʃɒt]	Schuss	
107	**fall in love**	sich verlieben	
	get married ['mærid]	heiraten	
	kill [kɪl]	töten, umbringen	
	turn around [tɜ:nə'raʊnd]	sich umdrehen →	Marshal Tucker *turned around* to see who was behind him.
	★fight [faɪt]	bekämpfen	
	gunfight ['gʌnfaɪt]	Schießerei	
	★shoot (at) [ʃu:t]	schießen (auf); erschießen →	The men hunted buffaloes because it was easy to *shoot* them.
108	**myth** [mɪθ]	Mythos	
	reality [ri'æləti]	Wirklichkeit, Realität	
	each other [i:tʃ'ʌðə]	einander, sich →	You're good at French and I'm good at maths – we could help *each other* with our homework.
	cattle ['kætl]	Vieh, Rinder	
	move cattle	Vieh treiben, Rinder treiben	
	railway station ['reɪlweɪsteɪʃn]	Bahnhof	
	I could [kʊd]	ich konnte →	Carlos *couldn't* speak English when he was younger.
	railway ['reɪlweɪ]	(Eisen-)Bahn; Bahnstrecke	
	change [tʃeɪndʒ]	(sich) ändern, (sich) verändern →	There's nothing we can do to *change* the rules. ⚠ she change**s** – they're chang**ing** – she change**d**
	forever [fər'evə]	für immer	
	tradition [trə'dɪʃn]	Tradition	
	gas [gæs]	Gas	
	casino [kə'si:nəʊ]	(Spiel-)Kasino	
	independence [ɪndɪ'pendəns]	Unabhängigkeit, Unabhängig-keits-	
	language ['læŋgwɪdʒ]	Sprache →	Julie is learning a very difficult *language*. – Which one? – I think it's Chinese.
	hogan ['həʊgən]	*(traditionelles achtseitiges Navajo-Haus)*	
109	**public holiday** ['pʌblɪk'hɒlədeɪ]	gesetzlicher Feiertag	
	celebrate ['selɪbreɪt]	feiern →	We'll have a big party to *celebrate* my 18th birthday.
	fireworks ['faɪəwɜ:ks]	Feuerwerk	
	flag [flæg]	Fahne, Flagge	
	everywhere ['evriweə]	überall	
	they're in love	sie sind verliebt	
	costume ['kɒstju:m]	Kostüm →	We all wore clowns' *costumes* in the *parade* last year.
	parade [pə'reɪd]	Parade, Umzug →	
	★throw [θrəʊ]	werfen	
	beads [bi:dz]	Perlenkette, -ketten	
	Thanksgiving [θæŋks'gɪvɪŋ]	Erntedankfest	
	turkey ['tɜ:ki]	Truthahn, Pute	
	dinner ['dɪnə]	Festessen	
	disguise [dɪs'gaɪz]	verkleiden →	She *disguised* herself *as* a reporter to get into the firm.
	as [əz]	als →	
	ghost [gəʊst]	Gespenst, Geist	
	witch [wɪtʃ]	Hexe	

Marshal Tucker *turned around* to see who was behind him.

OHNE "THE"
go to church
go to college
go to hospital
go to prison
go to school
go to town

army
soldier
gun
shot
fight
shoot
kill

We all wore clowns' *costumes* in the *parade* last year.

everybody
everything
everywhere

SOME SPECIAL DAYS
carnival ['kɑ:nɪvl]
Easter ['i:stə]
Ascension Day [ə'senʃndeɪ]
Whitsun ['wɪtsn]
Christmas ['krɪsməs]
New Year's Eve [nju:jɪəz'i:v]

EXTRA UNIT TWO

110	**Dear ...** [dɪə]	Liebe/Lieber ...
	mirror ['mɪrə]	Spiegel
111	**apartment** [ə'pɑ:tmənt]	(AE) Wohnung
	lorry ['lɒri]	Lastwagen →
	truck [trʌk]	(AE) Lastwagen →
	mailman ['meɪlmæn]	(AE) Briefträger, Postbote
	You know, ...	Du weißt schon, ... →
	shoe [ʃu:]	Schuh
	slow [sləʊ]	langsam
	camel ['kæml]	Kamel
	war [wɔ:]	Krieg

a *lorry* (BE)

a *truck* (AE)

... and there I met Andy. – Andy?
– Andy, *you know*, the boy from "Supersound".

★ IRREGULAR VERBS

INFINITIVE FORM	SIMPLE PAST FORM	PRESENT PERFECT FORM
fight [faɪt]	I fought [fɔ:t]	I've fought [fɔ:t]
put [pʊt]	I put [pʊt]	I've put [pʊt]
shoot [ʃu:t]	I shot [ʃɒt]	I've shot [ʃɒt]
throw [θrəʊ]	I threw [θru:]	I've thrown [θrəʊn]

AMERICAN ENGLISH VOCABULARY

AE (AMERICAN ENGLISH)	BE (BRITISH ENGLISH)	
apartment [ə'pɑ:tmənt]	flat	Wohnung
mailman ['meɪlmæn]	postman	Briefträger, Postbote
truck [trʌk]	lorry	Lastwagen

TEST YOURSELF

a LOVE
fall in love
get ?
?

b ANIMALS
buffalo
?
?
?

c -I- OR -Y-?
tr?be
arm?
m?th
real?t?
turke?

d Ergänze.
1 I ... speak English very well before I went to England.
2 You can't just ... the rules – that's unfair!
3 What ... do they speak in South Africa? – I'm not sure.
4 Let's ... Thanksgiving together this year.
5 He ... himself as a cowboy at our last carnival party.

USING A DICTIONARY

In der englischen Sprache werden die Wörter oft ganz anders geschrieben als ausgesprochen. Deshalb ist es so wichtig, sich die Aussprache immer genau anzuschauen. Finde nun heraus, ob sich die folgenden Wörter reimen. Suche die jeweilige Aussprache rechts in den eckigen Klammen und vergleiche sie miteinander.
Beispiel: 1 could – should: [kʊd] und [ʃʊd] reimen sich; 2 desert – dessert: ['dezət] und [dɪ'zɜ:t] reimen sich nicht.

DICTIONARY ■ Do these words rhyme?

1 could – should
2 desert – dessert
3 disguise – surprise
4 love – move
5 parade – salad
6 throw – slow
7 war – bar
8 witch – which

bar [bɑ:]	move [mu:v]	throw [θrəʊ]
could [kʊd]	parade [pə'reɪd]	war [wɔ:]
desert ['dezət]	salad ['sæləd]	which [wɪtʃ]
dessert [dɪ'zɜ:t]	should [ʃʊd]	witch [wɪtʃ]
disguise [dɪs'gaɪz]	slow [sləʊ]	
love [lʌv]	surprise [sə'praɪz]	

EXTRA UNIT THREE VOCABULARY

112	**web site** ['websaɪt]	Website *(Gesamtangebot eines Anbieters im Internet bzw. im World Wide Web)*
	1960s [naɪnti:n'sɪkstiz]	sechziger Jahre →
	parking ['pɑ:kɪŋ]	Park-
	parking lot ['pɑ:kɪŋlɒt]	(AE) *(großer)* Parkplatz
	parking space ['pɑ:kɪŋspeɪs]	Parkplatz, Parklücke →
	cheerleader ['tʃɪəli:də]	*Person, die das Publikum bei einem Wettkampf zum Beifall anfeuert*
	join [dʒɔɪn]	beitreten, Mitglied werden →
	practise ['præktɪs]	üben, trainieren
	regular ['regjələ]	regelmäßig →
	uniform ['ju:nɪfɔ:m]	Uniform
	I'll buy you a coke. [baɪ]	Ich spendiere dir eine Cola.
	***beat: I beat** [bi:t]	schlagen: ich schlug / ich habe geschlagen →
	play-off ['pleɪɒf]	Entscheidungsspiel
	coach [kəʊtʃ]	Trainer/Trainerin
	homepage ['həʊmpeɪdʒ]	Ausgangsseite *(einer Website im Internet)*
113	**frankfurter** ['fræŋkfɜ:tə]	(Frankfurter) Würstchen
	***lose** [lu:z]	verlieren
	Turkish ['tɜ:kɪʃ]	türkisch; Türkisch; Türke/Türkin
114	**tall** [tɔ:l]	groß (gewachsen); hoch →
	talent ['tælənt]	Talent
	ordinary ['ɔ:dnri]	gewöhnlich, normal
	***teach** [ti:tʃ]: **I taught** [tɔ:t]	beibringen, unterrichten: ich brachte bei / ich habe beigebracht →
	report [rɪ'pɔ:t]	Zeugnis
	at 16	mit 16 (Jahren) →
	sportsman, sportsmen ['spɔ:tsmən]	Sportler
	make [meɪk]	*(Geld)* verdienen →
	dream [dri:m]	Traum
	laugh at ['lɑ:fət]	auslachen →
	he's proud of himself	er ist stolz auf sich
115	**Slovakia** [sləʊ'vɑ:kiə]	Slowakische Republik
	Switzerland ['swɪtsələnd]	Schweiz
	Czech Republic [tʃekrɪ'pʌblɪk]	Tschechische Republik
	interest ['ɪntrəst]	Interesse
	horse [hɔ:s]	Pferd
	Canadian [kə'neɪdiən]	kanadisch; Kanadier/Kanadierin
	basket ['bɑ:skɪt]	Korb
	bread [bred]	Brot
116	**bar** [bɑ:]	Bar, Kneipe
	president ['prezɪdənt]	Präsident
	season ['si:zn]	Saison
	net [net]	Netz →
	professional [prə'feʃənl]	Profi-, Berufs- →
	kick [kɪk]	kicken; treten
	rough [rʌf]	hart, rauh →
	clothing ['kləʊðɪŋ]	Kleidung
	ice hockey ['aɪshɒki]	Eishockey
	ice-rink ['aɪsrɪŋk]	Eisbahn, Schlittschuhbahn
	indoors [ɪn'dɔ:z]	in der Halle, drinnen
	professionally [prə'feʃənli]	berufsmäßig →

In the *1980s* more people started to think about the environment.

It's so difficult to find a *parking space* in town.

Why don't you *join* our new inline-skating club – it's great fun!
Jenny phones her parents *regularly.*

⚠ practise (BE)
practice (AE)

The poor dog was *beaten* regularly by the children.

computer
homepage
web site
Internet
surf the Internet

I'm small, but my friend is a really *tall* girl.

⚠ German "groß":
people: **tall**
things: **big**

He *teaches* his children English.

At 75 she's still a good hiker.

It's a great job – he *makes* $50,000 a year!

Now go and do your rap – people won't *laugh at* you.

small
tall
high
long
big

Canada	–	Canadian
Czech Republic	–	Czech
Slovakia	–	Slovak
Switzerland	–	Swiss
Turkey	–	Turkish

interest
interested
interested in

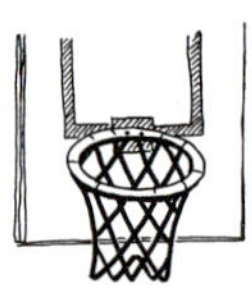

a basketball *net*

FARM ANIMALS
chicken
cows
horses
pigs
sheep
dogs
cats
mice

Tim is very good at football. He'll probably become a *professional* player.
The other boys were *rough.* They were always fighting each other.

My sister started to sing *professionally* after leaving college.

EXTRA UNIT THREE

117	**invention** [ɪn'venʃn]	Erfindung
	answer the phone	ans Telefon gehen, einen Anruf entgegennehmen
	dry [draɪ]	trocknen, abtrocknen
	hair [heə]	Haar, Haare →
	toast [təʊst]	toasten
	fax [fæks]	Fax
	wash dishes ['dɪʃɪz]	Geschirr spülen
	microwave ['maɪkrəweɪv]	Mikrowelle
	fax machine [fæksmə'ʃi:n]	Faxgerät
	washing-machine ['wɒʃɪŋmə'ʃi:n]	Waschmaschine
	answerphone ['ɑ:nsəfəʊn]	Anrufbeantworter
	helpful ['helpfl]	hilfreich →

⚠ he dr**ies** – they're dr**ying** – he dr**ied**

Of course you know Robin. He's the boy with the long, dark *hair*.

I asked the officer, but he wasn't very *helpful*.

-FUL
beautiful
careful
helpful
useful

★ IRREGULAR VERBS

INFINITIVE FORM	SIMPLE PAST FORM	PRESENT PERFECT FORM
beat [bi:t]	I beat [bi:t]	I've beaten ['bi:tn]
lose [lu:z]	I lost [lɒst]	I've lost [lɒst]
teach [ti:tʃ]	I taught [tɔ:t]	I've taught [tɔ:t]

AMERICAN ENGLISH VOCABULARY

AE (AMERICAN ENGLISH)	BE (BRITISH ENGLISH)	
parking lot ['pɑ:kɪŋlɒt]	car park	*(großer)* Parkplatz

TEST YOURSELF

a HE'S/SHE'S/IT'S ...
tall
?
?
?
?

b -EA-, -OA-, -AU- OR OU?

cheerl??der	pr??d
b??t	l??gh
c??ch	br??d
t??ch	s??son
t??ght	r??gh
dr??m	t??st

c Ergänze.
1 Come and ... the new school swimming club.
2 Our team is really bad – they were ... again!
3 My friend isn't very ..., but I'm small, too.
4 I was a ... child. I was always fighting the others.
5 I'm good at football. I want to play it ...
6 Do you like long ...? I think it looks great.

Dictionary

Alphabetische Liste der Wörter aus den Bänden 1 – 4

(AE): Angegeben sind grundsätzlich Schreibweise und Aussprache des britischen Englisch; Wörter, die vorwiegend im amerikanischen Englisch benutzt werden, sind mit (AE) gekennzeichnet.

A

a [ə] ein/eine; **£2 a week** 2 Pfund pro Woche
about [ə'baʊt] **1.** über, von; **2.** wegen; **3.** ungefähr; **The programme is about ...** Die Sendung handelt von ...; **What about ...?** Wie wäre es mit ...? Was ist mit ...?
above [ə'bʌv] über
accent ['æksənt] Akzent
accommodation [əkɒmə'deɪʃn] Unterkunft
across [ə'krɒs] (quer) durch, über
act [ækt] sich benehmen, sich verhalten
action ['ækʃn] Handlung, Tätigkeit
activity [æk'tɪvəti] Tätigkeit, Aktivität; Unternehmung
address [ə'dres] Adresse
adult ['ædʌlt] Erwachsene/r
Africa ['æfrɪkə] Afrika
after ['ɑ:ftə] **1.** nach; **after school** nach der Schule; **2.** nachdem
afternoon ['ɑ:ftə'nu:n] Nachmittag; **Good afternoon.** Guten Tag. *(nachmittags)*; **in the afternoon(s)** nachmittags; am Nachmittag; **this afternoon** heute Nachmittag
again [ə'gen] (schon) wieder; noch einmal
against [ə'genst] gegen
agency ['eɪdʒənsi]**: travel agency** Reisebüro
ago [ə'gəʊ]**: 400 years ago** vor 400 Jahren
ahead [ə'hed]**: straight ahead** [streɪtə'hed] geradeaus
aim [eɪm] Ziel
airport ['eəpɔ:t] Flughafen
Albania [æl'beɪniə] Albanien
alcohol ['ælkəhɒl] Alkohol
all [ɔ:l] alle; alles; **all day/month/...** den ganzen Tag/Monat/... (lang); **all over** überall in/auf; **all the time** die ganze Zeit
almost ['ɔ:lməʊst] fast, beinahe
alone [ə'ləʊn] allein
along [ə'lɒŋ] entlang
already [ɔ:l'redi] schon
always ['ɔ:lweɪz] immer
am [æm]**: I am** ich bin
am ['eɪ'em] morgens, vormittags
America [ə'merɪkə] Amerika
American [ə'merɪkən] amerikanisch; Amerikaner/in; **American Indian** (amerikanische/r) Indianer/Indianerin; indianisch
amputate ['æmpjuteɪt] amputieren
an [ən] ein/eine
and [ænd, ənd] und
angry ['æŋgri] böse, wütend
animal ['ænɪməl] Tier; **animal home** Tierheim
another [ə'nʌðə] ein anderer / eine andere / ein anderes; noch ein/eine/eins
answer ['ɑ:nsə] **1.** antworten, beantworten; **answer the phone** ans Telefon gehen, einen Anruf entgegennehmen; **2.** Antwort
answerphone ['ɑ:nsəfəʊn] Anrufbeantworter
any ['eni]**: not ... any** kein/keine; keine/keiner/keines
anybody ['enibɒdi]**: not ... anybody** niemand
anything ['eniθɪŋ]**: not ... anything** nichts
apart [ə'pɑ:t]**: miles apart** meilenweit voneinander entfernt
apartment [ə'pɑ:tmənt] (AE) Wohnung
apple ['æpl] Apfel
April ['eɪprəl] April
are [ɑ:]**: you are** du bist; ihr seid; Sie sind; **we/they are** wir/sie sind
arm [ɑ:m] Arm
army ['ɑ:mi] Armee, Heer
around [ə'raʊnd]**: around Manhattan** um Manhattan herum; **turn around** sich umdrehen
arrive [ə'raɪv] ankommen
art [ɑ:t] Kunst
article ['ɑ:tɪkl] Artikel
as [æz, əz] als; **as near as** so nah wie
Asian ['eɪʃn] asiatisch; Asiat/Asiatin
ask [ɑ:sk] fragen; bitten; **ask a question** eine Frage stellen; **ask about** fragen nach
asleep [ə'sli:p]**: I was asleep** ich schlief / ich habe geschlafen
assistant [ə'sɪstənt]**: shop assistant** Verkäufer/Verkäuferin
at [æt, ət] bei; an; in; **at 6 o'clock** um 6 Uhr / 18 Uhr; **at 16** mit 16 (Jahren); **at Dave's house / Asif's flat** bei Dave/Asif zu Hause; **at home** zu Hause, daheim; **at least** [ət'li:st] zumindest; mindestens; **at night** nachts, in der Nacht; **at school** in der Schule; **at the moment** zurzeit, im Augenblick; **at the top** auf der Spitze; **at the weekend** am Wochenende; **at work** bei der Arbeit
ate [et]**: I ate** ich aß / ich habe gegessen
Atlantic [ət'læntɪk] Atlantik; **Atlantic Ocean** Atlantischer Ozean
attack [ə'tæk] angreifen
auction ['ɔ:kʃn] Versteigerung
audience ['ɔ:dɪəns] Publikum
August ['ɔ:gəst] August
aunt [ɑ:nt] Tante
autumn ['ɔ:təm] Herbst
avenue ['ævənju:] Straße *(in einer Stadt)*
awake [ə'weɪk]**: I'm awake** ich bin wach
away [ə'weɪ] weg, entfernt; fort

B

baby ['beɪbi] Baby
back [bæk] **1.** zurück; **2.** Rücken
backcountry ['bækʌntri] „Hinterland" *(unerschlossenes Gelände)*
backpack ['bækpæk] Rucksack

backwards ['bækwədz] rückwärts; nach hinten
bacon ['beɪkən] Speck
bad [bæd] schlecht, schlimm; **too bad** schade
badge [bædʒ] Abzeichen; Anstecker, Button
bag [bæg] (Schul-)Tasche, Tüte
ball [bɔ:l] Ball
banana [bə'nɑ:nə] Banane
band [bænd] Band, (Musik-)Gruppe
bank [bæŋk] Bank, Sparkasse; **bank clerk** Bankangestellte/r
bar [bɑ:] Bar, Kneipe
barbecue ['bɑ:bɪkju:] Grill; Grillfest
baseball ['beɪsbɔ:l] Baseball
basket ['bɑ:skɪt] Korb
basketball ['bɑ:skɪtbɔ:l] Basketball
bathroom ['bɑ:θru:m] Bad(ezimmer)
battery ['bætəri] Batterie
be [bi:] sein
beach [bi:tʃ] Strand; **beach walk** *(asphaltierter)* Strandweg
beads [bi:dz] Perlenkette, -ketten
bean [bi:n] Bohne
bear [beə] Bär; **black bear** ['blækbeə] Schwarzbär; **grizzly bear** ['grɪzlibeə] Grislibär
beat [bi:t] schlagen; **I beat** ich schlug / ich habe geschlagen
beaten ['bi:tn]**: I've beaten** ich habe geschlagen
beautiful ['bju:tɪfl] schön, wunderschön
became [bɪ'keɪm]**: I became** ich wurde / ich bin geworden
because [bɪ'kɒz] weil; **because of** wegen
become [bɪ'kʌm] werden; **I've become** ich bin geworden
bed [bed] Bett; **go to bed** ins Bett gehen; **in bed** im Bett; **bed and breakfast** [bedən'brekfəst] Zimmer mit Frühstück *(in kleiner Frühstückspension)*
bedroom ['bedru:m] Schlafzimmer
been [bi:n, bɪn]**: I've been** ich bin gewesen
before [bɪ'fɔ:] **1.** vor; **2.** bevor; **3.** vorher, schon einmal
behind [bɪ'haɪnd] hinter
believe [bɪ'li:v] glauben
bell [bel] Glocke
belong to [bɪ'lɒŋtu:, bɪ'lɒŋtə] gehören (zu)
bench [bentʃ] (Garten-, Park-)Bank
bend [bend] Kurve
best [best] beste/bester/bestes; der/die/das Beste
better ['betə] besser
between [bɪ'twi:n] zwischen
big [bɪg] groß
bike [baɪk] Fahrrad; **ride a bike** Rad fahren; **bike path** Fahrradweg
bingo ['bɪŋgəʊ] Bingo(spiel)
bird [bɜ:d] Vogel
biro ['baɪrəʊ] Kugelschreiber
birthday ['bɜ:θdeɪ] Geburtstag; **Happy birthday (to you)!** Herzlichen Glückwunsch zum Geburtstag!
black [blæk] schwarz; **black bear** ['blækbeə] Schwarzbär
block [blɒk] Häuserblock
blue [blu:] blau
board [bɔ:d] Tafel
boat [bəʊt] Schiff, Boot
body ['bɒdi] Körper
bomb [bɒm] Bombe
book [bʊk] **1.** Buch; Heft; **2.** buchen, reservieren (lassen), vorbestellen
boring ['bɔ:rɪŋ] langweilig
born [bɔ:n]**: I was born** ich wurde geboren
borrow ['bɒrəʊ] (sich) borgen, (sich) ausleihen
Bosnia ['bɒzniə] Bosnien
bottle ['bɒtl] Flasche
bought [bɔ:t]**: I bought** ich kaufte / ich habe gekauft; **I've bought** ich habe gekauft
box [bɒks] Kiste, Karton, Schachtel, Dose
boy [bɔɪ] Junge
boyfriend ['bɔɪfrend] (fester) Freund
brain [breɪn] Gehirn
bread [bred] Brot
break [breɪk] **1.** brechen, zerbrechen, kaputtmachen; **2.** Pause; **have a break** (eine) Pause machen; **lunch break** Mittagspause
breakfast ['brekfəst] Frühstück; **for breakfast** zum Frühstück; **have breakfast** frühstücken
bricklayer ['brɪkleɪə] Maurer/in
bridge [brɪdʒ] Brücke
bring [brɪŋ] bringen, mitbringen
Britain ['brɪtn] Großbritannien
British ['brɪtɪʃ] britisch; Brite/Britin
brochure ['brəʊʃə] Broschüre
broken ['brəʊkən] gebrochen, zerbrochen, kaputt
brother ['brʌðə] Bruder
brought [brɔ:t]**: I brought** ich brachte (mit) / ich habe (mit)gebracht
brown [braʊn] braun
budgie ['bʌdʒi] Wellensittich
buffalo, buffaloes ['bʌfələʊ, 'bʌfələʊz] Büffel
buffet ['bʊfeɪ] Büffet
build [bɪld] bauen
built [bɪlt]**: I built** ich baute / ich habe gebaut; **I've built** ich habe gebaut
bus [bʌs] Bus; **bus station** Bushof, Busbahnhof
bus-stop ['bʌstɒp] Bushaltestelle
busy ['bɪzi] beschäftigt; hektisch, belebt
but [bʌt] aber
buy [baɪ] kaufen; **I'll buy you a coke.** Ich spendiere dir eine Cola.
by [baɪ] von, durch; **by bike/bus/car/...** mit dem Rad/Bus/Auto/...
Bye. / Bye-bye. [baɪ, baɪ'baɪ] Tschüs. Wiedersehen.

C

cab [kæb] Taxi
café ['kæfeɪ] Café
cafeteria [kæfə'tɪəriə] Selbstbedienungsrestaurant, Cafeteria
cake [keɪk] (kleiner) Kuchen
calculator ['kælkjuleɪtə] Taschenrechner
California [kælɪ'fɔ:niə] Kalifornien
call [kɔ:l] nennen; **a man called ...** ein Mann, der ... heißt
came [keɪm]**: I came** ich kam / ich bin gekommen
camel ['kæml] Kamel
camera ['kæmrə] Fotoapparat, Kamera
camp [kæmp] zelten; **go camping** zelten gehen
camp-site ['kæmpsaɪt] Campingplatz; Zeltplatz
can [kæn] Dose, Büchse
can [kæn, kən] können, dürfen; **can't** [kɑ:nt] (= **cannot** ['kænɒt]) nicht können, nicht dürfen
Canada ['kænədə] Kanada

Canadian [kə'neɪdiən] kanadisch; Kanadier/Kanadierin
cancer ['kænsə] Krebs
canoe [kə'nu:] **1.** Kanu; **2.** Kanu fahren
canyon ['kænjən] Cañon
capital ['kæpɪtl] Hauptstadt
car [kɑ:] Auto; **car park** *(großer)* Parkplatz, Parkhaus
caravan ['kærəvæn] Wohnwagen
card [kɑ:d] (Spiel-, Post-)Karte; **youth hostel card** Jugendherbergsausweis
careful ['keəfl] vorsichtig; sorgfältig
carry ['kæri] tragen; befördern
casino [kə'si:nəʊ] (Spiel-)Kasino
cassette [kə'set] Cassette
castle ['kɑ:sl] Burg; Schloss
cat [kæt] Katze
Catholic ['kæθlɪk] Katholik/Katholikin
cattle ['kætl] Vieh, Rinder
cave [keɪv] Höhle
CD [si:'di:] CD
celebrate ['selɪbreɪt] feiern
cent (¢) [sent] Cent *(amerik. Geld)*
centimetre ['sentɪmi:tə] Zentimeter
centre ['sentə] Zentrum, Mitte
cereal ['sɪəriəl] Getreide-, Frühstücksflocken
chair [tʃeə] Stuhl
change [tʃeɪndʒ] **1.** (sich) ändern, verändern; **change (trains/...)** umsteigen; (den Zug/...) wechseln; **2.** Veränderung
cheap [tʃi:p] billig, preiswert
check [tʃek] (über)prüfen, kontrollieren
cheer [tʃɪə]: **Cheer up!** Kopf hoch!
cheerleader ['tʃɪəli:də] *Person, die das Publikum bei einem Wettkampf zum Beifall anfeuert*
cheese [tʃi:z] Käse
cheeseburger ['tʃi:zbɜ:gə] Cheeseburger
chemist ['kemɪst] Apotheker/in, Drogist/in; **at the chemist's** in der Apotheke/Drogerie
chewing gum ['tʃu:ɪŋgʌm] Kaugummi
chicken ['tʃɪkɪn] Huhn; (Brat-)Hähnchen
chief [tʃi:f] Häuptling
child, children [tʃaɪld, 'tʃɪldrən] Kind, Kinder
Chinese [tʃaɪ'ni:z] chinesisch; Chinesisch; Chinese/Chinesin

chip shop ['tʃɪpʃɒp] Pommes-frites-Bude
chips [tʃɪps] Pommes frites
chocolate ['tʃɒklət] Trinkschokolade; Schokolade
choose [tʃu:z] aussuchen, auswählen, wählen
Christmas ['krɪsməs] Weihnachten
church [tʃɜ:tʃ] Kirche, Kirchen-
cinema ['sɪnəmə] Kino
city ['sɪti] Stadt, Großstadt
class [klɑ:s] Klasse
classroom ['klɑ:sru:m] Klassenzimmer
claw [klɔ:] Kralle
clean [kli:n] **1.** sauber machen, putzen; **I clean my teeth.** Ich putze mir die Zähne. **2.** sauber
clear ['klɪə]: **clear the table** den Tisch abräumen
clerk [klɑ:k]: **bank clerk** Bankangestellte/Bankangestellter
clever ['klevə] schlau, klug
climb [klaɪm]: **climb a tree** auf einen Baum klettern
clock [klɒk] Uhr
close [kləʊz] zumachen, schließen
closed [kləʊzd] geschlossen, zu
clothes [kləʊðz] Kleidung, Kleider
clothing ['kləʊðɪŋ] Kleidung
cloudy ['klaʊdi] bewölkt
club [klʌb] Club, Verein
coach [kəʊtʃ] Trainer/Trainerin
coal [kəʊl] Kohle
coffee ['kɒfi] Kaffee
coke [kəʊk] Cola
cola ['kəʊlə] Cola
cold [kəʊld] **1.** kalt; **I'm cold** ich friere; **2.** Erkältung
collect [kə'lekt] (ein)sammeln
college ['kɒlɪdʒ] Hochschule *(in den USA)*
colour ['kʌlə] Farbe; **What colour is ...?** Welche Farbe hat ...?
come [kʌm] kommen; **I've come** ich bin gekommen; **Come on!** Komm/Kommt schon! Los! **they come in boxes** sie sind in Schachteln erhältlich
comic ['kɒmɪk] Comic(heft)
company ['kʌmpəni] Gesellschaft, Firma
computer [kəm'pju:tə] Computer, Rechner
concert ['kɒnsət] Konzert
cook [kʊk] kochen

cool [ku:l] kühl; ruhig, überlegen
copy ['kɒpi] kopieren; **copy room** Fotokopierraum
cornflakes ['kɔ:nfleɪks] Cornflakes
cost [kɒst] *(Geld)* kosten
costume ['kɒstju:m] Kostüm
couch [kaʊtʃ] Couch, Sofa
cough [kɒf] Husten
could [kʊd]: **I could 1.** ich könnte; **2.** ich konnte
count [kaʊnt] zählen
country ['kʌntri] Land; **in the country** auf dem Land
course [kɔ:s]: **of course** natürlich, selbstverständlich
cousin ['kʌzn] Cousin/Cousine, Vetter
cow [kaʊ] Kuh
cowboy ['kaʊbɔɪ] Cowboy
crime [kraɪm] Verbrechen
crisps [krɪsps] Kartoffelchips
Croatia [krəʊ'eɪʃə] Kroatien
cross [krɒs] überqueren
cry [kraɪ] weinen
cup [kʌp] Tasse
cupboard ['kʌbəd] Schrank
curved [kɜ:vd] gekrümmt
customer ['kʌstəmə] Kunde/Kundin
cycle ['saɪkl] Rad fahren
cycling ['saɪklɪŋ] Radfahren
Czech Republic [tʃekrɪ'pʌblɪk] Tschechische Republik

D

dad [dæd] Papa, Vati
dance [dɑ:ns] **1.** tanzen; **2.** Tanz; Tanzveranstaltung, Ball
dancer ['dɑ:nsə] Tänzer/Tänzerin
dangerous ['deɪndʒərəs] gefährlich
dark [dɑ:k] dunkel
date [deɪt] Datum
daughter ['dɔ:tə] Tochter
day [deɪ] Tag; **day return** Tagesrückfahrkarte; **open day** Tag der offenen Tür
dead [ded] tot
Dear ... [dɪə] Liebe/Lieber ...
December [dɪ'sembə] Dezember
decoration [dekə'reɪʃn] Dekoration, Verzierung
degree [dɪ'gri:] Grad
deliver [dɪ'lɪvə] austragen, zustellen; liefern

dentist ['dentɪst] Zahnarzt/Zahnärztin; **at the dentist's** beim Zahnarzt / bei der Zahnärztin
deodorant [di'əʊdərənt] Deodorant
department store [dɪ'pɑːtməntstɔː] Kaufhaus
desert ['dezət] Wüste
dessert [dɪ'zɜːt] Nachtisch, -speise
destroy [dɪ'strɔɪ] zerstören
detention [dɪ'tenʃn] Nachsitzen
dialogue ['daɪəlɒg] Dialog, Gespräch
did [dɪd]: **I did** ich tat / ich habe getan
die [daɪ] sterben
different ['dɪfrənt] andere/anderer/anderes; verschieden, anders; **different from** anders als
difficult ['dɪfɪkəlt] schwierig, schwer
dinner ['dɪnə] Festessen
disaster [dɪ'zɑːstə] Katastrophe
disc jockey (DJ) ['dɪskdʒɒki, 'diː'dʒeɪ] Diskjockey
disco ['dɪskəʊ] Disko(thek)
discrimination [dɪskrɪmɪ'neɪʃn] Diskriminierung, Benachteiligung
disguise [dɪs'gaɪz] verkleiden
dishes ['dɪʃɪz]: **wash dishes** Geschirr spülen
dishwasher ['dɪʃwɒʃə] Geschirrspülmaschine
divide [dɪ'vaɪd] teilen
do [duː] tun, machen; schaffen; **do sports** Sport treiben
doctor ['dɒktə] Arzt/Ärztin, Doktor
dog [dɒg] Hund
dollar ($) ['dɒlə] Dollar *(amerik. Geld)*
done [dʌn]: **I've done** ich habe getan
door [dɔː] Tür
doughnut ['dəʊnʌt] Doughnut *(eine Art Krapfen oder Berliner)*
down [daʊn] hinunter/herunter, hinab/herab
downhill [daʊn'hɪl] bergab
drank [dræŋk]: **I drank** ich trank / ich habe getrunken
draw [drɔː] zeichnen
drawn [drɔːn]: **I've drawn** ich habe gezeichnet
dream [driːm] Traum
dress [dres] Kleid
drew [druː]: **I drew** ich zeichnete / ich habe gezeichnet
drink [drɪŋk] **1.** trinken; **2.** Getränk
drive [draɪv] fahren
driver ['draɪvə] Fahrer/Fahrerin
driving test ['draɪvɪŋtest] Führerscheinprüfung; **take a driving test** die Führerscheinprüfung machen
drop [drɒp] fallen lassen
drove [drəʊv]: **I drove** ich fuhr / ich bin gefahren
drug [drʌg] **1.** Droge, Rauschgift; **2.** Medikament
drunk [drʌŋk]: **I've drunk** ich habe getrunken
dry [draɪ] trocknen, abtrocknen
dump [dʌmp] Müllkippe

E

e-mail ['iːmeɪl] (= **electronic mail** [ɪlek'trɒnɪk'meɪl]) E-Mail (= elektronische Post)
each [iːtʃ] jede/jeder/jedes; je; **each other** einander, sich
early ['ɜːli] früh; vorzeitig, zu früh
east [iːst] Ost-; (nach) Osten; östlich
easy ['iːzi] einfach, leicht
eat [iːt] essen
eaten ['iːtn]: **I've eaten** ich habe gegessen
egg [eg] Ei
elevator ['elɪveɪtə] (AE) Aufzug
empty ['empti] **1.** leer; **2.** leeren, ausräumen
end [end] Ende
engineer [endʒɪ'nɪə] Techniker/Technikerin; Ingenieur/Ingenieurin
England ['ɪŋglənd] England
English ['ɪŋglɪʃ] englisch; Englisch; Engländer/Engländerin
enjoy [ɪn'dʒɔɪ] genießen, Spaß haben an, gern haben/tun; **I'm enjoying myself** ich amüsiere mich, ich habe viel Spaß
enough [ɪ'nʌf] genug
entrance ['entrəns] Eingang
environment [ɪn'vaɪrənmənt] Umgebung; Umwelt
equipment [ɪ'kwɪpmənt] Ausrüstung
especially [ɪ'speʃəli] besonders
Europe ['jʊərəp] Europa
European [jʊərə'piːən] europäisch; Europäer/Europäerin
even ['iːvn] sogar; **not even** nicht einmal
evening ['iːvnɪŋ] Abend; **Good evening.** Guten Abend. **in the evening(s)** abends; am Abend; **this evening** heute Abend
ever ['evə] schon einmal, jemals
every ['evri] jede/jeder/jedes
everybody ['evribɒdi] jeder, alle
everything ['evriθɪŋ] alles
everywhere ['evriweə] überall
example [ɪg'zɑːmpl] Beispiel; **for example** zum Beispiel
except [ɪk'sept] außer
exciting [ɪk'saɪtɪŋ] aufregend, spannend
excuse [ɪk'skjuːz]: **Excuse me, ...** Entschuldigen Sie, ...
exercise ['eksəsaɪz] **1.** Übung; **2.** Bewegung
exhibition ['eksɪ'bɪʃn] Ausstellung
expensive [ɪk'spensɪv] teuer
explain [ɪk'spleɪn] erklären
extra ['ekstrə] extra, zusätzlich

F

face [feɪs] Gesicht
factory ['fæktri] Fabrik
fair [feə] fair, gerecht
fair [feə] Markt
fall [fɔːl] fallen; umstürzen; **fall over** umfallen, hinfallen; **fall in love** sich verlieben
fall [fɔːl] (AE) Herbst
fallen ['fɔːlən]: **I've fallen** ich bin gefallen
false [fɔːls]: **false leg** künstliches Bein
family ['fæmli] Familie
famous ['feɪməs] berühmt
fan [fæn] Fan, Anhänger/Anhängerin
fantastic [fæn'tæstɪk] fantastisch
far [fɑː] weit
farm [fɑːm] Bauernhof, Farm
farmer ['fɑːmə] Landwirt/Landwirtin
fast [fɑːst] schnell; **fast food** [fɑːst'fuːd] Fastfood *(schnell verzehrbare kleinere Gerichte)*
father ['fɑːðə] Vater
fault [fɔːlt] Schuld
favour ['feɪvə]: **she owes me a favour** sie schuldet mir einen Gefallen
favourite ['feɪvrət] Lieblings-
fax [fæks] Fax; **fax machine** [fæksmə'ʃiːn] Faxgerät
February ['februəri] Februar
fed up [fed'ʌp]: **I'm fed up** ich habe die Nase voll
feed [fiːd] füttern, zu essen geben

feel [fiːl] (sich) fühlen
fell [fel]: **I fell** ich fiel / ich bin gefallen
felt [felt]: **I felt** ich fühlte (mich) / ich habe (mich) gefühlt
felt-tip ['felttɪp] Filzstift
few [fjuː]: **a few** ein paar, einige
field [fiːld] Feld, Wiese
fight [faɪt] **1.** bekämpfen; **2.** Kampf; Schlägerei
fighting ['faɪtɪŋ] Kämpfe
film [fɪlm] Film; **film-maker** Filmemacher/Filmemacherin
find [faɪnd] finden; **find out (about)** herausfinden, sich erkundigen (nach)
finger ['fɪŋgə] Finger; **fish finger** Fischstäbchen
finish ['fɪnɪʃ] aufhören (mit); beenden
fire ['faɪə] Feuer
fireworks ['faɪəwɜːks] Feuerwerk
firm [fɜːm] Firma
first [fɜːst] **1.** erste/erster/erstes; **2.** zuerst
fish [fɪʃ] **1.** fischen, angeln; **2.** Fisch, Fische; **fish and chips** Fisch und Pommes frites; **fish finger** Fischstäbchen
fit [fɪt] fit
flag [flæg] Fahne, Flagge
flashlight ['flæʃlaɪt] (AE) Taschenlampe
flat [flæt] Wohnung
Flatiron Building ['flætaɪənbɪldɪŋ] „Bügeleisengebäude"
flew [fluː]: **I flew** ich flog / ich bin geflogen
floor [flɔː] Stock(werk); **on the first floor** im ersten Stock(werk)
flower ['flaʊə] Blume
flower-bed ['flaʊəbed] Blumenbeet
flown [fləʊn]: **I've flown** ich bin geflogen
flu [fluː] Grippe
fly [flaɪ] fliegen
follow ['fɒləʊ] folgen, verfolgen; befolgen
food [fuːd] Essen; Lebensmittel; Futter
foot, feet [fʊt, fiːt] **1.** Fuß, Füße; **on foot** zu Fuß; **2.** *Längenmaß (= 30,48 cm)*
football ['fʊtbɔːl] Fußball
for [fɔː, fə] für; zu; **for 15 years** 15 Jahre lang; seit 15 Jahren; **for a long time** lange; **for breakfast / for lunch** zum Frühstück / zum Mittagessen; **for example** zum Beispiel; **for meeting friends** um Freunde zu treffen; **for miles and miles** meilenweit; **for the first time** zum ersten Mal; **I'm late / in time for school.** Ich komme zu spät / rechtzeitig zur Schule. **look for** suchen
forecast ['fɔːkɑːst]: **weather forecast** Wettervorhersage
forest ['fɒrɪst] Wald
forever [fər'evə] für immer
forget [fə'get] vergessen
forgot [fə'gɒt]: **I forgot** ich vergaß / ich habe vergessen
forgotten [fə'gɒtn]: **I've forgotten** ich habe vergessen
fork [fɔːk] Gabel
forward ['fɔːwəd]: **I'm looking forward to meeting you.** Ich freue mich darauf, Sie kennen zu lernen.
fought [fɔːt]: **I fought** ich bekämpfte / ich habe bekämpft; **I've fought** ich habe bekämpft
found [faʊnd]: **I found** ich fand / ich habe gefunden; **I've found** ich habe gefunden
frankfurter ['fræŋkfɜːtə] (Frankfurter) Würstchen
free [friː] frei; kostenlos; **free time** Freizeit
French [frentʃ] französisch; Französisch; Franzose/Französin; **French fries** [frentʃ'fraɪz] Pommes frites
Friday ['fraɪdeɪ, 'fraɪdi] Freitag
friend [frend] Freund/Freundin
friendly ['frendli] freundlich
fries [fraɪz]: **French fries** [frentʃ'fraɪz] Pommes frites
frighten ['fraɪtn] erschrecken
frightened ['fraɪtnd]: **I'm frightened** ich erschrecke, ich habe Angst
from [frɒm, frəm] von; aus; **from 8 till 10** von 8 (Uhr) bis 10 (Uhr); **from $59** ab $59
front [frʌnt] Vorder-; **front of the train** vorn im Zug; **in front of** vor
fruit [fruːt] Obst, Früchte
full [fʊl] voll; vollständig
fun [fʌn] Spaß; **... is/are fun** ... macht/machen Spaß; **She's great fun.** Es macht großen Spaß, mit ihr zusammen zu sein. **fun park** Vergnügungspark, Freizeitpark
funny ['fʌni] lustig, komisch
future ['fjuːtʃə] Zukunft

G

gallon ['gælən] Gallone *(in den USA = 3,8 Liter)*
game [geɪm] Spiel
garage ['gærɑːʒ] Garage
garbage ['gɑːbɪdʒ] (AE) Abfall, Müll
garden ['gɑːdn] Garten
gas [gæs] **1.** Gas; **2.** (AE) Benzin; **gas station** ['gæsteɪʃn] (AE) Tankstelle
gate [geɪt] Tor; Sperre, Schranke
gave [geɪv]: **I gave** ich gab / ich habe gegeben (usw.)
geography [dʒi'ɒgrəfi] Erdkunde, Geographie
German ['dʒɜːmən] deutsch; Deutsch; Deutsche/Deutscher
Germany ['dʒɜːməni] Deutschland
get [get] **1.** bekommen; **2.** besorgen, holen; **3.** werden; **get married** heiraten; **get off the train/bus/...** aus dem Zug/Bus/... aussteigen; **get on** aufsteigen, einsteigen; **get out of the car/taxi** aus dem Auto/Taxi aussteigen; **get to** kommen zu; **get up** aufstehen, sich erheben
ghost [gəʊst] Gespenst, Geist
girl [gɜːl] Mädchen
girlfriend ['gɜːlfrend] (feste) Freundin
give [gɪv] geben; schenken; spenden; **give up** aufgeben
given ['gɪvn]: **I've given** ich habe gegeben (usw.)
glass [glɑːs] Glas, Trinkglas
go [gəʊ] gehen, fahren; führen; **go for a walk** spazieren gehen; **go home** nach Hause gehen; **go out** aus-gehen, weggehen; **go out (together)** miteinander gehen; **go to bed** ins Bett gehen; **go to Dave's house** zu Dave (nach Hause) gehen; **go to school** zur Schule gehen; **go to the**

shops / **go shopping** einkaufen gehen; **go to town** in die Stadt gehen; **go to work** arbeiten gehen; **go window-shopping** einen Schaufensterbummel machen
going to ['gəʊɪŋtu, 'gəʊɪŋtə]**: I'm going to win** ich werde gewinnen / ich gewinne
gold [gəʊld] Gold
golden ['gəʊldən] golden
gone [gɒn]**: I've gone** ich bin gegangen, gefahren
good [gʊd] gut; **good at** gut in, geschickt in; **Good afternoon.** Guten Tag. *(nachmittags)*; **Good morning/evening/night.** Gute/n Morgen/Abend/Nacht. **Good luck!** Viel Glück!
Goodbye. [gʊd'baɪ] Auf Wiedersehen.
gossip ['gɒsɪp] Klatsch, Tratsch
got [gɒt]**: I got** ich bekam / ich habe bekommen (usw.); **I've got** ich habe bekommen (usw.)
grade [greɪd] (AE) Klasse(nstufe)
gram [græm] Gramm
grandfather ['grænfɑːðə] Großvater
grandma ['grænmɑː] Oma, Großmutter
grandmother ['grænmʌðə] Großmutter
grandparents ['grænpeərənts] Großeltern
grass [grɑːs] Gras; Rasen
great [greɪt] toll, großartig
great [greɪt]**: great-great grandparents** Ururgroßeltern
Greece [griːs] Griechenland
green [griːn] grün
greetings ['griːtɪŋz] Grüße
grew [gruː]**: I grew** ich wuchs / ich bin gewachsen
grizzly bear ['grɪzlibeə] Grislibär
ground [graʊnd] (Erd-)Boden
group [gruːp] Gruppe
grow [grəʊ] wachsen
grown [grəʊn]**: I've grown** ich bin gewachsen
guest [gest] Gast
guest-house ['gesthaʊs] Pension
guide [gaɪd] (Fremden-)Führer/in
guitar [gɪ'tɑː] Gitarre; **play the guitar** Gitarre spielen
gun [gʌn] Gewehr; Schußwaffe
gunfight ['gʌnfaɪt] Schießerei
guy [gaɪ] (AE) Typ, Kerl

H

had [hæd]**: I had** ich hatte / ich habe gehabt; **I've had** ich habe gehabt
hair [heə] Haar, Haare
hair-drier ['heədraɪə] Föhn
half [hɑːf] halb; **half an hour** eine halbe Stunde; **half past two** halb drei
hall [hɔːl]**: school hall** Aula; **town hall** Rathaus
Hallo. [hə'ləʊ] Hallo. Guten Tag.
ham [hæm] Schinken
hamburger ['hæmbɜːgə] Hamburger
hamster ['hæmstə] Hamster
hand [hænd] Hand
handball ['hændbɔːl] Handball
hang (from) [hæŋ] aufhängen (an), hängen (an)
happen ['hæpən] passieren, geschehen
happy ['hæpi] glücklich, froh; **happy with** zufrieden mit; **Happy birthday (to you)!** Herzlichen Glückwunsch zum Geburtstag!
hard [hɑːd] hart; schwer
hate [heɪt] hassen; **hate to wait** sehr ungern warten
have [hæv] haben; **have a break** Pause machen; **have a shower** duschen; **have a wash** sich waschen; **have breakfast** frühstücken; **have lunch** zu Mittag essen; **have sandwiches** / **have a cola** Sandwiches essen / eine Cola trinken
have to ['hævtu, 'hævtə] müssen
he [hiː] er
headache ['hedeɪk] Kopfschmerzen
healthy ['helθi] gesund
hear [hɪə] hören
heard [hɜːd]**: I heard** ich hörte / ich habe gehört; **I've heard** ich habe gehört
helmet ['helmɪt] Helm
help [help] **1.** helfen; **Help yourselves (to coffee)!** Bedient euch! Nehmt euch selbst Kaffee! **2.** Hilfe
helpful ['helpfl] hilfreich
her [hɜː] **1.** ihr/ihre; **2.** ihr/sie
here [hɪə] hier; hierhin/hierher; **Here you are.** Hier, bitte.
hers [hɜːz] ihre/ihrer/ihres
herself [hɜː'self] sich (selbst); selbst
Hi. [haɪ] Hallo.
high [haɪ] hoch; **high school** ['haɪskuːl] Oberschule *(in den USA)*
highlight ['haɪlaɪt] Höhepunkt
hike [haɪk] wandern
hiker ['haɪkə] Wanderer/Wanderin
hill [hɪl] Hügel, *(kleiner)* Berg
him [hɪm] ihm/ihn
himself [hɪm'self] sich (selbst); selbst
hind leg [haɪnd'leg] Hinterbein
hire ['haɪə] **1.** mieten; **2.** vermieten
his [hɪz] **1.** sein/seine; **2.** seine/seiner/seines
Hispanic [hɪ'spænɪk] Hispano-Amerikaner/in; hispanisch; spanischsprachig
history ['hɪstri] Geschichte
hobby ['hɒbi] Hobby
hockey ['hɒki] Hockey
hogan ['həʊgən] *traditionelles achtseitiges Navajo-Haus*
holiday ['hɒlədeɪ] Feiertag; Ferien, Urlaub; **on holiday** in/im Urlaub; **public holiday** gesetzlicher Feiertag
home [həʊm] **1.** Heim, Zuhause; **2.** nach Hause, heim; **at home** zu Hause, daheim
homeless ['həʊmləs] heimatlos; obdachlos
homepage ['həʊmpeɪdʒ] Eingangsseite *(einer Website im Internet)*
homework ['həʊmwɜːk] Hausaufgaben, Schularbeiten
hope [həʊp] **1.** hoffen; **2.** Hoffnung
horror ['hɒrə] Horror
horse [hɔːs] Pferd
hospital ['hɒspɪtl] Krankenhaus
hostel ['hɒstl]**: youth hostel** Jugendherberge
hot [hɒt] heiß; **hot dog** ['hɒt'dɒg] Hot Dog *(heißes Würstchen mit Ketchup im Brötchen)*
hotel [həʊ'tel] Hotel
hour ['aʊə] Stunde
house [haʊs] Haus; **Come to my house.** Komm zu mir (nach Hause).

how [haʊ] wie; **How long?** Wie lange? Wie lang? **How many?** Wie viele? **How much?** Wie viel? **How much is/are ...?** Was kostet/ kosten ...? **How old are you?** Wie alt bist du / sind Sie?
hump [hʌmp] Höcker, Buckel
hung [hʌŋ]: **I hung** ich hängte (auf) / ich habe (auf)gehängt; **I've hung** ich habe (auf)gehängt
hungry ['hʌŋgri] hungrig; **I'm hungry.** Ich habe Hunger.
hunt [hʌnt] jagen
hurry ['hʌri] sich beeilen; **in a hurry** in (großer) Eile
hurt [hɜ:t] verletzen; wehtun; **I hurt** ich verletzte / ich habe verletzt; **I've hurt** ich habe verletzt

I

I [aɪ] ich; **I'd** [aɪd] (= **I would**): **I'd like ...** Ich möchte ... / Ich hätte gern ...; **I'd like to go.** Ich möchte gehen.
ice [aɪs] Eis *(gefrorenes Wasser)*; **ice hockey** ['aɪshɒki] Eishockey
ice-cream [aɪs'kri:m] (Speise-)Eis
ice-rink ['aɪsrɪŋk] Eisbahn, Schlittschuhbahn
idea [aɪ'dɪə] Idee, Einfall; Meinung
if [ɪf] wenn, falls
ill [ɪl] krank
imagine [ɪ'mædʒɪn] sich vorstellen
immigrant ['ɪmɪgrənt] Immigrant/in, Einwanderer/Einwanderin
important [ɪm'pɔ:tnt] wichtig
in [ɪn] **1.** in; **2.** hinein/herein; **in 1850** (im Jahre) 1850; **in English** auf Englisch; **in front of** vor; **in my photo** auf meinem Foto; **in October** im Oktober; **in the country** auf dem Land; **in the morning(s)/afternoon(s)/ evening(s)** morgens/nachmittags/ abends; am Morgen/Nachmittag/ Abend; **in the world** auf der (ganzen) Welt; **in time** rechtzeitig; **in town** in der (Innen-)Stadt
independence [ɪndɪ'pendəns] Unabhängigkeit, Unabhängigkeits-
independent [ɪndɪ'pendənt] unabhängig
Indian ['ɪndiən] Indianer/Indianerin; indianisch
indoors [ɪn'dɔ:z] in der Halle, drinnen
industry ['ɪndəstri] Industrie
information [ɪnfə'meɪʃn] Informationen, Auskunft
inline-skates ['ɪnlaɪnskeɪts] Inline Skates
inline-skating ['ɪnlaɪn'skeɪtɪŋ] Inline-Skating
inner city ['ɪnə'sɪti] Innenstadt
interest ['ɪntrəst] Interesse
interested ['ɪntrəstɪd] interessiert; **interested in** interessiert an
interesting ['ɪntrəstɪŋ] interessant
interstate ['ɪntəsteɪt] Autobahn *(durch mehrere US-Bundesstaaten)*
interview ['ɪntəvju:] Interview
interviewer ['ɪntəvju:ə] Interviewer/ Interviewerin
into ['ɪntu, 'ɪntə] in (... hinein/herein)
invention [ɪn'venʃn] Erfindung
invitation [ɪnvɪ'teɪʃn] Einladung
invite [ɪn'vaɪt] *(Gäste)* einladen
Ireland ['aɪələnd] Irland
Irish ['aɪrɪʃ] irisch; Irisch; Ire/Irin
is [ɪz]: **he/she/it is** er/sie/es ist
it [ɪt] es (er/sie; *nicht bei Personen*)
Italian [ɪ'tæliən] italienisch; Italienisch; Italiener/Italienerin
Italy ['ɪtəli] Italien
its [ɪts] sein/seine; ihr/ihre

J

January ['dʒænjuəri] Januar
Japanese [dʒæpə'ni:z] japanisch; Japanisch; Japaner/Japanerin
jazz [dʒæz] Jazz(musik)
jeans [dʒi:nz] Jeans
Jewish ['dʒu:ɪʃ] jüdisch
job [dʒɒb] Arbeit, Beruf; Arbeitsstelle; Aufgabe
jogger ['dʒɒgə] Jogger/Joggerin
jogging ['dʒɒgɪŋ] Jogging
join [dʒɔɪn] beitreten, Mitglied werden
joke [dʒəʊk] Witz, Scherz; **practical joke** Streich
joking ['dʒəʊkɪŋ]: **You must be joking!** Du machst wohl Witze!
journalism ['dʒɜ:nəlɪzəm] Journalismus
journey ['dʒɜ:ni] Fahrt, Weg, Reise
judo ['dʒu:dəʊ] Judo
juggle ['dʒʌgl] jonglieren
juice [dʒu:s] Saft
July [dʒu'laɪ] Juli
jump [dʒʌmp] springen
junction ['dʒʌŋkʃn] Kreuzung
June [dʒu:n] Juni
just [dʒʌst] **1.** gerade, soeben; **2.** nur; **3.** einfach

K

keep [ki:p] halten, behalten
kept [kept]: **I kept** ich (be)hielt / ich habe behalten, gehalten
ketchup ['ketʃəp] Ketchup
kick [kɪk] kicken; treten
kill [kɪl] töten, umbringen
kilometre ['kɪləmi:tə] Kilometer; **kilometres per hour (km/h)** Kilometer pro Stunde
kilt [kɪlt] Kilt *(Schottenrock)*
king [kɪŋ] König
kiss [kɪs] **1.** (sich) küssen; **2.** Kuss
kitchen ['kɪtʃɪn] Küche
knee [ni:] Knie
knee-pad ['ni:pæd] Knieschoner
knew [nju:]: **I knew** ich wusste, kannte / ich habe gewusst, gekannt
knife, knives [naɪf, naɪvz] Messer
know [nəʊ] wissen; kennen; **You know, ...** Du weißt schon, ...
known [nəʊn]: **I've known** ich habe gewusst, gekannt

L

lake [leɪk] (Binnen-)See
land [lænd] Land
language ['læŋgwɪdʒ] Sprache
large [lɑ:dʒ] groß
lasagne [lə'zænjə] Lasagne
last [lɑ:st] letzte/letzter/letztes
late [leɪt] spät; zu spät, verspätet; **I'm late.** Ich bin spät dran; Ich habe mich verspätet. **I'm late for school.** Ich komme zu spät zur Schule.
laugh [lɑ:f] lachen; **laugh at** auslachen
lay [leɪ]: **I lay** ich lag / habe gelegen
layout ['leɪaʊt] Layout *(Gestaltungsskizze)*
leaf, leaves [li:f, li:vz] Blatt, Blätter
learn [lɜ:n] lernen
least [li:st]: **at least** zumindest; mindestens
leave [li:v] (liegen/stehen) lassen; verlassen, weggehen von, abfahren

left [left] linke/linker/linkes; (nach) links; **on the left** links, auf der linken Seite
left [left]**: I left** ich ließ / ich habe gelassen (usw.); **I've left** ich habe gelassen (usw.)
leg [leg] Bein
lemonade [lemə'neɪd] Limonade
lesson ['lesn] (Unterrichts-)Stunde
let [let]**: Let's go!** Lass/Lasst uns gehen. / Gehen wir!
letter ['letə] **1.** Buchstabe; **2.** Brief
library ['laɪbrəri] Bücherei
lie [laɪ] liegen
life, lives [laɪf, laɪvz] Leben
lift [lɪft] Aufzug
light [laɪt] Licht, Lampe
lights [laɪts] Ampel
like [laɪk] mögen, gern haben; **like to swim / like swimming** gern schwimmen; **I'd like ...** Ich möchte ... / Ich hätte gern ...; **I'd like to go.** Ich möchte gehen. **Would you like ...?** Möchtest du / Möchten Sie ...?
like [laɪk] (ähnlich) wie; **What's it like?** Wie ist es?
line [laɪn] **1.** Linie; **2.** Zeile; **3.** (AE) (Warte-)Schlange
list [lɪst] Liste
listen ['lɪsn] zuhören; **listen to** hören, sich anhören
litre ['li:tə] Liter
little ['lɪtl]**: a little** ein wenig; **Little Italy** [lɪtl'ɪtəli] „Klein-Italien"
live [lɪv] wohnen, leben
living-room ['lɪvɪŋru:m] Wohnzimmer
load [ləʊd] (be)laden; einräumen
long [lɒŋ] lang; **a long way** weit; **How long?** Wie lange? Wie lang?
look [lʊk] **1.** schauen, sehen; **2.** aussehen; **3.** Blick; **look after** sich kümmern um, aufpassen auf; **look at** (sich) ansehen; **look for** suchen; **I'm looking forward to meeting you.** Ich freue mich darauf, Sie kennen zu lernen.
lorry ['lɒri] Lastwagen
lose [lu:z] verlieren
lost [lɒst]**: I'm lost** ich habe mich verlaufen, verirrt; **I lost** ich verlor / ich habe verloren; **I've lost** ich habe verloren
lot [lɒt]**: a lot (of) / lots (of)** viele; viel

loud [laʊd] laut
love [lʌv] lieben, sehr mögen; **love to sing / love singing** sehr gern singen; **fall in love** sich verlieben; **they're in love** sie sind verliebt
luck [lʌk]**: Good luck!** Viel Glück!
lucky ['lʌki]**: you're lucky** du hast Glück / ihr habt Glück
lunch [lʌntʃ] Mittagessen; **for lunch** zum Mittagessen; **have lunch** zu Mittag essen; **lunch break** Mittagspause

M

machine [mə'ʃi:n]**: fax machine** Faxgerät
made [meɪd]**: I made** ich machte / ich habe gemacht; **I've made** ich habe gemacht; **it was made in Japan** er/sie/es wurde in Japan hergestellt; **made of plastic** aus Plastik
magazine [mægə'zi:n] Zeitschrift
mailbox ['meɪlbɒks] „Mailbox" *(eine Art Computerbriefkasten)*
mailman ['meɪlmæn] (AE) Briefträger, Postbote
major ['meɪdʒə] bedeutende/bedeutender/bedeutendes, wichtige/r/s, große/r/s
make [meɪk] machen, herstellen; *(Geld)* verdienen; erzielen
man, men [mæn, men] Mann, Männer
many ['meni] viele; **How many?** Wie viele?
map [mæp] Stadtplan, Landkarte; **subway map** (AE) U-Bahn-Plan
marathon ['mærəθən] Marathon
March [mɑ:tʃ] März
market ['mɑ:kɪt] Markt
married ['mærid]**: get married** heiraten
marshal ['mɑ:ʃl] Marshal
match [mætʃ] Spiel, Wettkampf
maths [mæθs] Mathe(matik)
matter ['mætə]**: What's the matter?** Was ist los?
May [meɪ] Mai
maybe ['meɪbi] vielleicht
mayonnaise [meɪə'neɪz] Majonäse
me [mi:] mir/mich; **older than me** älter als ich; **Me, too.** Ich auch.
meal [mi:l] Mahlzeit, Speise, (zubereitetes) Essen

mean [mi:n] bedeuten; meinen
meant [ment]**: I meant** ich meinte / ich habe gemeint; **I've meant** ich habe gemeint
medium ['mi:diəm] mittel(groß)
meet [mi:t] (sich) treffen (mit); kennen lernen
message ['mesɪdʒ] Mitteilung
messy ['mesi] schmutzig, dreckig; unordentlich
met [met]**: I met** ich traf / ich habe getroffen (usw.); **I've met** ich habe getroffen (usw.)
metal ['metl] Metall
meter ['mi:tə] Fahrpreisanzeiger
metre ['mi:tə] Meter
Mexican ['meksɪkən] mexikanisch; Mexikaner/Mexikanerin
Mexico ['meksɪkəʊ] Mexiko
microwave ['maɪkrəweɪv] Mikrowelle
might [maɪt]**: I might ask her ...** Vielleicht bitte ich sie, ...
mile [maɪl] Meile *(= ca. 1,6 km)*; **miles per hour (mph)** [maɪlzpər'aʊə] Meilen pro Stunde
milk [mɪlk] Milch
million ['mɪljən] Million
mine [maɪn] meine/meiner/meines
minute ['mɪnɪt] Minute
mirror ['mɪrə] Spiegel
miss [mɪs] vermissen; versäumen, verpassen; **missing** fehlend
mistake [mɪ'steɪk] Fehler
mixed [mɪkst] gemischt
model ['mɒdl] Modell; Nachbildung
modem ['məʊdem] Modem
modern ['mɒdən] modern
mom [mɒm] (AE) Mama, Mutti
moment ['məʊmənt]**: at the moment** zurzeit, im Augenblick
Monday ['mʌndeɪ, 'mʌndi] Montag; **on Monday** am Montag; montags
money ['mʌni] Geld
monster ['mɒnstə] Monster
month [mʌnθ] Monat
monument ['mɒnjumənt] Denkmal
more [mɔ:] mehr, weitere; **one more** noch ein/eine; **more expensive** teurer
morning ['mɔ:nɪŋ] Morgen, Vormittag; **Sunday morning** Sonntagmorgen; **Good morning.** Guten Morgen. **in the morning(s)** morgens, vormittags; am Morgen; **this morning** heute Morgen

most [məʊst] der/die/das meiste, die meisten; **most dangerous** gefährlichste/gefährlichster/gefährlichstes, am gefährlichsten
motel [məʊ'tel] Motel
mother ['mʌðə] Mutter
mountain ['maʊntən] Berg; **mountain bike** Mountainbike; **mountain biking** Mountainbikefahren
mouse, mice [maʊs, maɪs] Maus, Mäuse
move [mu:v] **1. move (to)** umziehen (nach), ziehen (nach); **2.** (sich) bewegen; **move cattle** Vieh treiben, Rinder treiben
movie ['mu:vi] (AE) Film
Mr ['mɪstə] Herr *(vor Namen)*
Mrs ['mɪsɪz] Frau *(vor Namen bei verheirateten Frauen)*
Ms [məz] Frau *(vor Namen bei unverheirateten oder verheirateten Frauen)*
much [mʌtʃ] viel; **How much?** Wie viel? **How much is/are …?** Was kostet/kosten …?
mug [mʌg] Becher, große Tasse
mum [mʌm] Mama, Mutti
museum [mju'zi:əm] Museum
music ['mju:zɪk] Musik
must [mʌst] müssen; **mustn't** ['mʌsnt] nicht dürfen
my [maɪ] mein/meine
myself [maɪ'self] mir/mich (selbst); selbst
myth [mɪθ] Mythos

N

nachos ['nɑ:tʃəʊz] Nachos *(Tortillachips mit geschmolzenem Käse)*
name [neɪm] Name
national park ['næʃnəl'pɑ:k] Nationalpark
Natural History Museum [nætʃrəl'hɪstrimju'zi:əm] Naturgeschichtliches Museum
nature ['neɪtʃə] Natur
near [nɪə] in der Nähe (von); nah
nearest ['nɪərɪst] nächste/nächster/nächstes
need [ni:d] brauchen
needn't ['ni:dnt] nicht brauchen, nicht müssen
neighbour ['neɪbə] Nachbar/Nachbarin
nervous ['nɜ:vəs] nervös, ängstlich
net [net] Netz
never ['nevə] nie, niemals
new [nju:] neu
New Yorker [nju:'jɔ:kə] New Yorker / New Yorkerin
news [nju:z] Nachricht(en), Neuigkeit(en); **this was bad news** dies war eine schlechte Nachricht
newspaper ['nju:speɪpə] Zeitung
next [nekst] nächste/nächster/nächstes
next to ['nekstu, 'nekstə] neben
nice [naɪs] nett; schön
night [naɪt] Nacht, (später) Abend; **at night** nachts, in der Nacht; **Good night.** Gute Nacht.
nineteensixties (1960s) [naɪnti:n'sɪkstiz] sechziger Jahre
no [nəʊ] **1.** nein; **2.** kein/keine
nobody ['nəʊbədi] niemand
north [nɔ:θ] Nord-; (nach) Norden; nördlich
North Sea [nɔ:θ'si:] Nordsee
Northern Ireland ['nɔ:ðən'aɪələnd] Nordirland
Northern Irish ['nɔ:ðən'aɪrɪʃ] nordirisch; Nordire/Nordirin
not [nɒt] nicht; **not … yet** [jet] noch nicht
note [nəʊt] Notiz, Briefchen
nothing ['nʌθɪŋ] nichts
November [nəʊ'vembə] November
now [naʊ] nun, jetzt
number ['nʌmbə] Nummer; Zahl; Ziffer
nurse [nɜ:s] Krankenpfleger/Krankenschwester

O

ocean ['əʊʃn] Ozean; Meer
o'clock [ə'klɒk]**: 6 o'clock** 6 Uhr / 18 Uhr; **at 6 o'clock** um 6 Uhr / 18 Uhr
October [ɒk'təʊbə] Oktober
of [ɒv, əv] von; **a cup of tea** eine Tasse Tee; **of course** [əv'kɔ:s] natürlich, selbstverständlich
off [ɒf]**: get off the train/bus/…** aus dem Zug/Bus/… aussteigen
office ['ɒfɪs] Büro
officer ['ɒfɪsə]**: (police) officer** (Polizei-)Beamter/Beamtin, Polizist/Polizistin
often ['ɒfn] oft
oil [ɔɪl] Öl
OK [əʊ'keɪ] okay, (schon) gut, in Ordnung; **I'm OK.** Mir geht's gut.
old [əʊld] alt
on [ɒn] **1.** auf; **2.** an, eingeschaltet; **on March 20th** am 20. März; **on Monday** am Montag; montags; **on Tuesdays** dienstags; **on foot** zu Fuß; **on holiday** in/im Urlaub; **on the beach/ocean** am Strand/Meer; **on the bus/train/plane** im Bus/Zug/Flugzeug; **on the first floor** im ersten Stock(werk); **on the left/right** links/rechts, auf der linken/rechten Seite; **on the road** unterwegs; **on the stall** am Stand; **on TV / on the radio** im Fernsehen / im Radio
one [wʌn] ein/eine; eine/einer/eines; **the green one** der/die/das grüne
only ['əʊnli] nur, bloß; erst; **the only** der/die/das einzige
open ['əʊpən] **1.** (sich) öffnen, aufmachen; **2.** offen, geöffnet; **open day** Tag der offenen Tür
opposite ['ɒpəzɪt] **1.** gegenüber (von); **2.** Gegenteil
or [ɔ:] oder
orange ['ɒrɪndʒ] Orange, Apfelsine
ordinary ['ɔ:dnri] gewöhnlich, normal
organise ['ɔ:gənaɪz] organisieren; veranstalten
origin ['ɒrɪdʒɪn] Ursprung, Herkunft; Abstammung
other ['ʌðə] andere, weitere; **each other** einander, sich
our ['aʊə] unser/unsere
ours ['aʊəz] unsere/unserer/unseres
ourselves [aʊə'selvz] uns (selbst); selbst
out [aʊt] hinaus/heraus, aus; **out of** ['aʊtəv] aus (…hinaus/heraus); **out of work** [aʊtəv'wɜ:k] arbeitslos
outside [aʊt'saɪd] außerhalb (von); (nach) draußen
over ['əʊvə] **1.** vorbei, zu Ende; **2.** über; **all over** überall (in/auf); **over there** da drüben, dort drüben
owe [əʊ]**: she owes me a favour** sie schuldet mir einen Gefallen
own [əʊn]**: my own** mein eigener / meine eigene / mein eigenes

P

Pacific [pə'sɪfɪk]**: Pacific Ocean** Pazifischer Ozean
page [peɪdʒ] Seite
paid [peɪd]**: I paid** ich zahlte / ich habe gezahlt (usw.); **I've paid** ich habe gezahlt (usw.)
pain [peɪn] Schmerz
Pakistan [pɑ:kɪ'stɑ:n] Pakistan
pancake ['pænkeɪk] *(kleiner)* Pfannkuchen
panic ['pænɪk] in Panik geraten
parade [pə'reɪd] Parade, Umzug
parent, parents ['peərənt, 'peərənts] Elternteil, Eltern
park [pɑ:k] **1.** parken; **2.** Park; **car park** *(großer)* Parkplatz
parking ['pɑ:kɪŋ] Park-; **parking lot** ['pɑ:kɪŋlɒt] (AE) *(großer)* Parkplatz; **parking space** ['pɑ:kɪŋspeɪs] Parkplatz, Parklücke
part [pɑ:t] Teil; Abschnitt
part-time job ['pɑ:ttaɪm'dʒɒb] Teilzeitarbeitsstelle
partner ['pɑ:tnə] Partner/Partnerin
party ['pɑ:ti] **1.** Party, Fest, Feier; **2.** Partei
passenger ['pæsɪndʒə] Fahrgast
past [pɑ:st] **1.** nach; **half past two** halb drei; **quarter past** Viertel nach; **2.** vorbei; **past the house** am Haus vorbei
path [pɑ:θ] Weg, Pfad
pay [peɪ] zahlen, bezahlen
PE ['pi:'i:] (= **Physical Education** ['fɪzɪkledʒu'keɪʃn]) Turnen, Turnunterricht
pea [pi:] Erbse
pen [pen] Füller
pence (p) [pens, pi:] Pence *(britisches Geld)*
pencil ['pensl] Bleistift
pencil-case ['penslkeɪs] Federmäppchen, Schreibetui
penknife, penknives ['pennaɪf, 'pennaɪvz] Taschenmesser
people ['pi:pl] Leute, Menschen
per cent [pə'sent] Prozent
perfect ['pɜ:fɪkt] vollkommen, perfekt
perfume ['pɜ:fju:m] Parfüm
perhaps [pə'hæps] vielleicht
permit ['pɜ:mɪt] Genehmigung, Genehmigungsschein, (schriftliche) Erlaubnis
person ['pɜ:sn] Person, Mensch
pet [pet] zahmes Tier, Haustier; **pet shop** Kleintierhandlung, Zoohandlung
phone [fəʊn] **1.** anrufen, telefonieren; **2.** Telefon; **phone card** Telefonkarte
photo ['fəʊtəʊ] Foto; **in my photo** auf meinem Foto; **take photos** Fotos machen, fotografieren
photocopy ['fəʊtəʊkɒpi] Fotokopie
photography [fə'tɒgrəfi] Fotografie
phrase [freɪz] Redewendung, Ausdruck
pick [pɪk] wählen, aussuchen
picture ['pɪktʃə] Bild, Foto
pig [pɪg] Schwein
pink [pɪŋk] rosa, pink
pitch [pɪtʃ]**: pitch a tent** ein Zelt aufstellen
pity ['pɪti]**: That's a pity.** Das ist schade.
pizza ['pi:tsə] Pizza
place [pleɪs] Ort, Platz, Stelle
plan [plæn] **1.** planen, vorhaben; einplanen; **2.** Plan
plane [pleɪn] Flugzeug
plastic ['plæstɪk] Plastik
plate [pleɪt] Teller
platform ['plætfɔ:m] Bahnsteig, Gleis
play [pleɪ] spielen; **play dead** sich tot stellen; **play the guitar** Gitarre spielen
player ['pleɪə] Spieler/Spielerin
play-off ['pleɪɒf] Entscheidungsspiel
please [pli:z] bitte
pleased [pli:zd] zufrieden; erfreut
plural ['plʊərəl] Plural, Mehrzahl
pm ['pi:'em] nachmittags, abends
pocket-money ['pɒkɪt'mʌni] Taschengeld
police [pə'li:s] Polizei; **(police) officer** (Polizei-)Beamter/Beamtin, Polizist/Polizistin; **police station** Polizeiwache
Polish ['pəʊlɪʃ] polnisch; Polnisch; Pole/Polin
polite [pə'laɪt] höflich
pollution [pə'lu:ʃn] (Umwelt-)Verschmutzung
pool [pu:l] Becken, Teich
poor [pʊə] arm
pop [pɒp] Pop(musik)
popular ['pɒpjələ] beliebt
port [pɔ:t] Hafen, Hafenstadt
post [pəʊst] Post; **post office** ['pəʊstɒfɪs] Post(amt)
postcard ['pəʊstkɑ:d] Postkarte, Ansichtskarte
poster ['pəʊstə] Poster
postman ['pəʊstmən] Briefträger, Postbote
potato, potatoes [pə'teɪtəʊ, pə'teɪtəʊz] Kartoffel, Kartoffeln
pound (£) [paʊnd] Pfund *(britisches Geld)*
practical ['præktɪkl']**: practical joke** Streich
practise ['præktɪs] üben, trainieren *(AE: practice)*
prefer [prɪ'fɜ:]**: prefer to watch TV** lieber fernsehen
present ['preznt] Geschenk
president ['prezɪdənt] Präsident
price [praɪs] (Kauf-)Preis
print [prɪnt] drucken
prison ['prɪzn] Gefängnis
probably ['prɒbəbli] wahrscheinlich
problem ['prɒbləm] Problem
professional [prə'feʃənl] Profi-, Berufs-
professionally [prə'feʃənli] berufsmäßig
programme ['prəʊgræm] (Radio-, Fernseh-)Sendung
project ['prɒdʒekt] Projekt, Projektarbeit
protect [prə'tekt] schützen, beschützen
Protestant ['prɒtɪstənt] Protestant/Protestantin
proud [praʊd] stolz; **proud to be Scottish** stolz Schotte/ Schottin zu sein; **he's proud of himself** er ist stolz auf sich
PS ['pi:'es] PS *(Nachtrag zu einem Brief)*
pub [pʌb] Kneipe, Lokal
public ['pʌblɪk]**: public holiday** gesetzlicher Feiertag; **The Public Library** Öffentliche Bibliothek *(von New York)*
pullover ['pʊləʊvə] Pullover
pupil ['pju:pl] Schüler/Schülerin
push [pʊʃ] schieben, stoßen; drücken
put [pʊt] stellen; legen; *(an einen Platz)* tun; **I put** ich stellte / ich habe gestellt (usw.); **I've put** ich habe gestellt (usw.); **put down** niederlegen; **put in** einfügen, hinzufügen; **Put your hands up.** Hebt eure / Hebe deine Hände hoch.

Q

quarter ['kwɔ:tə] Viertel; **quarter past** Viertel nach; **quarter to** Viertel vor
queen [kwi:n] Königin
question ['kwestʃən] Frage; **ask a question** eine Frage stellen
queue [kju:] (Warte-)Schlange
quiet ['kwaɪət] still, ruhig, leise
quiz [kwɪz] Quiz

R

rabbit ['ræbɪt] Kaninchen
radio ['reɪdiəʊ] Radio
railway ['reɪlweɪ] (Eisen-)Bahn; Bahnstrecke; **railway station** Bahnhof
rain [reɪn] regnen
rainy ['reɪni] regnerisch
ran [ræn]: **I ran** ich rannte / ich bin gerannt
ranger ['reɪndʒə] Aufseher/in (in Nationalparks); **ranger station** Wache der Parkaufsicht
rap [ræp] **1.** Rap(musik); **2.** rappen
rapper ['ræpə] Rapper
RE ['ɑ:'ri:] (= **Religious Education** [rɪ'lɪdʒəsedʒu'keɪʃn]) Religionsunterricht
read [ri:d] lesen, vorlesen; **I read** [red] ich las / ich habe gelesen; **I've read** [red] ich habe gelesen
reality [ri'æləti] Wirklichkeit, Realität
really ['ri:əli] wirklich, eigentlich
record [rɪ'kɔ:d] aufnehmen, aufzeichnen
red [red] rot
refill ['ri:fɪl] „Nachfüllung" *(eine weitere Portion)*
regular ['regjələ] regelmäßig
remember [rɪ'membə] sich erinnern (an)
remind [rɪ'maɪnd] erinnern
rent [rent] mieten; **rent out** (AE) vermieten
repair [rɪ'peə] reparieren
report [rɪ'pɔ:t] **1.** Bericht; **2.** Zeugnis
reporter [rɪ'pɔ:tə] Reporter/in
republic [rɪ'pʌblɪk] Republik
research ['ri:sɜ:tʃ] Forschung
reservation [rezə'veɪʃn] (Indianer-)Reservation, Reservat
respect [rɪ'spekt] respektieren
restaurant ['restərɒnt] Restaurant
return [rɪ'tɜ:n] Rückfahrkarte; **day return** ['deɪrɪ'tɜ:n] Tagesrückfahrkarte
ride [raɪd]: **ride a bike** Rad fahren
right [raɪt] **1.** richtig; **You're right.** Du hast / Sie haben Recht. **2.** rechte/rechter/rechtes; (nach) rechts; **on the right** rechts, auf der rechten Seite
ring [rɪŋ] Ring
river ['rɪvə] Fluss
road [rəʊd] Straße; **on the road** unterwegs
rock [rɒk] *(großer)* Stein, Fels
rock [rɒk] Rock(musik)
role-card ['rəʊlkɑ:d] Rollenspielkarte
roll [rəʊl] Brötchen
roll up [rəʊl'ʌp] zusammenrollen
room [ru:m] Zimmer, Raum
rope [rəʊp] Seil
rough [rʌf] hart, rauh
rubber ['rʌbə] Radiergummi
rubbish ['rʌbɪʃ] Abfall, Müll
rugby ['rʌgbi] Rugby
rule [ru:l] Regel, Vorschrift
ruler ['ru:lə] Lineal
run [rʌn] **1.** rennen, laufen; **2.** Lauf
Russia ['rʌʃə] Russland

S

sad [sæd] traurig
safe [seɪf] sicher, in Sicherheit
said [sed]: **I said** ich sagte / ich habe gesagt; **I've said** ich habe gesagt
sailing ['seɪlɪŋ] Segeln
salad ['sæləd] Salat
same [seɪm]: **the same** derselbe/dieselbe/dasselbe; der/die/das gleiche
sandwich ['sænwɪtʃ] Sandwich *(belegtes Brot)*
sang [sæŋ]: **I sang** ich sang / ich habe gesungen
sat [sæt]: **I sat** ich setzte mich / ich habe mich gesetzt
Saturday ['sætədeɪ, 'sætədi] Samstag, Sonnabend
sausage ['sɒsɪdʒ] Wurst, Würstchen
save [seɪv] sparen
saw [sɔ:]: **I saw** ich sah / ich habe gesehen (usw.)
say [seɪ] sagen
school [sku:l] Schule; **after school** nach der Schule; **at school** in der Schule; **go to school** zur Schule gehen; **school hall** ['sku:lhɔ:l] Aula
science ['saɪəns] Naturwissenschaft
Scotland ['skɒtlənd] Schottland
Scottish ['skɒtɪʃ] schottisch; Schotte/Schottin
seaside ['si:saɪd] Küste
season ['si:zn] **1.** Jahreszeit; **2.** Saison
secret ['si:krət] heimlich, geheim
see [si:] sehen; sich ansehen, besichtigen; **See you.** Bis dann.
seem [si:m]: **he seems nice** er scheint nett zu sein
seen [si:n]: **I've seen** ich habe gesehen (usw.)
sell [sel] verkaufen
send [send] schicken, senden
sense [sens]: **sense of smell** Geruchssinn
sent [sent]: **I sent** ich schickte / ich habe geschickt; **I've sent** ich habe geschickt
sentence [sentəns] Satz
September [sep'tembə] September
set [set]: **set the table** den Tisch decken; **he set the table** er deckte den Tisch / er hat den Tisch gedeckt; **he has set the table** er hat den Tisch gedeckt
she [ʃi:] sie
sheep [ʃi:p] Schaf, Schafe
shift [ʃɪft] Schicht
ship [ʃɪp] Schiff
shirt [ʃɜ:t] Hemd
shoe [ʃu:] Schuh
shoot (at) [ʃu:t] schießen (auf); erschießen
shop [ʃɒp] Laden, Geschäft; **go to the shops** einkaufen gehen; **shop assistant** Verkäufer/Verkäuferin
shopping ['ʃɒpɪŋ]: **go shopping** einkaufen gehen; **shopping street** Einkaufsstraße
short [ʃɔ:t] kurz
shorts [ʃɔ:ts] Shorts
shot [ʃɒt] Schuss
shot [ʃɒt]; **I shot** ich (er)schoss / ich habe geschossen, erschossen; **I've shot** ich habe geschossen, erschossen

should [ʃʊd, ʃəd]: **you should** du solltest, du müßtest; **When should we ...?** Wann sollen wir ...?
shout (at) [ʃaʊt] (an)schreien, laut rufen
show [ʃəʊ] **1.** zeigen; **2.** Schau, Show, Vorführung, Aufführung
shower ['ʃaʊə]: **have a shower** duschen
shown [ʃəʊn]: **I've shown** ich habe gezeigt
side [saɪd] Seite
sight [saɪt] Sehenswürdigkeit
sign [saɪn] Schild; Zeichen
silly ['sɪli] dumm, albern
since [sɪns] seit
sing [sɪŋ] singen
single ['sɪŋgl] einfache Fahrkarte
sister ['sɪstə] Schwester
sit [sɪt] sitzen; sich setzen
skate [skeɪt] Inline Skates (Rollschuh/Schlittschuh) laufen
skater ['skeɪtə] Inline Skates (Rollschuh/Schlittschuh)-Läufer/Läuferin
ski [ski:] Ski fahren
skyscraper ['skaɪskreɪpə] Wolkenkratzer, Hochhaus
sleep [sli:p] schlafen
slogan ['sləʊgən] Slogan
Slovakia [sləʊ'vɑ:kiə] Slowakische Republik
slow [sləʊ] langsam
small [smɔ:l] klein
smell [smel] riechen
smelly ['smeli] stinkend
smile [smaɪl] lächeln
snack [snæk] Imbiss, Snack
snow [snəʊ] Schnee
snowy ['snəʊi]: **it's snowy** es schneit viel
so [səʊ] also, daher; so; **so that** [səʊ'ðæt] damit
soccer ['sɒkə] Fußball
sock [sɒk] Socke, Strumpf
soft [sɒft] weich; weichherzig, verweichlicht
sold [səʊld]: **I sold** ich verkaufte / ich habe verkauft; **I've sold** ich habe verkauft
soldier ['səʊldʒə] Soldat/Soldatin
some [sʌm] **1.** einige, ein paar; **2.** etwas
somebody ['sʌmbədi] jemand
something ['sʌmθɪŋ] etwas
sometimes ['sʌmtaɪmz] manchmal
son [sʌn] Sohn
song [sɒŋ] Lied
soon [su:n] bald
sore throat ['sɔ:'θrəʊt] Halsschmerzen
sorry ['sɒri]: **I'm sorry. / Sorry.** Tut mir Leid.
south [saʊθ] Süd-; (nach) Süden; südlich
southern ['sʌðən] Süd-, südlich
souvenir [su:və'nɪə] Souvenir, Andenken
spaghetti [spə'geti] Spaghetti
Spanish ['spænɪʃ] spanisch; Spanisch; Spanier/Spanierin
speak [spi:k] sprechen; **Spanish-speaking** spanischsprachig
special ['speʃl] besondere/besonderer/besonderes
speed limit ['spi:dlɪmɪt] Geschwindigkeitsbeschränkung
spell [spel] buchstabieren
spend [spend] verbringen
spent [spent]: **I spent** ich verbrachte / ich habe verbracht; **I've spent** ich habe verbracht
split up [splɪt'ʌp] sich trennen; **they split up** sie trennten sich / sie haben sich getrennt; **they've split up** sie haben sich getrennt
spoke [spəʊk]: **I spoke** ich sprach / ich habe gesprochen
spoken ['spəʊkn]: **I've spoken** ich habe gesprochen
spoon [spu:n] Löffel
sport [spɔ:t] Sport, Sportart; **do sports** Sport treiben; **sports centre** Sportzentrum
sportsman, sportsmen ['spɔ:tsmən] Sportler
spring [sprɪŋ] Frühling
stadium ['steɪdiəm] Stadion
stall [stɔ:l] (Verkaufs-)Stand
stamp [stæmp] Briefmarke
stand [stænd] stehen
star [stɑ:] Star *(berühmte Persönlichkeit)*
stare at ['steərət] anstarren
start [stɑ:t] **1.** anfangen, beginnen (mit); **Start here.** Fang/Fangt hier an. **2.** Anfang
state [steɪt] (Bundes-)Staat, Land
station ['steɪʃn] Bahnhof; **police station** Polizeiwache; **ranger station** Wache der Parkaufsicht
Statue of Liberty ['stætʃu:əv'lɪbəti] Freiheitsstatue
stay [steɪ] **1.** bleiben; **2.** übernachten
steak [steɪk] Steak
steal [sti:l] stehlen
steep [sti:p] steil
stepfather ['stepfɑ:ðə] Stiefvater
still [stɪl] (immer) noch
stole [stəʊl]: **I stole** ich stahl / ich habe gestohlen
stood [stʊd]: **I stood** ich stand / ich habe gestanden; **I've stood** ich habe gestanden
stop [stɒp] aufhören; anhalten, stoppen; **Stop it.** Lass das. Hör auf (damit).
store [stɔ:] (AE) Laden, Geschäft
storey ['stɔ:ri] Stockwerk
story ['stɔ:ri] Geschichte, Erzählung
straight [streɪt] gerade; **straight ahead** [streɪtə'hed] geradeaus
street [stri:t] Straße
stress [stres] Stress
student ['stju:dnt] Schüler/Schülerin; Student/Studentin
studio ['stju:diəʊ] Studio
style [staɪl] Stil
subject ['sʌbdʒɪkt] (Schul-)Fach
subway ['sʌbweɪ] (AE) U-Bahn; **subway token** (AE) U-Bahn-Münze, -Marke
suddenly ['sʌdnli] plötzlich
suggestion [sə'dʒestʃən] Vorschlag
suit [su:t] Anzug; Kostüm
summer ['sʌmə] Sommer
sun [sʌn] Sonne
Sunday ['sʌndeɪ, 'sʌndi] Sonntag
sunny ['sʌni] sonnig
super ['su:pə] super, toll
supermarket ['su:pəmɑ:kɪt] Supermarkt
sure [ʃʊə] sicher
surf [sɜ:f] surfen; **surf the Internet** „im Internet surfen" *(sich im weltweiten Computerdatennetz umschauen)*
surprise [sə'praɪz] Überraschung(s-)
surprised [sə'praɪzd] überrascht
sweatshirt ['swetʃɜ:t] Sweatshirt
sweet [swi:t] Süßigkeit, Bonbon
swim [swɪm] schwimmen
Switzerland ['swɪtsələnd] Schweiz

T

T-shirt ['ti:ʃɜ:t] T-Shirt
table ['teɪbl] Tisch
table-tennis ['teɪbltenɪs] Tischtennis
taco ['tɑ:kəʊ] Taco *(knuspriger, gefüllter Teigfladen)*
take [teɪk] **1.** nehmen, mitnehmen; **2.** dauern; **take a driving test** die Führerscheinprüfung machen; **take photos** Fotos machen, fotografieren; **take the dog for a walk** mit dem Hund rausgehen, mit dem Hund spazieren gehen
take-away pizza ['teɪkəweɪ] Pizza zum Mitnehmen
taken ['teɪkən]**: I've taken** ich habe (mit)genommen (usw.)
talent ['tælənt] Talent
talk [tɔ:k] reden, sprechen, sich unterhalten; **talk to** sprechen mit, reden mit
tall [tɔ:l] groß (gewachsen); hoch
tardy slip ['tɑ:dɪslɪp] Strafzettel fürs Zuspätkommen *(in den USA)*
taught [tɔ:t]**: I taught** ich brachte bei, ich unterrichtete / ich habe beigebracht, unterrichtet; **I've taught** ich habe beigebracht, unterrichtet
taxi ['tæksi] Taxi
tea [ti:] Tee; **(afternoon) tea** Tee *(Nachmittagsmahlzeit, frühes Abendbrot)*
teach [ti:tʃ] beibringen, unterrichten
teacher ['ti:tʃə] Lehrer/Lehrerin
team [ti:m] Team, Mannschaft
technology [tek'nɒlədʒi] Technik, Technologie
teenager ['ti:neɪdʒə] Teenager
telephone ['telɪfəʊn] Telefon
tell [tel] erzählen; sagen; angeben
temperature ['temprətʃə] Temperatur
tennis ['tenɪs] Tennis
tent [tent] Zelt
terrible ['terəbl] schrecklich, fürchterlich
terrorism ['terərɪzəm] Terrorismus
terrorist ['terərɪst] Terrorist/Terroristin
test [test] **1.** testen, prüfen; **2.** Test
than [ðæn]**: nicer than** schöner als
thank [θæŋk]**: Thank you.** Danke (schön).
Thanks. [θæŋks] Danke.
Thanksgiving [θæŋks'gɪvɪŋ] Erntedankfest
that [ðæt] **1.** das; der/die/das (da); **2.** dass; **3.** der/die/das *(in Relativsätzen)*; **That's £8.45.** Das macht 8 Pfund 45. **that's why** deshalb, darum; **so that** [səʊ'ðæt] damit
the [ðə, ði] der/die/das
their [ðeə] ihr/ihre
theirs [ðeəz] ihre/ihrer/ihres
them [ðem, ðəm] ihnen/sie
themselves [ðəm'selvz] sich (selbst); selbst
then [ðen] dann
there [ðeə] da, dort; dahin, dorthin; **there are** da sind, es gibt, es sind; **there's** (= **there is**) da ist, es gibt, es ist
these [ði:z] diese, die (hier)
they [ðeɪ] sie
thing [θɪŋ] Ding, Sache; **the same thing** dasselbe
think [θɪŋk] finden, meinen; glauben; (nach)denken; **think of** denken an; **I don't think so.** Das finde ich nicht. **I think so, too.** Das finde ich auch.
thirsty ['θɜ:sti] durstig; **I'm thirsty.** Ich habe Durst.
this [ðɪs] dies/das (hier); diese/dieser/dieses; **this morning/afternoon/evening** heute Morgen/Nachmittag/Abend
those [ðəʊz] diese, jene, die (da)
thought [θɔ:t]**: I thought** ich dachte / ich habe gedacht (usw.); **I've thought** ich habe gedacht (usw.)
threw [θru:]**: I threw** ich warf / ich habe geworfen
through [θru:] durch, hindurch
throw (at) [θrəʊ] werfen (nach)
thrown [θrəʊn]**: I've thrown** ich habe geworfen
Thursday ['θɜ:zdeɪ, 'θɜ:zdi] Donnerstag
ticket ['tɪkɪt] Fahrkarte; Eintrittskarte
tidy ['taɪdi] **1.** aufräumen; **2.** ordentlich, aufgeräumt
till [tɪl] bis
time [taɪm] **1.** Zeit; Uhrzeit; **(for) a long time** lange; **in time** rechtzeitig; **What time is it?** Wie spät ist es? **2.** Mal; **this time** diesmal
timetable ['taɪmteɪbl] Stundenplan; Fahrplan
tip [tɪp] Tipp, Hinweis
tired ['taɪəd] müde
to [tu:, tu, tə] **1.** zu, nach; an; in, bei; **2.** vor; **3.** bis; **to go** um zu fahren; **start to run** beginnen zu rennen; **quarter to** Viertel vor
toast [təʊst] **1.** toasten; **2.** Toast(brot)
toaster ['təʊstə] Toaster
today [tə'deɪ] heute
together [tə'geðə] zusammen
toilet ['tɔɪlət] Toilette
token ['təʊkən]**: subway token** (AE) U-Bahn-Münze, -Marke
told: [təʊld] **I told** ich erzählte / ich habe erzählt
tolerate ['tɒləreɪt] tolerieren, dulden; sich gefallen lassen
tomato, tomatoes [tə'mɑ:təʊ, tə'mɑ:təʊz] Tomate, Tomaten
tomorrow [tə'mɒrəʊ] morgen
tonight [tə'naɪt] heute Abend; heute Nacht
too [tu:] **1.** auch; **2. too late** zu spät; **too bad** schade
took [tʊk]**: I took** ich nahm (mit) / ich habe (mit)genommen (usw.)
tool [tu:l] Werkzeug
tooth, teeth [tu:θ, ti:θ] Zahn, Zähne
toothache ['tu:θeɪk] Zahnschmerzen
top [tɒp] Spitze, oberes Ende
torch [tɔ:tʃ] Taschenlampe
tour [tʊə] Tour, Reise; Rundgang
tourist ['tʊərɪst] Tourist/Touristin; **tourist office** Touristeninformation, Fremdenverkehrsbüro
towards [tə'wɔ:dz] auf ... zu, in Richtung
towel ['taʊəl] Handtuch
town [taʊn] Stadt; **go to town** in die Stadt gehen; **in town** in der (Innen-)Stadt; **town hall** Rathaus
toy [tɔɪ] Spielzeug
tradition [trə'dɪʃn] Tradition
traffic ['træfɪk] Verkehr
trail [treɪl] Wanderweg; Pfad
train [treɪn] Zug, Eisenbahn
train [treɪn] trainieren
trainer ['treɪnə] Sportschuh
tram [træm] Straßenbahn
travel ['trævl] reisen, fahren; **travel agency** ['trævleɪdʒənsi] Reisebüro
tree [tri:] Baum
tribe [traɪb] Stamm
trick [trɪk] Trick
trip [trɪp] Ausflug, Reise

truck [trʌk] (AE) Lastwagen
true [tru:] wahr
try [traɪ] versuchen, probieren
Tuesday ['tju:zdeɪ, 'tju:zdi] Dienstag
tunnel ['tʌnl] Tunnel
turkey ['tɜ:ki] Truthahn, Pute
Turkey ['tɜ:ki] Türkei
Turkish ['tɜ:kɪʃ] türkisch; Türkisch; Türke/Türkin
turn [tɜ:n] abbiegen, einbiegen; **turn left/right (into)** nach links/rechts abbiegen (in); **turn around** sich umdrehen
turn [tɜ:n]: **it's my turn** ich bin dran, ich bin an der Reihe
tuxedo [tʌk'si:dəʊ] (AE) Smoking
TV ['ti:'vi:] Fernsehen; Fernsehgerät; **on TV** im Fernsehen; **watch TV** fernsehen; **TV programme** Fernsehsendung
twice [twaɪs]: **twice the time** doppelt so lange

U

uncle ['ʌŋkl] Onkel
under ['ʌndə] unter
underground ['ʌndəgraʊnd] U-Bahn
understand [ʌndə'stænd] verstehen
understood [ʌndə'stʊd]: **I understood** ich verstand / ich habe verstanden
unfriendly [ʌn'frendli] unfreundlich
unhappy [ʌn'hæpi] unglücklich
uniform ['ju:nɪfɔ:m] Uniform
United Kingdom [ju'naɪtɪd'kɪŋdəm] Vereinigtes Königreich
United Nations [ju'naɪtɪd'neɪʃənz] Vereinte Nationen
United States of America [ju'naɪtɪd'steɪtsəvə'merɪkə] Vereinigte Staaten von Amerika
unlucky [ʌn'lʌki]: **we were unlucky** wir hatten Pech
unpack [ʌn'pæk] auspacken
untidy [ʌn'taɪdi] unordentlich, unaufgeräumt
up [ʌp] hinauf/herauf
uphill [ʌp'hɪl] bergauf
upset stomach ['ʌpset'stʌmək] Magenverstimmung
upstairs [ʌp'steəz] oben (im Haus); nach oben
us [ʌs] uns
use [ju:z] benutzen, verwenden
useful ['ju:sfl] nützlich
usually ['ju:ʒuəli] meistens, normalerweise, gewöhnlich

V

vacation [və'keɪʃn] (AE) Ferien, Urlaub
Valentine's Day ['væləntaɪnzdeɪ] Valentinstag
vanilla [və'nɪlə] Vanille
vegetarian [vedʒə'teəriən] Vegetarier/Vegetarierin
verb [vɜ:b] Verb, Zeitwort
very ['veri] sehr
video ['vɪdiəʊ] Videofilm, Video
video-recorder ['vɪdiəʊrɪ'kɔ:də] Videorecorder
view [vju:] Aussicht, Sicht
village ['vɪlɪdʒ] Dorf
vinegar ['vɪnɪgə] Essig
visit ['vɪzɪt] **1.** besuchen; besichtigen; **2.** Besuch, Aufenthalt
visitor ['vɪzɪtə] Besucher/Besucherin, Gast
volleyball ['vɒlibɔ:l] Volleyball

W

wait [weɪt] warten; **wait for** warten auf
waiter ['weɪtə] Kellner, Ober
walk [wɔ:k] (zu Fuß) gehen, laufen; wandern; **go for a walk** spazieren gehen; **take the dog for a walk** mit dem Hund rausgehen, spazieren gehen
walk [wɔ:k]: **beach walk** *(asphaltierter)* Strandweg
walkman ['wɔ:kmən] Walkman
wall [wɔ:l] Wand, Mauer
want [wɒnt] wollen; **want to go** gehen wollen
war [wɔ:] Krieg
warden ['wɔ:dn] Herbergsmutter/Herbergsvater
warm [wɔ:m] warm
warning ['wɔ:nɪŋ] Warnung, Vorwarnung
was [wɒz, wəz]: **I was** ich war; **I was invited** ich wurde eingeladen
wash [wɒʃ]: **wash dishes** Geschirr spülen; **wash up** abwaschen, spülen; **have a wash** sich waschen
washing-machine ['wɒʃɪŋmə'ʃi:n] Waschmaschine
watch [wɒtʃ] zusehen, sich anschauen, beobachten; **watch TV** fernsehen
water ['wɔ:tə] Wasser
way [weɪ] Weg; **a long way** weit
we [wi:] wir
wear [weə] tragen, anziehen
weather ['weðə] Wetter; **weather forecast** ['weðəfɔ:kɑ:st] Wettervorhersage
web [web]: **web site** ['websaɪt] Website *(Gesamtangebot eines Anbieters im Internet bzw. im World Wide Web)*; **word web** „Wortnetz“
Wednesday ['wenzdeɪ, 'wenzdi] Mittwoch
week [wi:k] Woche
weekday ['wi:kdeɪ] Wochentag
weekend ['wi:k'end] Wochenende; **at the weekend** am Wochenende
weigh [weɪ] wiegen
welcome ['welkəm]: **Welcome to ...** Willkommen in/im/bei ...
well [wel] gut
Well, ... [wel] Nun, ...
Welsh [welʃ] walisisch; Walisisch; Waliser/Waliserin
went [went]: **I went** ich ging, fuhr / ich bin gegangen, gefahren
were [wɜ:]: **you were** du warst; ihr wart; Sie waren
west [west] West-; (nach) Westen; westlich
western ['westən] Western
wet [wet] nass, feucht
what [wɒt] **1.** was; **2.** welche/welcher/welches; **What a ...!** Was für ein/eine ...! **What about ... ?** Wie wäre es mit ... ? Was ist mit ... ? **What colour is ...?** Welche Farbe hat ...? **What time is it?** Wie spät ist es? **What's it like?** Wie ist es? **What's the matter?** Was ist los? **What's the weather forecast?** Wie ist die Wettervorhersage? **What's this/... in English?** Was heißt dies/... auf Englisch? **What's your name?** Wie heißt du? / Wie heißen Sie?

wheelchair ['wi:ltʃeə] Rollstuhl
when [wen] **1.** wann; **2.** wenn; **3.** als; **When's the next train to Chester?** Wann fährt der nächste Zug nach Chester?
where [weə] wo; wohin; **Where are you from?** Wo kommst du her? / Wo kommen Sie her?
which [wɪtʃ] welche/welcher/welches
while [waɪl] während
whisky ['wɪski] Whisky
whistle ['wɪsl] pfeifen
white [waɪt] weiß
who [hu:] **1.** wer; **2.** der/die/das *(in Relativsätzen)*
why [waɪ] warum, weshalb; **that's why** deshalb, darum
wife, wives [waɪf, waɪvz] Ehefrau, Ehefrauen
will [wɪl]**: I will** (= **I'll** [aɪl]) ich werde
win [wɪn] gewinnen
wind [wɪnd] Wind
window ['wɪndəʊ] (Schau-)Fenster
window-shopping ['wɪndəʊʃɒpɪŋ]**: go window-shopping** einen Schaufensterbummel machen
windsurfing ['wɪndsɜ:fɪŋ] Windsurfen
windy ['wɪndi] windig
winter ['wɪntə] Winter
witch [wɪtʃ] Hexe
with [wɪð] mit; bei
without [wɪ'ðaʊt] ohne
woman, women ['wʊmən, 'wɪmɪn] Frau, Frauen
won [wʌn]**: I won** ich gewann / ich habe gewonnen; **I've won** ich habe gewonnen
won't [wəʊnt] (= **will not**)**: I won't** ich werde nicht
wood [wʊd] Holz
word [wɜ:d] Wort; **word web** „Wortnetz"
wore [wɔ:]**: I wore** ich trug, zog an / ich habe getragen, angezogen
work [wɜ:k] **1.** arbeiten; funktionieren; **2.** Arbeit; **at work** bei der Arbeit; **go to work** arbeiten gehen; **out of work** arbeitslos
world [wɜ:ld] Welt; **in the world** auf der (ganzen) Welt
World Trade Center [wɜ:ld'treɪdsentə] Welthandelszentrum
worn [wɔ:n]**: I've worn** ich habe getragen, angezogen
worried ['wʌrid]**: she was worried (about)** sie machte sich Sorgen (um)
worry ['wʌri]**: Don't worry.** Mach dir keine Sorgen.
worse [wɜ:s] schlimmer
would [wʊd]**: Would you like ...?** Möchtest du / Möchten Sie ...? **I'd like** [aɪd'laɪk] (= **I would like**) **...** Ich möchte ... / Ich hätte gern ... **I'd like to go.** Ich möchte gehen.
write [raɪt] schreiben
written ['rɪtn]**: I've written** ich habe geschrieben
wrong [rɒŋ] falsch
wrote [rəʊt]**: I wrote** ich schrieb / ich habe geschrieben

Y

yeah [jeə] (AE) ja
year [jɪə] Jahr; Jahrgang
yellow ['jeləʊ] gelb
yes [jes] ja
yesterday ['jestədeɪ, 'jestədi] gestern
yet [jet]**: not ... yet** noch nicht
yoghurt ['jɒgət] Joghurt
you [ju:] **1.** du; ihr; Sie; **2.** man
young [jʌŋ] jung
your [jɔ:] dein/deine; euer/eure; Ihr/Ihre
yours [jɔ:z] deine/deiner/deines, eure/eurer/eures, Ihre/Ihrer/Ihres
yourself [jɔ:'self] dir/dich (selbst); selbst
yourselves [jɔ:'selvz] euch (selbst); sich (selbst); selbst
youth [ju:θ] Jugend-; **youth club** Jugendclub; **youth hostel** Jugendherberge; **youth hostel card** Jugendherbergsausweis

Z

zoo [zu:] Zoo

List of names

GIRLS/WOMEN

Amy ['eɪmi]
Angela ['ændʒələ]
Ashley ['æʃli]
Beth [beθ]
Dawn [dɔ:n]
Eileen ['aɪli:n]
Erica ['erɪkə]
Gail [geɪl]
Haley ['heɪli]
Helen ['helən]
Isabel ['ɪzəbel]
Jade [dʒeɪd]
Jennifer ['dʒenɪfə]
Kate [keɪt]
Kay [keɪ]
Kelly ['keli]
Laura ['lɔ:rə]
Maria [mə'ri:ə]
Melissa [mə'lɪsə]
Michelle [mɪ'ʃel]
Nicola ['nɪkələ]
Rachel ['reɪtʃəl]
Rita ['ri:tə]
Sadie ['seɪdi]
Sandra ['sændrə]
Sarah ['seərə]
Shyrette [ʃɪ'ret]
Stella ['stelə]
Susan ['su:zən]
Sylvia ['sɪlviə]
Tara ['tɑ:rə]
Tatyana [tʌt'jɑ:nə]
Tina ['ti:nə]

BOYS/MEN

Ali ['æli]
Arthur ['ɑ:θə]
Bob [bɒb]
Brad [bræd]
Chuck [tʃʌk]
Clifford ['klɪfəd]
Costa ['kɒstə]
Craig [kreɪg]
Daniel ['dænjəl]
Danny ['dæni]
David ['deɪvɪd]
Eric ['erɪk]
Frank [fræŋk]
Freddy ['fredi]
Jack [dʒæk]
James [dʒeɪmz]
Jerry ['dʒeri]
Larry ['læri]
Marvin ['mɑ:vɪn]
Matt [mæt]
Michael ['maɪkəl]
Mike [maɪk]
Pete [pi:t]
Ray [reɪ]
Richard ['rɪtʃəd]
Rick [rɪk]
Robert ['rɒbət]
Ron [rɒn]
Ryan [raɪən]
Shaun [ʃɔ:n]
Steve [sti:v]
Tony ['təʊni]
Troy [trɔɪ]
Vince [vɪns]
Walt [wɔ:lt]
Will [wɪl]

FAMILIES

Alvarez ['ælvərez]
Bird [bɜ:d]
Bond [bɒnd]
Brennan ['brenən]
Breuer ['brɔɪə]
Brown [braʊn]
Burns [bɜ:nz]
Chan [tʃæn]
Chang [tʃæŋ]
Connell ['kɒnl]
Davey ['deɪvi]
Delano [də'leɪnəʊ]
Devine [də'vaɪn]
Dobson ['dɒbsən]
Dooley ['du:li]
Ferguson ['fɜ:gəsən]
Fowler ['faʊlə]
Frommer ['frɒmə]
Fujito [fʊ'dʒɪtəʊ]
Garcia [gɑ:'si:ə]
Gonzalez [gɒn'zɑ:lɪs]
Grant [grɑ:nt]
Heffer ['hefə]
Hendricks ['hendrɪks]
Hernandez [hɜ:'nændez]
Kane [keɪn]
Khan [kɑ:n]
Kline [klaɪn]
Lehman ['li:mən]
Lewis ['lu:ɪs]
Lopez ['ləʊpez]
Malkin ['mælkɪn]
Mayer ['meɪə]
Miller ['mɪlə]
Morales [mɒ'rɑ:les]
Murphy ['mɜ:fi]
Ortega [ɔ:'teɪgə]
Pepaj [pe'pɑ:dʒ]
Perez ['peres]
Rackowsky [rə'kaʊski]
Rice [raɪs]
Russell ['rʌsl]
Sachse ['sæksə]
Sands [sændz]
Smith [smɪθ]
Soldano [sɒl'dɑ:nəʊ]
Stone [stəʊn]
Tanios ['tʌnjɒs]
Vandermolen ['vændəməʊlən]
Vu [vu:]
Wilson ['wɪlsən]

FAMOUS PEOPLE

Mary Austin ['meəri'ɒstɪn]
Terry Fox ['teri'fɒks]
Martina Hingis [mɑ:'ti:nə'hɪŋgɪs]
Magic Johnson ['mædʒɪk'dʒɒntsən]
Michael Jordan ['maɪkəl'dʒɔ:dən]
James Naismith ['dʒeɪmz'neɪsmɪθ]
Ogden Nash ['ɒgdən'næʃ]
Shaquille O'Neal [ʃæ'ki:ləʊ'ni:l], **Shaq** [ʃæk]
Levi Strauss ['li:vaɪ'straʊs]

STATES IN THE USA

Alaska [ə'læskə]
Arizona [ærɪ'zəʊnə]
California [kælɪ'fɔ:niə]
Hawaii [hə'waii]
Idaho ['aɪdəhəʊ]
Massachusetts [mæsə'tʃu:sɪts]
Missouri [mɪ'zʊəri]
Montana [mɒn'tænə]
New Jersey [nju:'dʒɜ:zi]
New Mexico [nju:'meksikəʊ]
Texas ['teksəs]
Wyoming [waɪ'əʊmɪŋ]

CITIES AND TOWNS IN NORTH AMERICA

Amarillo [æmə'rɪləʊ]
Amboy ['æmbɔɪ]
Atlanta [ət'læntə]
Barstow ['bɑ:stəʊ]
Boston ['bɒstən]
Brownsville ['braʊnzvɪl]
Cameron ['kæmərən]
Chicago [ʃɪ'kɑ:gəʊ]
Cody ['kəʊdi]
Dallas ['dæləs]
Denver ['denvə]
Detroit [də'trɔɪt]
Flagstaff ['flægstɑ:f]
Gallup ['gæləp]
Hadleyville ['hædlivɪl]
Houston ['hju:stən]
Kingman ['kɪŋmən]
Los Alamos [lɒs'æləmɒs]
Los Angeles [lɒs'ændʒɪlɪz]
Miami [maɪ'æmi]
Miles City ['maɪlz'sɪti]
Mormon Lake ['mɔ:mən'leɪk]
New Orleans [nju:'ɔ:liənz]
New York City [nju:jɔ:k'sɪti],
New York [nju:'jɔ:k]
Oklahoma City [əʊklə'həʊmə'sɪti]
Phoenix ['fi:nɪks]
Salt Lake City [sɔ:ltleɪk'sɪti]
San Antonio [sænæn'təʊniəʊ]
San Bernardino [sænbɜ:nə'di:nəʊ]
San Diego [sændi'eɪgəʊ]
San Francisco [sænfrən'sɪskəʊ]
Santa Barbara [sæntə'bɑ:bərə]
Santa Fe [sæntə'feɪ]
Seattle [si'ætl]
Sedona [sə'dəʊnə]
St. John's [sənt'dʒɒnz]
St. Louis [sənt'lu:ɪs]
Thunder Bay [θʌndə'beɪ]
Toronto [tə'rɒntəʊ]
Tucson ['tu:sɒn]
Washington, D.C. ['wɒʃɪŋtən'di:'si:]
Window Rock ['wɪndəʊ'rɒk]
Winona [wɪ'nəʊnə]

PARTS OF NEW YORK CITY

Bronx [brɒŋks]
Brooklyn ['brʊklɪn]
Manhattan [mæn'hætən]
Queens [kwi:nz]
Staten Island ['stætn'aɪlənd]

SIGHTS IN NORTH AMERICA

Big Bend [bɪg'bend]
Brooklyn Bridge ['brʊklɪn'brɪdʒ]
Central Park ['sentrəl'pɑ:k]
Chinatown ['tʃaɪnətaʊn]
Chrysler Building ['kraɪzlə'bɪldɪŋ]
CN Tower ['si:'entaʊə]
Death Valley ['deθ'væli]
Empire State Building ['empaɪə'steɪtbɪldɪŋ]
Everglades ['evəgleɪdz]
Flatiron Building ['flætaɪənbɪldɪŋ]
Grand Canyon [grænd'kænjən]
Hollywood ['hɒliwʊd]
Humboldt Redwoods ['hʌmbəʊlt'redwʊdz]
Little Italy [lɪtl'ɪtəli]
Mammoth Mountain ['mæməθ'maʊntən]
Monument Valley ['mɒnjəmənt'væli]
Rockefeller Center ['rɒkəfelə'sentə]
Rocky Mountains ['rɒki'maʊntənz]
Route 66 ['ru:t'sɪksti'sɪks]
Skydome ['skaɪdəʊm]
Statue of Liberty ['stætʃu:əv'lɪbəti]
Times Square ['taɪmz'skweə]
United Nations [ju'naɪtɪd'neɪʃənz]
Yellowstone National Park ['jeləʊstəʊn'næʃnəl'pɑ:k]

OTHER PLACES IN THE USA

Abbey High School ['æbi'haɪsku:l]
Calle Rosales ['kʌlərəʊ'zɑ:ləs]
Cedar Ridge ['si:də'rɪdʒ]
Church Avenue [tʃɜ:tʃ'ævənju:]
City High School ['sɪti'haɪsku:l]
Colorado River [kɒlə'rɑ:dəʊ'rɪvə]
East Houston Street ['i:st'hju:stənstri:t]
Fifth Avenue [fɪfθ'ævənju:]
Fishing Bridge ['fɪʃɪŋ'brɪdʒ]
Fishing Village ['fɪʃɪŋ'vɪlɪdʒ]
Fresh Kills [freʃ'kɪlz]
Giants Stadium ['dʒaɪənts'steɪdiəm]
Grand Central Station ['grændsentrəl'steɪʃn]
Ground Zero [graʊnd'zɪərəʊ]
Heart Lake ['hɑ:tleɪk]
Main Street ['meɪnstri:t]
Myers Park ['maɪəz'pɑ:k]
Porter High ['pɔ:tə'haɪ]
Rivera High School [rɪ'veərə'haɪsku:l]
Springsville ['sprɪŋsvɪl]
West End Avenue ['westend'ævənju:]
Westbrook ['westbrʊk]
World Trade Center [wɜ:ld'treɪdsentə]
Wounded Knee ['wu:ndɪd'ni:]

OTHER COUNTRIES AND CITIES

Albania [æl'beɪniə]
Bosnia ['bɒzniə]
Canada ['kænədə]
China ['tʃaɪnə]
Croatia [krəʊ'eɪʃə]
Czech Republic [tʃekrɪ'pʌblɪk]
Greece [gri:s]
Holland ['hɒlənd]
Italy ['ɪtəli]
Japan [dʒə'pæn]
Kosice ['kɔ:ʃi:tseɪ]
Mexico ['meksɪkəʊ]
Pisa ['pi:zə]
Portugal ['pɔ:tʃʊgl]
Russia ['rʌʃə]
Slovakia [sləʊ'vɑ:kiə]
Switzerland ['swɪtsələnd]
Tel Aviv [telə'vi:v]
Turkey ['tɜ:ki]
Vietnam [viet'næm]

OTHER NAMES

American Airlines [ə'merɪkən'eəlaɪnz]
Beachwatch ['bi:tʃwɒtʃ]
Betta Burger ['betə'bɜ:gə]
Black Katt [blæk'kæt]
Black Sounds [blæk'saʊndz]
Boston Celtics ['bɒstən'seltɪks]
Braun's [braʊnz]
Canada's Wonderland ['kænədəz'wʌndəlænd]
Celsius ['selsiəs]
Chicago Bulls [ʃɪ'kɑ:gəʊ'bʊlz]
City Scene ['sɪti'si:n]
Exxon ['eksɒn]
Fahrenheit ['færənheɪt]
Gumbos ['gʌmbəʊz]
Halloween ['hæləʊ'i:n]
Harlem Globetrotters ['hɑ:ləm'gləʊbtrɒtəz]
High Noon [haɪ'nu:n]
Internet ['ɪntənet]
Jellystone Park ['dʒelistəʊn'pɑ:k]
Katz's Delicatessen ['kætsɪzdelɪkə'tesn]
Kids' Club ['kɪdzklʌb]
King Kong [kɪŋ'kɒŋ]
Lassie ['læsi]
Los Angeles Lakers [lɒs'ændʒɪlɪz'leɪkəz]
Macy's ['meɪsiz]
Mardi Gras ['mɑ:di'grɑ:]
McBurger [mək'bɜ:gə]
Mega Movies ['megə'mu:viz]
Metrocard ['metrəʊkɑ:d]
Mr Tux [mɪstə'tʌks]
Navajo ['nævəhəʊ]
Nick's Burger Joint [nɪks'bɜ:gədʒɔɪnt]
Paseo Nuevo [pæ'seɪəʊ'nweɪvəʊ]
Roxy ['rɒksi]
Roy's [rɔɪz]
Santa Fe Railroad ['sæntə'feɪ'reɪlrəʊd]
Sioux [su:]
Smokey ['sməʊki]
Steuben Day Parade ['stɔɪbəndeɪpə'reɪd]
Supersound ['su:pəsaʊnd]
Texaco ['teksəkəʊ]
The Strawberries [ðə'strɔ:bəriz]
Yogi Bear ['jəʊgi'beə]

Ordinal numbers

1st **first** [fɜːst]

2nd **second** ['sekənd]

3rd **third** [θɜːd]

4th **fourth** [fɔːθ]

5th **fifth** [fɪfθ]

6th **sixth** [sɪksθ]

7th **seventh** ['sevnθ]

8th **eighth** [eɪtθ]

9th **ninth** [naɪnθ]

10th **tenth** [tenθ]

11th **eleventh** [ɪ'levnθ]

12th **twelfth** [twelfθ]

13th **thirteenth** [θɜː'tiːnθ]

14th **fourteenth** [fɔː'tiːnθ]

15th **fifteenth** [fɪf'tiːnθ]

16th **sixteenth** [sɪks'tiːnθ]

17th **seventeenth** [sevn'tiːnθ]

18th **eighteenth** [eɪ'tiːnθ]

19th **nineteenth** [naɪn'tiːnθ]

20th **twentieth** ['twentiəθ]

21st **twenty-first** [twenti'fɜːst]

22nd **twenty-second** [twenti'sekənd]

23rd **twenty-third** [twenti'θɜːd]

24th **twenty-fourth** [twenti'fɔːθ]

25th **twenty-fifth** [twenti'fɪfθ]

26th **twenty-sixth** [twenti'sɪksθ]

27th **twenty-seventh** [twenti'sevnθ]

28th **twenty-eighth** [twenti'eɪtθ]

29th **twenty-ninth** [twenti'naɪnθ]

30th **thirtieth** ['θɜːtiəθ]

The English alphabet

a [eɪ]

b [biː]

c [siː]

d [diː]

e [iː]

f [ef]

g [dʒiː]

h [eɪtʃ]

i [aɪ]

j [dʒeɪ]

k [keɪ]

l [el]

m [em]

n [en]

o [əʊ]

p [piː]

q [kjuː]

r [ɑː]

s [es]

t [tiː]

u [juː]

v [viː]

w [ˈdʌbljuː]

x [eks]

y [waɪ]

z [zed]

English sounds

[iː] team, see, he
[ɑː] ask, class, start
[ɔː] or, ball, four, door
[uː] ruler, blue, too, two, you
[ɜː] girl, her, early, work
[ɪ] in, big, enough
[e] yes, bed
[æ] cat, black
[ʌ] bus, colour
[ɒ] on, dog, what
[ʊ] put, good, woman
[ə] again, sister, today
[i] radio, video, coffee, happy
[u] July, usually

[eɪ] eight, name, play, great
[aɪ] I, time, right, my
[ɔɪ] boy, toilet
[əʊ] old, no, road, yellow
[aʊ] house, now
[ɪə] near, here, we're
[eə] there, repair
[ʊə] you're, plural

[b] bike,hobby, table, job
[p] pen, pupil, shop
[d] day, window, good
[t] ten, matter, at
[k] car, lucky, book
[g] go, again, bag
[ŋ] wrong, morning
[l] like, old, small
[r] ruler, friend, biro
[v] very, seven, have
[w] we, where, quarter
[s] six, poster, yes
[z] zoo, present, his
[ʃ] she, station, English
[tʃ] child, teacher, match
[dʒ] jeans, German, badge
[ʒ] garage, usually
[j] yes, you, young
[θ] thing, maths, tooth
[ð] the, father, with

Classroom phrases

What YOU can say in the classroom

You need help
Sorry, I don't understand.
Can you speak louder, please?
What's '...' in English / in German?
What does '...' mean?
Is '...' the right word for ...?
Can you explain this exercise/word/..., please?

How do you spell '...'?
How do you say the second word in line 5?
Can you write it on the board, please?
Sorry, I can't find it. What page are we on?

Can I say it in German?

Listening and reading
I can't hear the cassette/CD.
Can we listen to that again, please?
I think the story is nice/interesting/boring/terrible/...

It was funny/boring/... when ...
I was frightened/happy/sad/... when ...
I liked it / didn't like it when ...
I think Michelle is right/wrong because ...
I'm not sure. Perhaps ...
I think so, too. / I don't think so.

You and your partners
It's my/your turn (to write/ask questions).

I think we should/could ...
I don't think we should ...
I'd like to make a video/...
Why don't we write ... / ask ...?
What about a poster/...?
Couldn't we stick this photo here?

Was DU im Klassenzimmer sagen kannst

Du brauchst Hilfe
Tut mir Leid, das verstehe ich nicht.
Können Sie bitte lauter sprechen?
Was heißt „...“ auf Englisch / auf Deutsch?
Was bedeutet „...“?
Ist „...“ das richtige Wort für ...?
Können Sie bitte diese Übung / dieses Wort / ... erklären?
Wie buchstabiert man „...“? Wie schreibt man „...“?
Wie spricht man das zweite Wort in Zeile 5 aus?
Können Sie es bitte an die Tafel schreiben?
Tut mir Leid, ich kann es nicht finden. Auf welcher Seite sind wir?
Kann ich es auf Deutsch sagen?

Beim Zuhören und beim Lesen
Ich kann die Cassette/CD nicht hören.
Können wir das noch einmal hören, bitte?
Ich finde die Geschichte nett/interessant/langweilig/schrecklich/...
Es war lustig/langweilig/..., als ...
Ich hatte Angst / war glücklich/traurig/..., als ...
Ich fand es gut / nicht gut, als ...
Ich meine, Michelle hat Recht/Unrecht, weil ...
Ich bin nicht sicher. Vielleicht ...
Das finde ich auch. / Das finde ich nicht.

Du und deine Partner/innen
Ich bin an der Reihe / Du bist an der Reihe (zu schreiben / Fragen zu stellen).
Ich finde, wir sollten/könnten ...
Ich finde, dass man nicht ... sollte.
Ich möchte gern ein Video machen/...
Warum schreiben wir nicht ... / fragen wir nicht ...?
Wie wäre es mit einem Poster/...?
Könnten wir dieses Foto nicht hierhin kleben?

What YOUR TEACHER says

Open your books at page 24, please.
Close your books.
Look at line 8 / at the picture on page 24. / Look at the board.
Finish the word web.
Correct the mistakes.
Put in the right words.
Put the words in the right order.
Take notes.
Walk around the classroom and ask other students.

Read out your answers.
Do exercise 3 for homework, please.
Have you finished?
Bring some photos/... to school.
Well done!
Not quite right. Try again.
Let me help you.

Was DEIN/E LEHRER/IN sagt

Schlagt bitte eure Bücher auf Seite 24 auf.
Macht eure Bücher zu.
Seht euch Zeile 8 / das Bild auf Seite 24 an. / Schaut an die Tafel.
Vervollständigt das Wortnetz.
Verbessert die Fehler.
Setzt die richtigen Wörter ein.
Bringt die Wörter in die richtige Reihenfolge.
Macht euch Notizen.
Geht im Klassenzimmer umher und fragt andere Schüler und Schülerinnen.
Lies deine Antworten vor.
Macht bitte Übung 3 als Hausaufgabe.
Seid ihr fertig? / Bist du fertig?
Bringt Fotos/... mit zur Schule.
Gut gemacht!
Nicht ganz richtig. Versuch/Versucht es noch einmal.
Lasst mich euch helfen.

Irregular verbs

INFINITIVE FORM (Grundform)	SIMPLE PAST FORM (Einfache Vergangenheit)	PRESENT PERFECT FORM (Vollendete Gegenwart)	
be	I was, you were, she was	I've been	sein
have	I had	I've had	haben
do	I did	I've done [dʌn]	tun, machen
beat	I beat	I've beaten	schlagen
become	I became	I've become	werden
break	I broke	I've broken	brechen, zerbrechen
bring	I brought	I've brought	bringen, mitbringen
build	I built	I've built	bauen
buy	I bought	I've bought	kaufen
come	I came	I've come	kommen
cost	it cost	it has cost	kosten
draw	I drew	I've drawn	zeichnen
drink	I drank	I've drunk	trinken
drive	I drove	I've driven ['drɪvn]	fahren
eat	I ate [et]	I've eaten	essen
fall	I fell	I've fallen	fallen
feed	I fed	I've fed	füttern
feel	I felt	I've felt	(sich) fühlen
fight	I fought	I've fought	bekämpfen
find	I found	I've found	finden
fly	I flew	I've flown	fliegen
forget	I forgot	I've forgotten	vergessen
get	I got	I've got	bekommen; besorgen
give	I gave	I've given	geben; schenken
go	I went	I've gone [gɒn]	gehen, fahren
grow	I grew	I've grown	wachsen
hang	I hung	I've hung	aufhängen, hängen
hear	I heard [hɜːd]	I've heard [hɜːd]	hören
hurt	I hurt	I've hurt	verletzen; wehtun
keep	I kept	I've kept	halten, behalten
know	I knew	I've known	wissen; kennen
leave	I left	I've left	lassen; verlassen
lie	I lay	I've lain	liegen
lose	I lost	I've lost	verlieren
make	I made	I've made	machen
mean	I meant [ment]	I've meant [ment]	bedeuten; meinen
meet	I met	I've met	treffen; kennen lernen
pay	I paid	I've paid	zahlen, bezahlen
put	I put	I've put	stellen; legen
read	I read [red]	I've read [red]	lesen, vorlesen
ride	I rode	I've ridden	(Rad) fahren
run	I ran	I've run	rennen, laufen

INFINITIVE FORM (Grundform)	SIMPLE PAST FORM (Einfache Vergangenheit)	PRESENT PERFECT FORM (Vollendete Gegenwart)	
say	I said [sed]	I've said [sed]	sagen
see	I saw	I've seen	sehen; besichtigen
sell	I sold	I've sold	verkaufen
send	I sent	I've sent	senden, schicken
set the table	I set the table	I've set the table	den Tisch decken
shoot	I shot	I've shot	schießen; erschießen
show	I showed	I've shown	zeigen
sing	I sang	I've sung	singen
sit	I sat	I've sat	sitzen; sich setzen
sleep	I slept	I've slept	schlafen
speak	I spoke	I've spoken	sprechen
spend	I spent	I've spent	verbringen
split up	they split up	they've split up	sich trennen
stand	I stood	I've stood	stehen
steal	I stole	I've stolen	stehlen
swim	I swam	I've swum	schwimmen
take	I took	I've taken	(mit)nehmen; dauern
teach	I taught	I've taught	beibringen, unterrichten
tell	I told	I've told	erzählen; sagen
think	I thought	I've thought	finden; glauben; denken
throw	I threw	I've thrown	werfen
understand	I understood	I've understood	verstehen
wear	I wore	I've worn	tragen, anziehen
win	I won	I've won	gewinnen
write	I wrote	I've written	schreiben

Quellen

BILDQUELLEN

Arizona-Sonora Desert Museum, Tuscon/AZ (G. C. Kenny S. 28 u-re); Gary Barber, Dallas/TX (6 u-re; 83 mi-li; 84; 85; 86 o; 90 o, mi; 91 o; 92 D, E; 93 u-li; 96 o-re, u-re; 112 G); Bavaria, Gauting (D. Ball 46 o-li, 79 C; G. French 11 mi-li; H. Manfred 101: 4; Messerschmidt 100 o; Mollenhauer 11 o-li; PP 7 u-re, 64 mi-re, 79 A, 83 o-li; TCL 94); Tom Bean, Flagstaff/AZ (40); John Berthelot, Santa Barbara/CA (6 mi; 47 u-li; 48 o, mi-re; 50; 51; 56); John Birdsall, Nottingham (100 mi; 102 o); Millie Burns, New York (6 o-li; 12; 13; 14 o; 15; 18 u); Circle Line Cruises, New York (20 A); Consultwebs.com, Raleigh/NC (D. Tincher 11 u-re); Corel-Library (Hintergründe 21, 28f, 42, 46f, 64f, 82f; 10 u-li, o-re; 28 o-re, u-li; 29 o-li; 30 u; 32: 1,2,4, u; 39 mi-li; 43 A; 46 o-re, u-re; 49; 54 mi außer ham, beans, cereal; 57; 59; 64 u-li; 65 o-li; 75; 77; 79 E; 82 u-re; 83 mi-re; 91 mi-re; 93 o; 96 o-li; 105 D, E; 107 mi; 109 D, E; 110; 112 alle außer B, G; 115 u alle außer 2a; 116 u-re; 117); Roderick Cox, Aachen (7 o-re; 24 u-li; 25 B; 43 B; 74 C; 83 u-li); dpa, Berlin (AFD Photo/Buck 116 u-li); EMI Music Canada (103); Angelika Fischer, Berlin (36 u); Focus, Hamburg (N. Benn 102 mi; M. Yamashita 14 mi); Das Fotoarchiv, Essen (S. Winter 116 o); The Terry Fox Foundation, Toronto (60 o-re); Dwight Haigh, Flagstaff/AZ (6 o-re, u-li; 7 o-li; 29 mi-re, u-re; 30 o; 31 o; 33; 36 o; 37; 38; 39 o; 43 C; 54 o, u; 55 o; 66; 67; 68; 72; 73; 74 B, D, E); Birgit Herrmann, Aachen (43 D; 92 B, C); Bruce Hucko, Moab/UT (108 mi); IFA Bilderteam, Frankfurt (Chromosohm 101: 5; Deuter 41; Disc 29 u-li; Donnezan 42 mi; International Stock 100 mi-re); Image Bank, Berlin (L. Castañeda 64 o-li; A. Caufield 42 u-re; A. Choisnet 14 mi-li; J. Kelly 65 o-re; S. Krongard 61 B; R. Maas 54 cereal; J. Mahaux 109 A; M. Melford 105 B; P. Miller 64 o-re; J. van Os 78; H. Sund 83 o-re; 105 C; A. Pistolesi 109 B; Yellow Dog Prods 92 A); International Stock, New York (S. Barrow 101: 3; S. Bly 82 o-li; M. Bolster 61 E; C. Ehlers 32: 3; B. Firth 39 mi-re; J. Greenberg 92 F; M. & T. Grimm 7 mi, 74 A; M. Ikeda 74 F; A. Jenny 91 mi-li; B. Mays 64 u-re; M. Paras 18 o, mi, 24 o-re, 100 mi-li, 101: 1, 2; P. Picardi 96 u-li; Johnny Stockshooter 10 u-re; P. Thompson 31 mi; C. Szymanski 11 u-li; P. Wallick 83 u-re, 90 u; D. Willison 82 o-re, 116 mi-re; B. Wolf 47 o-re; K. Wood 82 u-li); Todd James, New York (23); Barbara Jung, Berlin (79 B); Kenji Kawano, Window Rock/AZ (108 u); Kinoarchiv Engelmeier, Hamburg (107 o); Lufthansa, Köln (61 A); Mary Evans Picture Library, London (47 u-re); Mauritius, Berlin (AGE 48 li; Canstock 55 mi; Kord 7 u-li; 10-11 Hintergrund; Lindner 29 o-re; Mulvehill 109 C; SST 14 mi-re); Ministry of Transportation, Ontario, Canada (G. Sawiak 60 u); Museum f. Verkehr und Technik, Berlin (AEG 86 u); National Park Service, Washington D.C. (65 u-re); NBA Properties Inc., USA (114 li); Pictor, Hamburg (47 o-li, mi; 61 D; 112 B); Pop-Eye, Berlin (102 u); pwe-Verlag, Hamburg (105 A); Reisig + Taylor (114 re); Rivera High School, Brownsville/TX (93 re); Paul Robson, York (54 beans); Sportimage, Hamburg (Dunking 114 o; Roland Garros 115 o; Sportschrome 116 mi-li); Bob Strong, New York (11 o-re; 19; 20; 24 u-re, mi-li; 25 A, C, D; 54 ham; 61 C; 91 mi; 104 o); Thomas J. Snyder, New York (42 o-re); Studio X, Paris (Benali/Liaison 104 mi-li); Süddeutscher Verlag, München (106 o); Tony Stone, Hamburg (D. Hiser 28 o-li; Jess Stock 46 u-li); Ullstein Bilderdienst, Berlin (115: 2a); Visitor Guide Publishing, Inc., New York (20 F); Vista Point Archiv, Köln (42 u-li)

Einband Michael Paras/International Stock, New York

LIEDQUELLEN

California dreamin' (Text und Musik: J. Phillips/M. Gilliam) © MCA Music GmbH, Hamburg (57)
Deep in the Heart of Texas (T.: J. Hershey, M.: D. Swander) © Peer Musikverlag GmbH, Hamburg (93)
Jamaican in New York (T.: Sting/E. C.Aiken Jr., M.: G. M. Sumner) © EMI Music Publishing Germany GmbH, Hamburg (21)
(Get your Kicks on) Route 66 (T. u. M.: B. Troup) © Chappell & Co. GmbH, Hamburg (39)

TEXTQUELLEN

"Grizzly Bear" from THE CHILDREN SING IN THE FAR WEST by Mary Austin. © 1928 by Mary Austin, renewed 1956 by Kenneth M. Chapman and Mary C. Wheelwright. Reprinted by permission of Houghton Mifflin Co. All rights reserved. (53)
Ogden Nash "Adventures of Isabel" © Little, Brown & Co. Inc., Boston/MA (53)
Wesley Curtright "Heart of the Woods" (53)

Nicht alle Copyrightinhaber konnten ermittelt werden; deren Urheberrechte werden hiermit vorsorglich und ausdrücklich anerkannt.

Für die freundliche Unterstützung bedanken wir uns bei: Linda Gregg, New York, und Susan Shields, Santa Barbara.